Due Date	Due Date	Due Date

Haig's Tower of Strength

Haig's Tower of Strength

General Sir Edward Bulfin – Ireland's Forgotten General

John Powell

Foreword by
General the Lord Dannatt GCB, CBE, MC, DL

Pen & Sword
MILITARY

First published in Great Britain in 2018
by Pen & Sword Military
An imprint of Pen & Sword Books Limited
47 Church Street
Barnsley
South Yorkshire
S70 2AS

ISBN 978 1 52672 260 7

A CIP catalogue record for this book is
available from the British Library.

Typeset in Ehrhardt
by Mac Style

Printed and bound in the UK
by TJ International Ltd, Padstow, Cornwall

Pen & Sword Books Limited incorporates the imprints of Atlas,
Archaeology, Aviation, Discovery, Family History, Fiction, History,
Maritime, Military, Military Classics, Politics, Select, Transport,
True Crime, Air World, Frontline Publishing, Leo Cooper,
Remember When, Seaforth Publishing, The Praetorian Press,
Wharncliffe Local History, Wharncliffe Transport,
Wharncliffe True Crime and White Owl.

For a complete list of Pen & Sword titles please contact
PEN & SWORD BOOKS LIMITED
47 Church Street, Barnsley, South Yorkshire, S70 2AS, England
E-mail: enquiries@pen-and-sword.co.uk
Website: www.pen-and-sword.co.uk

Contents

Maps

Family Tree

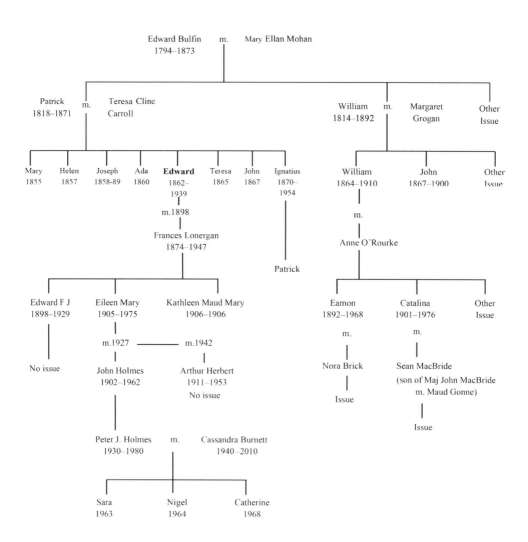

Edward Bulfin   m.   Mary Ellan Mohan
1794–1873

Patrick   m.   Teresa Cline
1818–1871   Carroll

William   m.   Margaret   Other
1814–1892   Grogan   Issue

Mary   Helen   Joseph   Ada   **Edward**   Teresa   John   Ignatius
1855   1857   1858–89   1860   1862–   1865   1867   1870–
                                              1939   1954

m.1898

Frances Lonergan
1874–1947

Patrick

William   John   Other
1864–1910   1867–1900   Issue

m.

Anne O'Rourke

Edward F J   Eileen Mary   Kathleen Maud Mary
1898–1929   1905–1975   1906–1906

No issue

m.1927 ——————— m.1942

John Holmes   Arthur Herbert
1902–1962   1911–1953

No issue

Peter J. Holmes   m.   Cassandra Burnett
1930–1980   1940–2010

Sara   Nigel   Catherine
1963   1964   1968

Eamon   Catalina   Other
1892–1968   1901–1976   Issue

m.   m.

Nora Brick   Sean MacBride
(son of Maj John MacBride
Issue   m. Maud Gonne)

Issue

Glossary

AA&QMG	Assistant Adjutant & Quartermaster General
ADC	Aide-de-Camp
AG	Adjutant General
ANZAC	Australian and New Zealand Army Corps
BEF	British Expeditionary Force
BGGS	Brigadier General, General Staff
BL	British Library
CB	Companion of the Order of the Bath
CGS	Chief of General Staff
CIGS	Chief of the Imperial General Staff
C-in-C	Commander-in-Chief
CO	Commanding Officer
COS	Chief-of-Staff
CRA	Commander Royal Artillery
CRE	Commander Royal Engineers
DAAG	Deputy Assistant Adjutant General
DSO	Distinguished Service Order
EEF	Egyptian Expeditionary Force
GHG	Green Howards Gazette
GHQ	General Headquarters
GOC	General Officer Commanding
GSO1	General Staff Officer Grade 1
GSO2	General Staff Officer Grade 2
IRA	Irish Republican Army
IWM	Imperial War Museum
KCB	Knight Commander of the Bath
KOSB	King's Own Scottish Borderers
KOYLI	King's Own Yorkshire Light Infantry
KRRC	King's Royal Rifle Corps

LHCMA	Liddell Hart Centre for Military Archives
MC	Military Cross
MGGS	Major General, General Staff
MGRA	Major General, Royal Artillery
NAM	National Army Museum
NCO	Non-Commissioned Officer
ODNB	Oxford Dictionary of National Biography
OH	Official History
QMG	Quartermaster General
RA	Royal Artillery
RE	Royal Engineers
RIC	Royal Irish Constabulary
RSM	Regimental Sergeant Major
RWF	Royal Welch Fusiliers
TA	Territorial Army
TCD	Trinity College Dublin
TF	Territorial Force
TNA	The National Archives, Kew
VC	Victoria Cross
Y&L	York & Lancaster Regiment

Foreword

Bookshelves are well supplied with volumes about the great and the good and their remarkable achievements. But it is rare to find a biography of one of those characters in history who might have been missed in the thick of the scrum or in the crush of life. John Powell has brought forward one such man, who demands our attention – Edward Bulfin. Not a household name liked Haig or Allenby, but General Sir Edward Bulfin was a distinguished soldier in his own right, and without his herculean efforts both Haig and Allenby might well have been consigned to the footnotes of history. Both generals recognised Bulfin's contribution to their success – Haig described him as his 'Tower of Strength', and Allenby acknowledged that he would never have succeeded in his great battles in Palestine without him. Here is a man who deserves our attention, and in this superbly researched biography, John Powell – an accomplished soldier and military historian himself – explains why this is so.

As this book recounts, Edward Bulfin stood out from the ranks of many early twentieth century soldiers for a variety of reasons. He was the most senior Irish Catholic soldier to serve in the British Army during and after the First World War. He was fiercely Irish *and* British, never forgetting the land of his birth but equally never forgetting under whose authority he served – that of God and King. His refusal, late in his career, to accept command of all police forces in Ireland as tension between Nationalists and Unionists mounted, demonstrated his priorities – to serve his God-given conscience first, and his King second. But ultimately, his heart lay with people – the people of his native Ireland, the people in uniform who were the soldiers under his command, and especially those in his beloved regiment, The Green Howards. Moreover, he was a family man, delighted to have his son, Eddie, serve as his ADC for many years and then desolate when that son predeceased him, not through enemy action but after a tragic illness.

Success on the battlefield, however, rarely comes about through chance. Napoleon Bonaparte might have admired 'lucky' generals, but for Edward Bulfin the hard grind of experience – battles fought, lessons learnt and wisdom derived – substituted for attendance at Sandhurst or Woolwich, or even at the Army Staff College. Bulfin was a graduate of the battle at Modder River in the Boer War, the retreat to the Marne in 1914 in steadfast command of 2nd Brigade, his crucial contribution to saving Ypres and a desperate pounding at Loos in 1915 in command of 28th Division at the hands of both the Germans and Hubert Gough, his own Corps Commander. Moreover, there was a period of reflection and dedication in his training of the superb 60th (London) Division in 1916 and his subsequent command of that division in France and Salonika – all these experiences resulting in Bulfin becoming the outstanding commander of XXI Corps in Palestine, when Allenby needed him most, to complete the defeat of the Turks. And then, as now, a soldier needs not just to be courageous and committed but worldly-wise too. Bulfin's early appointment as ADC to the Commander-in-Chief and sometime acting High Commissioner in South Africa had shown him that politics and soldiering are indivisible. This realization paid huge dividends when dealing with civil unrest in Egypt in 1919 and bred the caution that led him to refuse the overall police command role in Ireland in 1920 – the latter event, perhaps, coloured by the knowledge that it was his cousin's son who had raised the flag of Irish Nationalism on the roof of the GPO building in Dublin, on Easter Day 1916.

While this book will appeal to many readers on both sides of the Irish Sea, there is one group who will take particular pleasure and pride in turning these pages – those who have served in the Nineteenth of Foot. Edward Bulfin was Colonel of his Regiment for twenty-five years and, as John Powell records in his author's introduction, Bulfin's portrait has peered down on generations of Green Howard soldiers since his death in 1939. In regimental terms, his place in history is assured by his winning of the right from the Army Council to change the name of his regiment on New Year's Day 1921. This move would take nothing away from the very warm affection shown by Bulfin and his North Yorkshire soldiers for Princess, later Queen, Alexandra – Colonel-in-Chief from 1914 to 1925 – but it was a long awaited formalization of the nickname 'Green Howards', by which the Nineteenth of Foot had been known in peace and war since 1744.

In summary, this book gives both the military historian and the general reader alike an unusual opportunity to see behind the lives of some famous figures in history and find one of those supporting characters without whom the dramas of the early twentieth century might well have turned out differently. Edward Bulfin left few diaries or letters, which makes the writing of this comprehensive volume an even greater triumph for its author. John Powell is to be congratulated for his dedicated scholarship, and the reader will be delighted by its easily accessible outcome.

Richard Dannatt
General The Lord Dannatt GCB, CBE, MC, DL
Chief of the General Staff 2006–9 and Colonel, The Green Howards,
1994–2003

Introduction

The First World War left its mark on my family as it did on most. Both grandfathers, whom I was fortunate to know, were wounded; one great-uncle, after whom I am named, was killed at Loos; another was badly wounded the day after landing at Anzac Cove in Gallipoli; only one great-uncle escaped unscathed. In 2014, as the centenary of that war got underway, I became increasingly aware that I did not know as much as I should, even as an old soldier, about the course of that momentous period in our nation's – and empire's – history. In studying the early battles of 1914 I came across an excellent book, *Stemming the Tide*,[1] which includes a chapter by Michael LoCicero on one of Douglas Haig's brigade commanders, one Edward Bulfin from my regiment, the Green Howards. His staunch fighting spirit and calm fortitude under the most extreme pressure, as the German masses poured into Belgium and France, had deeply impressed his commander; so much so that he called Bulfin his 'tower of strength'.[2] On discovering that so little was known about him within the Army, let alone by the general public, I felt that this soldier deserved greater recognition.

Over the decades, whilst attending regimental meetings in our headquarters in the Yorkshire Dales town of Richmond, ensconced in a deep 'Mousey' Thompson oak chair, I had stared up at a full length portrait of an imposing First World War general. In many ways he looked the typical Edwardian senior officer: immaculately dressed, rows of campaign ribbons on his chest, full moustache and given character by his bushy eyebrows and somewhat lugubrious expression. In the way of the young, so often absorbed in their own lives and responsibilities, I had shown little curiosity about this formidable gentleman. All I knew was that this officer, Edward Bulfin, had been our Colonel for some twenty-five long years and in 1920 had pressured the Army Council into allowing us to be officially titled the Green Howards, our nickname since the 1740s, thereby incurring the displeasure of his Sovereign.

What I had failed to appreciate was that, after Bulfin's influential leadership at the Battle of the Aisne and then First Ypres, where his counter-attacks had helped to save the British line at a critical moment, he had been badly wounded. He had then led an infantry division through the bleak and often forgotten days of 1915 at Second Ypres and Loos. Picked out by Allenby to command a corps in Palestine, in his successful mobile campaign against the Turks later in the war, Bulfin, 'a staunch fighter',[3] provided the battering ram to break through the Turkish positions at Third Gaza in 1917, secure Jerusalem and gain the historic victory at Megiddo, Allenby's finest hour. His last operational command was as Commander-in-Chief in Egypt in 1919, when the British Empire was struggling to contain aspirations for independence which often turned violent, whilst balancing the urgent need to demobilize its vast imperial army.

It would be easy, but lazy, to pigeonhole General Sir Edward Stanislaus Bulfin as just another Great War general struggling with the immense challenges of modern industrial warfare, with little to distinguish him from his contemporaries and of no great significance to military or social historians.

What I hope to show is that Bulfin, an Irish Catholic, was not a typical product of the late Victorian Army. He did not follow a classic path to senior command in which birth, schooling, fashionable regiment and attendance at Sandhurst and Staff College, helped by patronage, were often essential requirements. Even more surprisingly, in an age when Irish Catholics were treated with a degree of suspicion in British society, Bulfin had relatives actively involved in the fight for Irish independence, a link of which the British establishment must have been aware. One of a very small band of Irish Catholics to reach general officer rank, his career was testament to sheer ability and merit, to the Army's great credit. Indeed, his war encompassed more than just the momentous events on the Western Front in 1914 and 1915; in particular, he was at the centre of the break-up of the Ottoman Empire in 1917 and 1918 and Egypt's early struggle for independence. A friend of Gertrude Bell and Sir Mark Sykes, his latter career had profound implications for the Middle East and our lives today.

Faced with the stimulating prospect of writing this, my first solo book, I was confronted with a considerable hurdle. It quickly became apparent that the usual sources of research for a biography were scant. Bulfin made clear, in a foreword to a junior officer's memoirs, that he disapproved of generals giving vent to their own outpourings. None of his personal papers and very few letters survive, with the exception of some correspondence with Sir James Edmonds and Cyril Falls, the official historians of the time. I have found only one diary of his, for 1914; it is difficult to believe he did not write further ones. His only son died a bachelor, on active service in 1929 in Palestine, and his daughter's descendants have only been able to provide family photographs. One stroke of fortune was tracking down the previously unread diaries of his ADC in 1915, Captain Hugh Carlton Cumberbatch, through his granddaughter.

In the case of better known officers who also left little trail of themselves, such as Field Marshal Herbert Plumer, much was written about them by their contemporaries. But Edward Bulfin is in many ways a harder man to get to know, and hence I have not attempted a biography in the traditional sense of the word.

Nevertheless, I trust that this study of the career and campaigns of an unusual and remarkable Irishman, almost unknown in Britain and his own country of birth, will ensure that Haig's 'tower of strength' is not forgotten by historians and those interested in the First World War and the origins of the modern Middle East.

One of the delights of researching and writing history is the generous help one receives from librarians, archivists, curators and fellow historians.

First, I must acknowledge the gracious permission of Her Majesty Queen Elizabeth in allowing me to use material from the Royal Archives, and thank Julie Crocker for her help at Windsor Castle.

I am especially grateful to members of the Bulfin family. Jane Bulfin, the granddaughter of Eamon Bulfin, and her mother Jane, welcomed me, with typical Irish warmth, to Derrinlough, the family's ancestral home in Co. Offaly; their assistance helped me greatly in understanding the wider Bulfin family history and its place in Ireland's struggle for independence. Eamon's daughter, Jeanne Bulfin Winder, and Michael, her brother, have also been indispensable with their knowledge of the Derrinlough side of the family. Sara Richer, the great-granddaughter of Edward Bulfin, and her sister Catherine, have also kindly loaned family photographs of their ancestor and encouraged me.

Without the generous help and advice of those who have studied and written about Bulfin I would not have been able to undertake this project. In particular, I would like to thank the following: Michael LoCicero, who not only opened my eyes to Bulfin's part in 1914 but has patiently answered my many subsequent enquiries, offering fresh ideas for research; Iris Oakey, whose MA dissertation on 28th Division is the only previous detailed analysis of Bulfin as a commander in 1915, generously read, with both cogent and robust comments, all of the draft; John Bourne and Gary Sheffield, whose deep knowledge of the Western Front and encouragement to write on Bulfin have been a huge fillip; Spencer Jones, who has been at the forefront of writing on the 'forgotten year' of 1915, has been of great assistance and led me to key sources; lastly, Simon Innes-Robbins, an archivist and author with an encyclopaedic knowledge of the Great War commanders, was an enormous help at the Imperial War Museum and kindly commented on some of my early chapters.

I would also like to thank other historians and authors whose support and advice has been much appreciated: Ian Beckett, John Dixon, Paul Kendall, Nick Perry, Steven O'Connor, Patrick McCarthy, Jan Foster and Wendy Hudson.

My thanks are also due to the following for allowing me to quote from material in their possession: the Green Howards Museum, Prince Consort's Library in Aldershot, Trinity College Dublin Library, the British Library, the National Archives at Kew, National Library of Scotland, National Library of Ireland, National Archives in Dublin, the Imperial War Museum, the National Army Museum, the Liddell Hart Centre for Military Archives, the Diocese of Westminster Archives, Stonyhurst College Archives, Downside Abbey Archives, Wiltshire and Swindon History Centre, and Hull History Centre. I am much indebted to their staffs for their advice and assistance. In particular, I would like to mention Lynda Powell and Steve Erskine of the Green Howards Museum, David Knight and Paul Garlington of Stonyhurst College, Steven Parsons of Downside Abbey, and Rob Tilley and Geoff Sear of Prince Consort's Library where I have spent many a fruitful hour.

Edward Pereira generously allowed me access to his grandfather's papers and gave permission for the fine illustration of Cecil Pereira to be included in this book.

Peter Clarke kindly welcomed me to Woodtown House, Edward's childhood home, and has been very helpful in providing historical details of the house and its previous owners.

A happy event, late in writing this book, was meeting Tim Moloney, who is working on a biography of Edward's cousin, William Bulfin. Our sharing of knowledge has been most rewarding and I wish him well with his endeavour.

I have turned to a number of long-standing friends for advice. Their help has been immeasurable and I would like to thank them, in particular: Richard Dannatt, a brother officer who followed me to Durham University and then command of our regiment, who has kindly written the Foreword; another brother officer of old, Roddy Bailey, who not only read most of the draft but put me in touch with some Irish historians, as well as looking after me so well whilst visiting Ireland; and Ros Grimes, whose research ability launched this novice on the road of discovery.

I must thank Dr Joseph Quinn, of Trinity College Dublin, who has carried out research for me and responded to my requests most helpfully.

I am immensely indebted to Hyacinth Cumberbatch, who entrusted me as a stranger with her grandfather's pocket diaries, meticulously filled out every day by him, tidily in fountain-pen ink. They have now been copied and are held in the Imperial War Museum.

My thanks are due to the publishers, Pen & Sword, for their confidence in commissioning this book, especially to Henry Wilson, Matt Jones and my editor, George Chamier.

Lastly, I would like to pay tribute to my wife, Jill, who has been forever patient and encouraging whilst I have been cossetted with Bulfin for the past four years.

John Powell
Farnham, Surrey

Chapter 1

1862–1898
Early Life

Early in the morning of 28 November 1899, the men of Lieutenant General Lord Methuen's two infantry brigades began to advance silently across the open veldt towards a line of trees marking the meandering course of the Modder River.

'They are not there', remarked Methuen to his companion as they rode forward, less than a mile from the poplar trees lining the bank.

'They are sitting uncommonly tight if they are, sir', he replied.[1]

Along the river, concealed by its steep bank, thousands of Boers waited to lay down the most devastating rifle fire since the South African War had started, some months before.

Amongst the tired British infantrymen, who had already fought two sharp battles at Belmont and Graspan a few days earlier in their advance from the Orange River, was a thirty-six-year-old captain, newly appointed as brigade-major to Major General Reggie Pole-Carew's 9 Infantry Brigade. His name was Edward Stanislaus Bulfin, of the Princess of Wales's Own (Yorkshire Regiment).

As Methuen's casualties mounted, his troops pinned down mercilessly in the open for ten scorching hours with no water and short of ammunition, Bulfin helped swing the pendulum of battle. With a keen tactical eye he brought his commander's attention to the crucial river crossing that allowed the Boer right flank to be enveloped. His brigade commander, gathering his men together, forged across the drift of the Modder River, cleared the settlement of Rosmead and, with it, forced the withdrawal of the Boers.

Bulfin's Irish Roots

Like many generals of the period, Bulfin came from Ireland; he was born in November 1862 outside Dublin. But Bulfin's background was exceptional.

He was not from the Protestant Ascendancy, that stable of 'Anglo-Irish' landed gentry which provided so many of these senior officers, Field Marshals French and Wilson being leading figures of the Great War, with Roberts, Wolseley and Kitchener before them. Indeed, Corelli Barnett, amongst others, has commented that the 'Anglo-Irish' were 'the nearest thing Britain ever possessed to the Prussian Junker class'.[2] Bulfin was not landed gentry and, moreover, was a Roman Catholic. Even more interestingly, he came from a family a close branch of which was strongly identified with the Irish nationalist cause. Most families involved in historical struggles towards independence have members taking different sides. Ireland was no exception, and the Bulfins could not have reflected this contradiction more sharply.

Edward Bulfin's family originated from Birr in Co. Offaly, then 'King's County', and they had an adventurous nature. His first cousin, William Bulfin, was a fervent nationalist. Like many Irish emigrants, he had settled in the Argentine in 1884. He made his name writing sketches and stories in the Buenos Aires weekly paper, the *Southern Cross,* about his fellow countrymen and their gaucho companions herding sheep on horseback across the vast grasslands; these sketches later reached the *United Irishman*, eventually being published in the New York *Daily News.* He later wrote *Rambles in Eirinn*, a well-regarded account of his travels around Ireland by bicycle in 1902. Two of William's children became well known Republican activists: his son Eamon gained fame by raising the flag of the Irish Republic above the General Post Office in Dublin during the 1916 Easter Rising; his daughter Catalina ('Kid') was also an active nationalist and would marry Sean MacBride, the son of Irish nationalist icons Major John MacBride and Maud Gonne, and later a leading figure in the IRA. Nevertheless, one of William's brothers, John (known as Jack) joined the British Army in India as a cavalry trooper and later served in the same division as his cousin Edward, five years older, during the Boer War. The reader will hear more of them later in the book.

Edward Bulfin's father, Patrick, took a very different path from his nephew William. He came to Dublin in 1846 as a young man of twenty-eight to make his fortune, setting up a wholesale grocery business at 50 Thomas Street, in an increasingly prosperous and confident Victorian city. Five years later, he went into partnership with a colleague, and the business expanded to such a degree that by 1871 Bulfin & Fay ('wholesale grocers, merchants and seedsmen') owned premises in Thomas Street, North King Street and City Quay. Patrick's homes reflected his growing wealth. In 1858 he had taken an early nineteenth century house in Raheny, Co. Dublin, and four years later, in December 1861, he bought the impressive 1830s mansion, Woodtown Park, in Rathfarnham, built by Judge Henry Joy; the purchase price of £5,000 was a considerable sum in those days.[3] Set in 48 acres of paddock and pasture, with extensive outbuildings, ornamental and walled gardens and 'commanding extensive views of Dublin Bay, Howth Head and 6 miles of Dublin' as the particulars of the day boasted, it was a statement of confident, self-made success. Woodtown House, as it was now titled, had an intriguing later history. In February 1916 Edward, by then a major general in the British Army, sold the property to James MacNeill, who shared it with his brother Eoin. A founder member of the Irish Volunteers, Eoin was considered one of the foremost Gaelic scholars in Europe. Many of the key figures involved in the Easter Rising frequented Woodtown, among them Patrick Pearse.

It was here that Edward was born on 6 November 1862. His father had married Teresa Carroll, from a well established Co. Offaly family, whose father had been Lord Mayor of Dublin. Edward had three elder sisters and his brother Joseph to look up to, and two more brothers and a younger sister to follow, in what must have been a lively and busy home. The grand sweeping staircase and formal rooms, with their ornate ceilings, would have witnessed much entertainment, as Patrick established himself in political and civic life. Elected to Dublin City Council in 1869 as the Conservative councillor for the Merchants Quay ward, he rose quickly in two years to be elected Lord Mayor of the 'second city of Empire', as Dublin was known before Glasgow assumed that title. Loyal to the British Crown, Patrick Bulfin would have been considered a 'Castle Catholic', although it was some time before this term was actually coined.[4] One of Ireland's leading newspapers of the time, *Freeman's Journal*, reported in fulsome prose:

> Yesterday Alderman Bulfin was duly installed Lord Mayor … The distinction is one of which the highest and most ambitious amongst us might be proud, and in offering our congratulations to his Lordship on the honourable position to which he has been elevated by the unanimous

vote of his brother corporators, we do so believing that he deserves the honour, and will honourably acquit himself in the performance of the duties of the office.

The paper went on to forecast:

Peering so far into the future as is permitted, everything seems to promise a year of official ease to his Lordship, the civic horizon does not just now appear clouded.[5]

Freeman's Journal's forecast could not have been less accurate. Just at a time when the Lord Mayor's standing was so high, tragedy struck the family. That very year, in June 1871, Bulfin died suddenly in office, reportedly from typhoid, although his descendants consider it was a heart attack, an affliction which struck many of the family in their prime. Lord Mayor Patrick Bulfin was only fifty-three, and young Edward just eight, a tender age at which to lose one's father.

With no offspring old enough to take on her husband's business, Teresa decided to move to England with her young brood of eight. Four years later she remarried, to another Irishman. Captain Richard Eustace was a Royal Navy surgeon, promoted the year before to Fleet Surgeon, and well known in medical circles for his work on dysentery and malaria (he had been Staff Surgeon during the Ashanti Wars on the Gold Coast three years earlier, when the disembarked Royal Marines were decimated by disease). He must have been devoted to Teresa to take on her large family in addition to his own son Alexander. In 1879 he retired from the service and they settled in the Bournemouth area; he died in 1908 aged seventy-five.

An English Education

Two years before his mother remarried, young Edward had been sent off with his elder brother Joseph to Stonyhurst College, the Jesuit public school in distant Lancashire. Many of the old Ascendancy families of Ireland, as well as prosperous Catholic parents, believed their sons would be best educated in English public schools. Arriving two months short of his eleventh birthday, Edward spent his first two years at the preparatory school there, Hodder. His progress was not impressive. At the end of his first year he was placed twenty-fourth out of a class of twenty-seven, but the following year he showed some improvement, albeit modest, rising to seventeenth place. In his third year, 1875/6, he moved to the College and finished the year twenty-ninth out of thirty-three. Schoolmasters at that time produced notes on their pupils' progress – or lack of it – which were for their own use rather than as formal reports for parents' eyes. Bulfin was described variously as: 'straightforward, fun, cheerful, giddy, buffooning, repugnance to Lat/Gr [Latin/Greek], good temper, slovenly, little study, unsettled'.[6] It would seem that Edward had much to learn, but it should be borne in mind that many other boys received similar comments in their early years, a fellow student, Arthur Conan Doyle, being one of them.

Stonyhurst had a history of sending its alumni to serve in the armed forces. Indeed, in his preface to the Stonyhurst War Record, Bulfin commented on the high number of old boys who had lost their lives in the Great War (out of 1,102 boys who served 207 died, and this from a small school in 1914 of only 382 pupils). 'These figures', he wrote, 'show the spirit animating the old school, and prove the high sense of duty and disregard for self inculcated by Stonyhurst.' He then added:

> May I be allowed to suggest, to those who follow after, a careful study of those words of the great Apostle: 'Honour all men, love the brotherhood, fear God, honour the King'. To my mind these contain the essentials to make us worthy of Stonyhurst and citizens of our glorious Empire.[7]

It is interesting to note that the Irish connection was strong: of Stonyhurst's seven Victoria Cross winners, three were Irish-born and two more had Irish parents.[8]

Then suddenly in 1876, at the age of fourteen, after only one year in the senior College and for reasons not recorded, young Edward was sent to London to attend the newly opened Kensington Catholic Public School at Earl's Court.[9] This school, which had a short and disastrous life, had been established as a limited company by Monsignor Capel, with a capital of £50,000 and these stated objects:

> The establishment and conduct of a School as nearly as possible on the model of the great public schools for the education of the sons of gentlemen … to prepare boys direct for the Universities, the Indian Civil Service and the Army, in strict conformity with the principles and doctrines of the Catholic Church in communion with the See of Rome.[10]

At that time there was still a degree of prejudice against Catholics. Some twenty years earlier, in 1859, Cardinal Newman had started the Oratory School as a Roman Catholic alternative to Eton; it was not tied to any monastic order, as was the case with Benedictine Ampleforth and Downside or Jesuit Stonyhurst. Capel, with a similar dream in mind, started his school in 1873 with five boys and two masters, using a spare kitchen in his private residence in Kensington. He established it more formally in February 1877, by which time it had grown to seventy-three pupils, eleven masters and a chaplain.[11] With grandiose plans in mind, he had commissioned George Goldie, who had been the architect of the magnificent Our Lady of Victories cathedral in Kensington (destroyed in 1940 by German incendiary bombs), to design a school and chapel of similar standing. Almost as soon as the school was underway, Cardinal Manning, the Archbishop of Westminster, was being drawn into questioning its future, and by 1879 the fledgling institution was in severe financial and management difficulties and forced to close. It cannot have been a settled education for young Bulfin, who had already faced so much turbulence in his life. He was only sixteen.

Then, in 1881, he followed his brother Joseph to Trinity College Dublin, to read for a degree.[12] One of the five most ancient universities in the United Kingdom, of which Ireland was then a part, it had a reputation, established in the previous century, of being the university of the Protestant Ascendancy; restrictions on Catholics studying there had only been lifted in 1873.

Soldier of the Queen

However, Bulfin never took his degree but decided instead to join the Army, taking the traditional 'back door' route of a commission in the Militia. It was to Armagh that he headed to join the 3rd Militia Battalion of the Royal Irish Fusiliers,[13] but it was in an English regiment that he gained his regular commission. The 2nd Battalion of the Princess of Wales's Own (Yorkshire Regiment) was then based in the Curragh, the military cantonment outside Dublin, and he joined them in November 1884 at the age of twenty-two.[14] It was not unusual for an Irishman to choose an English regiment, especially as Bulfin had been educated mostly in England. His new regiment, with the colourful informal title the 'Green Howards',[15] had returned from a long tour in India a few years earlier and was looking for new officers to refill its ranks after overseas service. The Green Howards were not considered a fashionable regiment like the Guards or the Rifle Brigade, but had the reputation of being a well respected and steady county infantry regiment, with their base in the North Riding of Yorkshire. The Princess of Wales in their title was Alexandra, the beautiful Danish wife of the future King Edward VII. She had first met the regiment in Sheffield in August 1875, when she presented new Colours and consented to the regiment being designated 'The Princess of Wales's Own'. It was the start of a close association with the royal houses of Denmark and later Norway. In 1914 the then widowed Queen Alexandra became the regiment's first Colonel-in-Chief, with whom Bulfin was later to have much contact as Colonel of the Regiment.

Thirteen years before Bulfin was commissioned, Edward Cardwell, the energetic Liberal Secretary of State, had introduced major reforms to the Army, much needed after the Crimean War, in order to create a coherent military system. The abolition of promotion by purchase was one of the more eye-catching, but he also placed regiments on a stable footing by the 'linked-battalion' system, whereby each infantry regiment consisted of two regular battalions, one serving at home and the other overseas. In order to improve recruiting, regimental depots were set up in the middle of their recruiting areas – regiments now had a home. For the Green Howards it was the lovely market town of Richmond, in the Yorkshire Dales.

Taking the 'back door' route to a regular commission through the Militia was not unusual. In the late 1870s there were nine applicants for every place at Sandhurst or Woolwich. Henry Wilson, who rose to be Field Marshal and Chief of the Imperial General Staff (later to be the only field marshal to be killed on duty, assassinated by Irish nationalists in 1922), made two unsuccessful attempts at Woolwich (then the Royal Military Academy) and three at Sandhurst (then the Royal Military College).[16] So Bulfin was in fine company. What efforts he made to enter Sandhurst are not known, but his unsettled academic record would not have put him in a strong position.

Bulfin served with the 2nd Battalion for six uneventful years, initially in Ireland and then in England, before sailing to India on New Year's Day in 1890, for what would be a nineteen-year tour for the battalion.[17] The year before, he suffered a personal tragedy in the loss of his elder brother Joseph, doubtless a father figure to him, who died in India aged only thirty-one while serving as an army surgeon.[18]

India was his first experience of the East. The battalion's station for the first three years was Bangalore, set 3,000ft above sea level on the Deccan Plateau of southern India and blessed by pleasant weather throughout the year. The cantonment was one of the largest British Army stations in India, covering some thirteen square miles outside the old city, the seat of the Maharajah of Mysore. It was a town in its own right, where the European population was self-contained, with all the sports and entertainment typical of garrison life in the Raj. It would have been a very comfortable, but untaxing, existence for the young lieutenant.

But in October 1892 the prospect of active service beckoned when orders were received to move to Upper Burma. Three small parties had sailed ahead of the main body for conversion to mounted infantry platoons, to carry out reconnaissance and patrolling tasks (the cavalry was trained as an *arme blanche* – a strike force – and was therefore unsuited to this lighter and more mobile role). Countrymen were plentiful in the regiment, so mounted work on the small local ponies came easily to them.

Since the Green Howards had last served in Burma, some twenty-four years earlier, the whole country had come under British rule. Upper Burma had been annexed after the Third Burma War in 1885, a conflict that had arisen because of the threat of French penetration from their colonial territory to the east in what is now Laos.

Since the occupation of Bhamo, a town close to the Chinese border, following this war, the indigenous Kachin Hills tribesmen had been reluctant to accept outside rule. Bands of armed bandits, locally termed *dacoits*, caused the local military police to send out punitive expeditions in an effort to control this unruly region. The *dacoits* were not easy to pin down in the hilly jungle, where they had the advantage of being able to seek refuge in nearby China. So once again the Green Howards were stationed on Burma's border, based upon Shwebo and Bhamo, places now well known to Western tourists visiting Mandalay and the surrounding countryside.

In December 1892 a British column was ambushed en route to Sima, north of Bhamo, near where an outpost was to be constructed. The column included Lieutenant Dent, a brother Yorkshire Regiment officer of Bulfin's, who was badly wounded in the neck. At the same time, the town of Myitkyina to the north-west was raided, its garrison commander Captain Morton falling mortally wounded; the surgeon who brought him into the fort received the Victoria Cross for his gallantry. In January 1893 a sizeable relieving force of some 1,200 British and Indian troops, organized into mobile columns, was dispatched to reinforce these threatened outposts, with some fierce fighting ensuing. Lieutenant Bulfin was selected to command one of these mobile columns of mounted infantry, and this expedition provided the excitement and responsibility any young officer would relish. The Green Howards journal of 1893 included a tongue-in-cheek report from Shwebo of a later expedition that year :

> Rather an amusing incident happened on the last column. Our men were toiling along the hilly jungle path which leads to Lower Palup, Thomas, with his collar well open and his helmet wrong way round, perspiring copiously and thinking of rations, relatives and rum. Suddenly came the sound of a ragged volley from the front. Our leader raised his hand, and we stood like carved images of stone. One man kept his head, a lance-corporal. He ran rapidly to our commander with a pocket-book and pencil, and, in a voice choking with suppressed excitement, gurgled: 'Sir, please note that at 4.45 p.m. on this 4th day of March, 1893, the 2nd Battalion Yorkshire Regiment first came into action since it was raised. We shall have a battle on our colours at last!' By the way, Bulfin says he *did* see fighting. The crossing of the Pakoi Khar and the storming of Warror Kran under heavy fire he declares knocks the Redan business[19] into pulp. There is no doubt about the heavy firing, but we only heard of one mule and seven pigs having been hit.[20]

Allowing for a degree of leg-pulling in this account, it is nevertheless clear that Bulfin had enjoyed the opportunity of independent command. Not for nothing was this campaign called the 'subalterns' war'. For this experience of active service, albeit in an unglamorous counter-insurgency role, he was awarded his first campaign medal, Kachin Hills 1892–93, with clasp.

A further couple of years followed back in Bangalore before Bulfin was promoted captain in January 1895, aged thirty-two. In the Mess he enjoyed the reputation of being 'a humorous companion with a merry wit', and he was a leading light in the battalion's dramatic club, where 'he sang a good song with a strong bass voice'.[21]

The next year he was invalided home to England, with an undisclosed illness, and posted to the regimental depot at Richmond. During this time he took the opportunity to return to Ireland to visit his family's ancestral home at Derrinlough, before taking up his new appointment as garrison adjutant in Dover, the headquarters of South East Command.

In every career officer's progress a degree of luck, coupled with fortunate timing, is essential in getting noticed outside the confines of regimental life. 1898 was to be Bulfin's year. Whilst fulfilling his routine but responsible job in Dover, a large and strategically important military base, he had the previous year come to the notice of the general commanding troops in the south-east of England, Sir William Butler.

Butler had his residence in Dover Castle and must have approved of this captain's ability. A fellow Irishman and Catholic, also educated by the Jesuits, there was an evident rapport between the two men. Although better known as the husband of the famous Victorian artist, Elizabeth Butler, the painter of 'The Roll Call', 'Quatre Bras', 'Scotland Forever' and 'The Defence of Rorke's Drift', amongst many other patriotic pictures, the general had had a full and colourful career to date. Brought up in Co. Tipperary, his earliest recollections were of the sufferings and evictions following the potato famine of the 1840s. One of the 'Wolseley Ring', sometimes known as the 'Ashanti Ring', he had taken part in many of Victoria's 'small wars'. He made his name in Canada on the Red River, then served in West Africa on the Ashanti expedition of 1873 and later in the relief of Khartoum. During his time in the Sudan he would have fought alongside the Green Howards, whilst commanding a brigade at the battle of Ginnis against the Mahdi's forces in 1885. Butler had had experience of the prejudice against Catholics when, as a lieutenant colonel, he had been selected by the Marquess of Ripon, the Viceroy of India, to be his private secretary, but was turned down by

Gladstone on the grounds of his faith.[22] He also got to know South Africa whilst serving on Wolseley's staff in Natal in 1875, at the time when the latter was governor and high commissioner. Even there, Butler was treated with some disapproval. Lady Wolseley, a Church of Ireland Protestant from Co. Cork, later referred to him as a 'very *imperfect* gentleman'.[23] One of his responsibilities was to report on the land system then in force in the colony, and this knowledge was shortly to become invaluable, as well as unwelcome.

Butler was a radical soldier and a fine writer with forthright views. A defender of the underdog throughout his life, it would land him in deep water on his next assignment. As Ian Beckett commented, 'To reach high rank as an Irish Catholic nationalist was unusual, but it was the more so given the sympathy Butler showed for the crown's opponents in many of his campaigns.'[24] When his wife was painting 'The Defence of Rorke's Drift', Butler remarked, 'One more painting like this and you will drive me mad.' Having served in the Zulu War, he admired this warrior nation; some suspected he preferred the Zulus to the English. Whilst he held the belief that 'obedience is the first duty of a soldier', he also thought the soldier had the right to know what he was fighting for. He wrote: 'The nation that will insist on drawing a broad line of demarcation between the fighting man and the thinking man is liable to find its fighting done by fools and its thinking done by cowards.'[25]

When General Goodenough, the Commander-in-Chief in South Africa, died suddenly in October 1898, Butler was selected to replace him. The High Commissioner at the time was Sir Alfred Milner, a brilliant public servant but somewhat in the mould of a Roman proconsul; he was coming to the belief that the only way to resolve the difficulties with Paul Kruger, the dour old President of the Boer Republic of Transvaal and an impediment to British territorial ambitions from Cairo to the Cape, was by war. Milner held the democratic process in some contempt and was determined to further his policy of pushing the Boers to war, often bullying Joseph Chamberlain, the Secretary for the Colonies, into supporting him. When he needed a new army commander he urged that the successor should be a man 'of energy and resource and of some political sense, rather than some worn-out Lieutenant-General'.[26] As events turned out, Butler could not have been a less suitable choice. Alarm bells should have been ringing even louder in Whitehall when Milner also decided to take three months' leave in England, leaving Butler as acting High Commissioner in Cape Town. In the little time available to acquaint himself, whilst in London, with the situation in South Africa, including an interview of less than half an hour with an unforthcoming Secretary for the Colonies, Butler was given no indication of any trouble brewing, or of Milner's home-coming.

South Africa with Butler

Bulfin's moment came when Butler set sail to Cape Town in November of that year, taking him as his aide-de-camp and assistant military secretary. It was a role which would allow this captain to witness, at close hand, the pressures of high command and political decision-making during a critical phase in Anglo-Boer relations.

Equally momentous events were taking place in Bulfin's personal life during that year of 1898. At the beginning of the year, on 11 January, at the age of thirty-five, he married Frances (known as Fanny) Mary Lonergan at the fashionable London church of St James's, Spanish Place. Also from an Irish family, but now living in London in Portman Square, Fanny was eleven years his junior. Both her parents had died some three years earlier, her father in Monaco. It was a very regimental wedding; the four bridesmaids were dressed in white satin dresses and green velvet hats adorned with white ostrich feathers, and their bouquets were also green and white, reflecting the bridegroom's regimental colours. The bride celebrated her ancestry with a flounce of old Irish lace on her wedding dress, given her by the groom's mother. The best man was Lieutenant Wilfred Dent, our gallant officer from Sima, and 'the presents were numerous and costly', carefully listed in the *Green Howards Gazette* report on the wedding.[27] That evening, the newly-weds set off on honeymoon to Paris, Rome and then the Riviera.

On 8 November their first child was born, Edward Francis Joseph, known as Eddie, a mere four days before Bulfin sailed to Cape Town with his new master, the sole staff officer to accompany him. Aboard the *Hawarden Castle*, three days out from Southampton, they passed the *Scot*, homeward bound carrying Sir Alfred Milner. Next morning they reached Madeira, where Butler found 'a long and very interesting letter from the home-going Governor … the mention of a likelihood of any trouble arising in South Africa during my temporary tenure of office was conspicuous by its absence'.[28]

The four-week voyage south gave the two men the opportunity to get to know each other better, as well as to savour some amusement provided by their fellow passengers. A gentleman dealing in gramophones and, somewhat strangely, stockings, offended Butler, who noted, 'One evening he gave us a performance in the saloon upon these excruciating instruments of torture'; he declined an invitation for them to dine with this passenger. The night before their arrival in Cape Town, Butler recorded:

> I said to my staff-officer [Bulfin], 'It is worth getting up at daylight to-morrow to see Table Mountain at sunrise.' We did so. The ship was anchored in the outer harbour; the great mountain was in all its superb glory flushed with rose pink. A solitary boat had already approached the ship, carrying a couple of police-officers. While my staff-officer was regarding with admiration the glory of the Cape Peninsula, he saw the police-officers leading out between them the gentleman of the gramophones, in handcuffs, over the ship's side. I signed his extradition papers the next morning.[29]

The miscreant turned out to be the absconding fraudulent secretary of a London company.

At noon Butler took the oaths of office and, with his ADC, began work immediately. On 12 December he set off with Bulfin by special train on a forty-eight-hour journey to Grahamstown, through the vast open spaces of the Karoo, with distant glimpses of the blue Drakensberg mountains. It was Butler's third time in South Africa, yet he was as excited by the huge skies of Africa as was his ADC. The purpose of the journey was to open a large exhibition, to which all the states of South Africa were invited. At a public lunch on the 17th for some 250 guests Butler gave a largely impromptu speech extolling the virtues of peace. This was applauded by the Boers, as well as by the Prime Minister of Cape Colony, but denounced by those foreigners, mostly British, who had flocked in massive numbers to the Transvaal since gold was discovered. The Boers called these foreigners 'Uitlanders', and tensions were growing fast between the two communities. Butler was on a collision course, not only with the Uitlanders, but also with those who had vested political interests in provoking confrontation.

On his return to Cape Town, two days before Christmas, the acting High Commissioner was presented with a clear manifestation of Uitlander trouble-making. As Butler described the matter in his autobiography, 'The year was not destined to close without further complications. A man of British nationality had been shot by a policeman in a midnight brawl in a low quarter of Johannesburg'.[30] The killing of Tom Edgar by a Boer policeman precipitated a petition demanding British intervention, which Butler refused to forward to London. Relations now worsened further. For Bulfin, being close to the corridors of power for the first time in his career and helping Butler to draft his reports to London, this tense prelude to war must have been a most formative experience.

Whilst at Grahamstown, his cousin Jack almost ran into 'Ned', as Edward was called by his Irish relatives. Jack had been attending the same exhibition. Having left the British Army, he had headed to South Africa a few years earlier to seek his fortune, starting in Port Elizabeth, where he was enjoying the freedom and opportunities of this blossoming country. He had held a colourful range of jobs, from cab driver to racehorse trainer and ostrich dealer, but was soon to become fatally involved in 'a damn good row' as he called the forthcoming war.[31]

January was spent more pleasantly visiting the old Dutch settlements of Paarl and Stellenbosch to open agricultural shows, before Milner returned in mid-February. Initially, relations were cordial between the two men, Milner writing home that Butler 'has behaved perfectly well towards me on my return. He does not meddle in political affairs in any way.'[32] Butler returned gladly to his military duties and took himself off with Bulfin, as a single staff officer, to inspect the frontiers of the British colonies of the Cape and Natal, in order to prepare a scheme of defence in the event of hostilities. But the War Office also wanted Butler to investigate the option of a more offensive response – crossing the frontier into Boer territory, something which, with the weak forces available to him, would in Butler's judgement be courting disaster. By withholding his report from the War Office until June he did not help his position in Whitehall. When it was received, there was evident frustration that Butler had not answered the questions posed to him.

Some of the strain of political life in Cape Town was relieved for Butler and Bulfin by the arrival of their respective wives and children in mid-March, a month after Milner had returned. Lady Butler, her maid and nurse, plus three daughters, had sailed from Southampton on 18 February on the *Carisbrook Castle*. They were accompanied by Fanny Bulfin, her son Eddie (two months old) and her maid (the last three listed on the ship's manifest as Irish, unlike her husband). Once in Cape Town, settling into their home at Rosebank, where 'Table Mountain rises square and precipitous above our garden', Lady Butler became quickly aware of the pressures with which her husband was dealing: 'Would that all the evil brought to South Africa by the finding of gold could be gathered together and burnt on that altar as a peace-offering.'[33]

Bulfin still found time to continue his enjoyment of amateur dramatics, in which he 'played the villain with unparalleled zest and humour'.[34] Moreover, both families succeeded in getting out of Cape Town and relaxing together. Lady Butler's diary continued:

On Whitsun-eve we had a most enchanting expedition to Stellenbosch and the Paarl … W., I, the children and the B.'s formed the party. We left home just at sunrise, the heavy dew warning us of a very hot winter's day though it was then cold enough. We took the train to Stellenbosch, and I was in ecstasies over the perfect loveliness of the scenes we passed through as the train climbed towards those deeply serrated mountains.

From Stellenbosch they travelled on into the mountains in a cart drawn by a mixed team of six horses and mules:

We lit a fire and spread our repast under the shade of the oak at the edge of a wood that sloped down to a mountain stream. All around the solemn mountains, all about us fragrant aromatic flowers and the call of wild African birds! I can well understand the passionate love an Africander-born must feel for his country.[35]

May saw the annual Queen's Birthday Review on the plain at Green Point, where General Butler, accompanied by his ADC, rode up on his big grey to give the Governor the royal salute before leading 'Three cheers for Her Majesty the Queen!' As his wife wrote in her diary, 'A prophet might have seen the War Spectre moving through the ranks of red-coats behind the General.'[36]

Behind these customary scenes of colonial ritual Butler's relationship with Milner was deteriorating. After the Bloemfontein conference in early June, when old Kruger left the negotiations with tears in his eyes, repeating to Milner, 'It is our country you want', Milner decided he needed a new Commander-in-Chief, one with whom he could see eye to eye and in whom he could have confidence. Milner was further infuriated when Butler telegraphed the War Office on 23 June; having been asked for his observations on troop levels and stores, Butler stated: 'I believe that war between the white races coming as a sequel to the Jameson raid and the subsequent events of the last three years, *would be the greatest calamity that ever occurred in South Africa* [Butler's emphasis].'[37]

As Milner himself wryly commented to his general after another disagreement, 'It can never be said, Sir William Butler, that *you* precipitated a conflict with the Dutch';[38] Milner also recorded in his diary, 'Butler or I will have to go.'[39]

On 4 July Butler wrote to the War Office tendering his resignation as Commander-in-Chief. The War and Colonial Offices hesitated in their reply, worrying that, on the one hand, acceptance of Butler's resignation would signal a forthcoming war, whilst on the other, failure to support Milner would not only put him in an impossible position but also undermine Britain's strategic intentions towards South Africa. Butler had to go, however, and on 9 August his resignation was accepted by Her Majesty's Government.

Sir Hew Strachan's assessment of Butler's time is succinct:

Charged with political and military responsibilities at a time of high tension in Anglo-Boer relations, Butler had sought to appease rather than to confront. To him was passed some of the blame for Britain's unpreparedness for war.[40]

Butler wrote to William Schreiner, the Prime Minister of the Cape Colony, prior to his departure: 'Try to remember me as one who did his best, according to his lights, for South Africa and her peoples.'[41]

Lady Butler wrote sadly in her diary:

We left on the 23rd August '99 on a day of blinding rain, which, as the ship moved off, drew like a curtain across that country which I felt we were leaving to a fast-approaching trouble. The war cloud was descending. It burst in blood and fire a few weeks later and deepened the sense of melancholy with which I shall ever think of that far-away land.[42]

Accompanying the Butler family were Fanny Bulfin and Eddie, but Fanny's husband did not sail with her and their young son back to England. As Britain headed inexorably towards war through September and into October, Edward Bulfin, now bereft of job and family, remained in Cape Town awaiting a new post. This experienced captain's knowledge of the country and recent events would now be put to good use in his most testing appointment so far.

For Bulfin 'the association [serving under Butler] proved to be a happy one'.[43] Beyond the evident rapport between the two men and their families, the wonders of the Cape provided a heady time for Edward and Fanny to enjoy married life with their young son. Moreover, the nine months observing the unorthodox Butler at work furnished an object lesson for Bulfin about the tensions that frequently exist between the military and politicians, and the degree to which generals can afford to be 'political'. The late Victorian Army had an internal political culture of patronage and infighting amongst its generals, manifested in the competition between the Wolseley and Roberts 'rings'; this would shock a modern soldier, unaccustomed to the degree to which senior generals were then 'deeply politicized and well versed in the arts of political intrigue'.[44] Bulfin, whose previous experience had been limited mostly to the inward-looking tribalism of regimental soldiering, must have found his time in Cape Town a profoundly educational experience.[45]

Chapter 2

1899–1902
The Boer War – 'No end of a lesson'

After the failure of the Bloemfontein talks in the early summer of 1899, Britain and the Boer Republics had started making preparations for war. Butler's controversial report to the War Office had warned that 200,000 men would be required to defeat the Boers, whilst Field Marshal Wolseley, the Commander-in-Chief in London, had warned the Government of the need to mobilize and equip an expeditionary force in good time. He believed, unlike the Cabinet, that the Boers would stand and fight, although he was confident that, after a short campaign in Natal, the British would be on the march, even reaching Pretoria by Christmas. But, as so often happens, the response was that the costs of such a force would be prohibitive and that its mobilization might unnecessarily antagonize the Boers. Eventually, Britain dispatched its largest expeditionary force for nearly a century, bigger than that sent to the Crimea in 1854. The commander was to be the well respected but reluctant Sir Redvers Buller, who had won a Victoria Cross in the Zulu War. Even as late as 7 October, the Colonial Secretary had commented to the Chancellor of the Exchequer, 'My own opinion is, as it has always been, that both Milner and the military authorities greatly exaggerate the risks of this campaign.'[1]

Arrayed against the British were the Boers, burgher farmers who were expert horsemen, excellent shots and knew their country intimately. Their new-found wealth in gold and diamonds had enabled them to purchase modern weapons, both Mauser rifles and Krupp artillery. The Boers did not wait for Buller's corps to arrive but issued an ultimatum, which was welcomed with some delight in the corridors of power in London. After this expired on 11 October, in the small hours of the next day the Boer 'commandos' – mounted units raised from their towns and districts – rode across the border to invade Natal. The Boers were about to teach the British, in Kipling's famous words, 'no end of a lesson'.

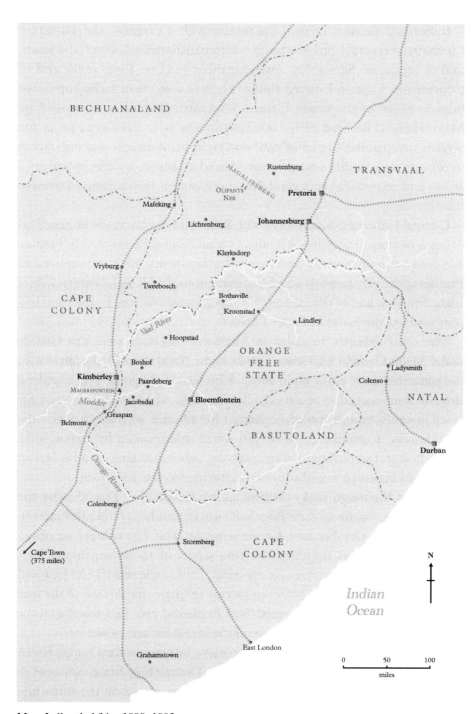

Map 1. South Africa 1899–1902.

Buller had decided to split his forces, with a division, the 1st under Lieutenant General Lord Methuen, which had disembarked in Cape Town, told to march on Kimberley. Awaiting them in Cape Town at the end of October was Captain Edward Bulfin. He was now about to be appointed brigade-major to the newly formed 9 Infantry Brigade, commanded by Major General Richard Fetherstonhaugh.[2] The post was a key one, as the brigade commander's chief of staff and right hand man; it was only given to officers with ability and promise. Ahead of Bulfin lay the prospect of action and responsibility, a good deal more serious than fighting Burmese bandits.

General Fetherstonhaugh was a 60th Rifles officer who would be ridiculed by some modern historians for foolhardy leadership at Belmont.[3] His brigade was drawn from renowned county infantry regiments: 1st Northumberland Fusiliers ('the Fighting 5th'), 2nd Northamptons, 2nd King's Own Yorkshire Light Infantry, half of the 1st Loyal North Lancashires (the Loyals) and two companies of the Royal Munster Fusiliers.

The other infantry brigades in Methuen's division were the Guards under Major General Sir Henry Colvile and a Naval Brigade, the latter with the added bonus of a few rapid-firing 4.7in naval field guns. The Highland Brigade was retained in reserve. Buller had refused Methuen's request for more mounted troops; hence he started his advance with about 800 – the 9th Lancers, a colonial corps of 150 scouts commanded by Major Mike Rimington and some mounted infantry. As Nelson had lamented his lack of frigates, so Methuen would suffer from having too few horsemen.

Amongst the tough ranks of Rimington's Guides (or 'Tigers', after the leopardskin hatbands on their Boer hats) was cousin John (Jack) Bulfin, who had joined that October as a farrier sergeant. The Tigers were recruited from Uitlanders and colonials, the elite scouts of the army, though 'not men I would invite to bivouac on my estate', as Colvile remarked.[4] Jack and Edward would be drawn together in a string of battles for the rest of the year and did their best to keep in touch: 'Ned Bulfin did poor Jack many a favour and of whom he [Jack] spoke in the very best and highest praise.'[5]

The 1st Division's initial task was to move by train to the Orange River, close to the border of Cape Colony and the Orange Free State. Adjacent to the railway station the regimental bell-tents were erected on the soft white sand, orders were issued and final preparations made for the dusty advance into Boer country. Although everyone was shocked by the recent news of the sieges of Kimberley and Mafeking, and the worse news of General White's blunders in being forced back to Ladysmith, morale remained high.

Their commander was a tall and determined Scots Guardsman, the youngest lieutenant general in the British Army. Paul Stanford, 3rd Baron Methuen, took his profession seriously and was not new to the challenges of fighting in Africa, with service behind him in Bechuanaland (now Botswana) as well as the Sudan and Cape Town. He knew the Boers and respected their fighting skill and mobility. For the next year Captain Bulfin's fortunes would be very much tied up with those of his divisional commander.

Although Methuen would have preferred to await the arrival of more mounted troops, Buller pressed him to get on, and by Monday, 20 November he was preparing to cross the river the following day. Ahead of his troops, many of them recently recalled reservists, lay a 74-mile march across the arid Great Karoo to Kimberley. In the heat of an African summer, the open veldt interspersed with blue-grey *kopjes* (hills) 'presented the very incarnation of the spirit of desolation'.[6] Holed up in Kimberley was the long-suffering Colonel Kekewich, constantly goaded by an impatient and interfering Cecil Rhodes. Methuen calculated it would take a week to relieve the garrison, with at least one battle. 'I shall breakfast in Kimberley on Monday', he told his wife.[7]

Methuen has often been criticized for marching north along the line of the railway towards Kimberley, openly heralding his approach to the Boers and showing little guile. But he did not have the logistic flexibility or the mounted troops to do much else than stick to the railway; water was scarce, he lacked animal transport and he needed to secure the railway in order to evacuate the non-combatants from Kimberley. As with most British commanders in this short conventional campaign, he suffered from poor maps, sketchy intelligence of the enemy and a strange unwillingness to make a detailed reconnaissance. Speed, coupled with trust in the numerical superiority and pluck of his troops, would hopefully carry the day. The 1st Division gained a reputation for endurance in marching long distances at speed, often at night, their equipment stripped down to the essentials. Later the division would gain the nicknames 'Beechams' ('because we relieve everybody'), 'Methuen's Moonlighters' or the 'Mobile Marvels'.[8] Officers had no special privileges and were ordered to take off any item of dress which would mark them out as such. Their commander led by example and slept in a Mexican poncho. On 19 November Methuen wrote home:

> As likely as not, I may have to see no more tents this side of January or my plum pudding. No officer has a sword, all rifles, no marks on their [uniforms], and [look] like the men. I am in a Boer hat, a pair of Norwegian slippers, khaki trousers, and short sleeves, looking the most disreputable man in camp.[9]

For Bulfin this would have been an exciting and hectic time, with a lot to learn in getting this new brigade organized and ready for action.

On the eve of battle Methuen turned to his intelligence officer and proclaimed: 'My good fellow, I intend to put the fear of God into these people.'[10] This late Victorian army, shackled by its long experience of colonial warfare, was about to receive a most rude awakening.

Belmont

Methuen expected to first encounter the Boers about 19 miles to the north, near the rail station at Belmont. Although the enemy were on ground of their own choice, 1st Division's speed of approach took them by surprise.

The Boers, led by the inexperienced Free Stater, Jacobus Prinsloo, had placed their commandos on two lines of *kopjes* which ran parallel to the east of the railway. The first objectives for the 1st Division were Gun Hill and, just to the north, Table Mountain. Once these were taken, the next range would be attacked, dominated by the higher Mont Blanc. The capture of the latter *kopje* was the key to unlocking the route north.

Methuen decided that the best method of getting close to the Boer positions would be a night march by his three brigades, followed by a dawn attack against the Boer right flank – tactics he had learned from Wolseley and Roberts.[11] He appreciated that such an approach would demand a great deal of skill from his troops and, from his experiences during the Tirah campaign on the North-West Frontier, knew the importance of his infantry keeping well dispersed and using any available cover once in view of the enemy. Indeed, Colonel Denny of the Northamptons had already drummed these tactical lessons into his men before the battle.[12]

'The lion's share of the fighting' was to be given to 9 Brigade. By 3.00 am on 23 November the battalions, supported by the Naval Brigade, had started their 2-mile night march across the open plain from Thomas's Farm, crossing the railway line and aiming for Table Mountain. The 9th Lancers and some mounted troops secured their left flank, whilst the Gunners were placed to shell the Boer positions. It was a sound plan and, with the Northumberlands on the left, the Northamptons on the right and the King's Own Yorkshire Light Infantry (KOYLI) and Munsters in reserve, the brigade advanced on Table Mountain in darkness. Navigation was good, and although the Northamptons were exposed to some heavy fire from Gun Hill, intense volley fire from their ranks allowed the crest of Table Mountain to be won. As the sun rose with its African urgency, the Northumberlands were able to advance, and by dawn the brigade had cleared the western side of Table Mountain. Their regimental history records:

> The men were in the best of spirits, cracking jokes while advancing under quite heavy fire. One very fat man, a greengrocer from Northampton and a Reservist, was carrying a rope round his waist which he said he had brought to hang Kruger.[13]

So far, all had gone to plan, and the 9th's commander and his brigade-major must have been pleased with their battalions' performance in this first contact with the enemy.

However, the advance by the Guards Brigade to the right met with immediate difficulties. Faulty map reading meant they ended up at the foot of a precipitous slope, not on the expected open flank of the Boers, and in full view of the enemy in daylight. Casualties, although heavy, were mitigated by the Grenadiers being well dispersed and hidden in dead ground as they climbed the steep incline, reaching the crest of Gun Hill with a bayonet charge and driving the Boers off the *kopje*. At 4.50 am the second phase of the battle opened with an artillery barrage on Mont Blanc. With no horse artillery yet available, a few field guns had been dragged up the slopes, but they made little impact on the Boer positions.

The advancing 9 Brigade, now in full view of the enemy, met punishing Boer fire from the north and south-east ridges of Table Mountain, supported by further fire from Mont Blanc, and their attempt to sweep across

Table Mountain to the northern side of Mont Blanc got bogged down. Fetherstonhaugh and Bulfin, still mounted, rode between the lines of infantry, encouraging them on but, to the irritation of the men, obscuring their line of fire as well as drawing the enemy's. A Geordie from the Northumberlands shouted out, 'Domn thee, Get thee to hell and let's fire.'[14] It was a while later that Bulfin lost his commander, shot in the right shoulder, and the brigade was handed over to Colonel Money of the Northumberlands. It was a lively time for the brigade-major, demanding a cool head under fire.

Methuen, well forward behind his leading troops, saw that the two brigades were diverging and had the presence of mind to correct their line of advance and adjust his plan. It now fell to the Guards Brigade, rather than supporting the 9th on to Mont Blanc, to bear the brunt of the battle and make an unexpected frontal assault on this final objective which they carried out with great *élan*.

Belmont dissolved very much into a soldier's battle, characterized by hard local skirmishes by small groups of determined men to seize the next *kopje* and drive off the enemy. As General Colvile wrote, 'The men did for themselves what no general would have dared ask of them.'[15] Frustratingly – and this would happen again and again – once these exhausted men had taken the final objective (Mont Blanc), they watched as hundreds of Boer horsemen cantered away on their ponies north across the veldt, unharmed by the overstretched cavalry and artillery. In the case of Belmont, Methuen had sent urgent messages to the 9th Lancers to cut off the Boers, but their horses were 'done in' and they were too few in number. The horse artillery were exhausted, their mounts not watered since the day started, and the naval guns, the only ones with the range to catch the Boers, could not be dragged up Mont Blanc in time.

By 7.30 am the Battle of Belmont was over, some three and a half hours after the first shots were fired. It was a British victory, albeit an expensive one,[16] which could have been decisive if Methuen had been given the assets to cut off the retreating Boers.

By 10.30 am the bloodied 9th Brigade was back in its bivouac area near the railway, and the wounded were evacuated to Orange River. For the Free Staters it was also a chastening initiation into modern warfare; a prisoner complained, 'What's the use of firing at you? You still come on.'[17]

Graspan

The division, with little delay, pushed on up the railway towards Kimberley, which Methuen was still confident of reaching on 27 November. He expected the main force of Boers to be north of the Modder River. The next day, he heard that about 400 of them were on the *kopjes* just north-east of Graspan Siding, some 11 miles north. In fact, many Free Staters, shaken by Belmont, had fallen back further north to Ramdam. This left Prinsloo and his remnants to support de la Rey with his Transvaal commando in taking up a defensive position at Graspan. Here a total of some 2,000–2,500 Boers were dug in on the *kopjes* awaiting the British advance.

At fifty-two, de la Rey, known as Koos, was two years younger than his British adversary. 'Deeply religious; a small pocket Bible rarely out of his hand … [he had] a prematurely patriarchal appearance. And he was a man of formidable silences.'[18] A veteran of the First Boer War, in which he was the youngest officer present, he was an indomitable fighter and one of the outstanding Boer commanders of the war. He and Methuen would earn each other's respect and, after the war, form a friendship.

Once again, Methuen was confronted with the problem of not being free to skirt the Boers. He also knew there was no water between Belmont and the Modder River, a distance of 32 miles. So he was faced with no option but to take on the enemy and in the late afternoon of the 24th he marched his troops towards Graspan. Methuen accompanied the reconnaissance party in person, finding nothing to change his view that he was only facing a small force.

Unlike Belmont, where Methuen had used the infantry to march by night to seize the *kopjes* at dawn with the bayonet, this time his plan was that an artillery barrage would drive the small enemy force off their positions, whilst his flanking mounted troops would sweep round and capture the fleeing Boers. The guns would be brought up at night, protected by the 9th and Naval Brigades accompanying them.

Having pushed his force forward through the night, the artillery came into action in the early hours of the 25th on another blistering day, the hottest of the war so far. It soon became apparent that Methuen, once again, was acting under woefully inaccurate information.

What he had hoped would be a short, sharp action, giving the Naval Brigade, frustrated at not firing a shot at Belmont, the chance to prove themselves, now turned out to be another hard-fought frontal assault for the infantry. Even more alarmingly, his flanking mounted troops to the east were attacked by a superior force of Boers, and Methuen hurriedly heliographed the Guards to come up and reinforce his right flank.

It fell to the Naval Brigade, a brigade only in name, being a mixed force of some 245 sailors and marines, to take centre stage. They were faced with storming the prominent *kopje* in full view of the enemy, with the KOYLI in close support and the rest of 9 Brigade attacking on the left. Tragically, the inexperienced Naval Brigade ignored Methuen's directive about dress and tactics so, with their CO waving his sword and leading his men in disciplined close order, they assaulted the Boer position with the sort of hopeless gallantry which the British public love: 'Their matchless charge was to thrill an England where eyes were moist on reading how a terrier followed a major of the Marines into battle and stood over his dying master.'[19] Although the KOYLI suffered badly, the remainder of the brigade escaped relatively lightly. Once again, the Boers trotted away unmolested to fight another day.

This was Bulfin's second battle, 'a trying fight' as Methuen described the brigade's work in his Dispatches.[20] Bulfin was to receive warm accolades in these dispatches, one from Colonel Money, his second commander in as many days : 'My staff Captain Bulfin and Lieutenant Taylor rendered me great assistance and were near me at the final assault.'[21] More importantly, Methuen reported: 'Captain Bulfin, the Brigade Major, on whose shoulders a great responsibility rested, did admirable work.'[22]

The British had paid a heavy price for these two small victories at Belmont and Graspan, and the reality of modern warfare had shaken many of Methuen's men. It was the same for the Boers, although their casualties were lighter; but their morale was fragile, and even some of de la Rey's men were 'streaming off to their homes'.[23]

After fighting two battles in three days, some officers of the 1st Division were expressing doubts about their commander's tactical judgement. 'It seems to be the habit of our commanding officers to find out the strongest position of the enemy and then attack him in front', remarked one; to which a Guards colonel responded with a certain clairvoyance, 'It appears to me we attack the enemy first and then find out his position.'[24]

But it was de la Rey who learnt the main lesson from these early encounters, appreciating that relying on holding hill tops only invited defeat; their crests offered excellent artillery targets and the steep slopes provided cover to any attacking force once it had reached the base. Concealment on level ground, away from obvious hill features, would also allow a more effective field of fire for the long-range, flat trajectory of modern rifles.

As the soldiers made what efforts they could to bivouac comfortably that night, without tents and short of clean water, for the first time a searchlight flashed against the sky to the north, a signal that Kimberley was holding out. The next day, Sunday, a day of rest, albeit suffered under flies and dust, brought a strange sight. 'Thus the appearance of the camp by daylight was that of a great gipsy encampment, where similar shelter, but on more extended and serviceable lines, suffices for the English Bedouin', observed the amused war correspondent Alfred Kinnear.[25] The division then set off on Monday and by the following afternoon they were at Wittekop, 6 miles south of the Modder River. They had marched and fought 50 of the 74 miles to Kimberley.

That Monday Bulfin received his third brigade commander, Major General Reggie Pole-Carew, newly promoted from holding a colonel's post on Buller's staff. A Coldstream Guardsman, he was a popular officer, called 'Polly' by his friends, and had accompanied Lord Roberts as his ADC on the famous march from Kabul to Kandahar. Known as a 'smart, dapper fellow even in the midst of battle … one of the few officers to shave every morning in camp … giving out orders at the same time',[26] more importantly he proved to be clear-headed and unruffled in action. Bulfin was to learn a great deal from him.

Modder River

Whilst the division were on the march, signals were being flashed to Methuen from Kimberley that the Boers intended to make their stand at Spytfontein, a line of *kopjes* ten miles south of the town. It seemed the Boers were moving away from their supply base at Jacobsdal and hence would not be holding the Modder river line to Methuen's front in any strength. He responded to this intelligence with a boldly ambitious plan: to carry out a 25-mile flanking march with five days of supplies, seize Jacobsdal, cross the Modder river and then turn north-west and attack the flanks of Spytfontein, the final obstacle before relieving Kimberley.

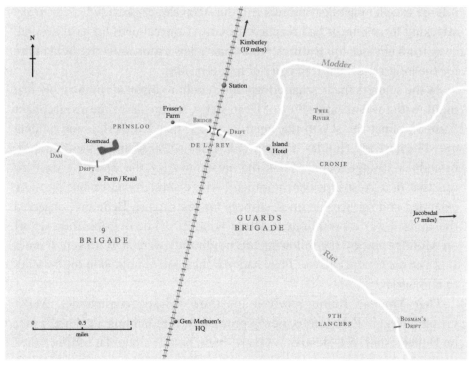

Map 2. Modder River.

Then Methuen received news from the mounted reconnaissance forays that the Boers were digging in along the banks of the Modder and Riet Rivers, the 9th Lancers putting the enemy strength at 4,000. This was shortly underlined by a loyal station-master's information that they were 'burrowing like rabbits'. Although Methuen seriously doubted the numbers, he realized he could not ignore this threat to his lines of communication. Once again he changed his plans at the very last moment and cancelled the flank march. Still convinced the main Boer force was at Spytfontein, he reckoned a sudden overwhelming frontal attack on this delaying rear-guard would easily rout them – as he wrote to Buller, 'It is a mere question of pluck.'[27]

In times of peace for the good citizens of Kimberley, the confluence of the Modder and Riet rivers had seemed the African equivalent of Henley, a delightful weekend retreat with a very nostalgic English feel. The tree-lined riverside, the Island Hotel and the dam at Rosmead were places for relaxation, family picnics and excursions in rowing boats, not for a clash of armies.

The only map and ground description Methuen had was a poorly drawn sketch made six weeks earlier by a Sapper captain. It was inaccurate in almost every detail, most critically in stating that the rivers were easily fordable and that both banks were dominated by higher covered ground to the south. It failed also to show that the line of the Riet ran parallel to Methuen's advance to his east.

Rather than the 600 Boers the British thought were facing the 1st Division, the Lancers' estimate of nearly 4,000 was nearer the mark. General Piet Cronje, the short, black-bearded veteran of the First Boer War, who had arrested Jameson and his raiders at Doornkop, had rushed south from Mafeking with his Transvaal commandos to join de la Rey and Prinsloo. At the *kriegsraad* (coucil of war) de la Rey persuaded his fellow generals, even the obstinate Cronje with whom he had strained relations, not to dig in on the hills at Spytfontein but to hold the river lines at Modder River and thus avoid the casualties of Belmont and Graspan – not what Methuen expected. So in preparation for defence, the railway bridge was dynamited and slit trenches were dug on both sides, whilst the steep banks of the rivers offered natural cover and wide fields of fire. The only crossing points were three: the old ford (drift) beside the railway, Bosman's Drift 3 miles to the east and another beside the dam at Rosmead, 2 miles downriver to the west. These were covered by Cronje's troops on the left flank, in the centre was de la Rey, and on their right (west) flank as far as Rosmead were Prinsloo's less steadfast Free Staters; all were backed by judicious deployment of the Free State regular gunners under the German Major Albrecht. Their right flank would prove to be the weak link in what was a strong and well concealed plan of defence.

The night before battle, Methuen cancelled his flanking march and with scant notice ordered two brigades to advance towards the Modder River in the early hours of the next morning, the 28th. The plan was simple: his objective was the railway bridge, with the Guards Brigade to the right and 9 Brigade along the railway and to the left, with the aim, in effect, of forcing the Boer to show his hand. His reserve brigade of the Highlanders was left some distance back to protect the railway. The new commander of 9 Brigade, with only a few hours' acquaintance with his brigade-major and units, would have relied heavily upon Bulfin as orders were hurriedly given out.

As the sun rose on another scorching African day, the men marched steadily and silently across the open veldt towards the trees marking the river course ahead. They had had no time to feed but were promised breakfast later and a swim in the Modder. Less than a mile short of the winding river banks, Methuen turned in his saddle to Major General Sir Henry Colvile, the Guards brigade commander, and remarked that the enemy were not there.

Colvile's reply, that they were 'sitting uncommonly tight if they are, Sir', was followed 'as if they had heard him … with a roar of musketry'.[28] The British had walked into an ambush, only saved from being a massacre because some of Cronje's burghers failed to hold their fire until the leading troops, fortunately well dispersed, were closer.

On the right of the railway 9 Brigade had started their advance with the Northumberlands, the KOYLI to the left of them across the line and the Loyal North Lancashires on the left flank; the night before, the brigade had been strengthened by the arrival of a battalion of Argyll and Sutherland Highlanders, placed in support. Pole-Carew and his brigade-major were close behind the leading elements. The left and the centre of the brigade was partly protected by a fold in the ground, but the Northumberlands as well as the Guards Brigade on the right took heavy casualties, caught in the open. Any prospect of outflanking the Boers to the east by the 1st Coldstream Guards and the 9th Lancers failed, as they came across the unexpected northern course of the Riet; the first wasted opportunity was due to ignorance of Bosman's Drift further east and the Lancers' failure to seek it out. Earlier, the Guards Brigade had been forced to adjust their angle of advance leftwards, causing 9 Brigade to shift over to the west, a difficult procedure but inadvertently providing better coverage of the Boers' left flank; the benefits would soon become evident. For Bulfin, this required him to move about ceaselessly organizing these adjustments. His opposite number in the Guards Brigade, Captain Harold Ruggles-Brise, had already been felled by a shell fragment.

For many soldiers, the Battle of Modder River was remembered for being pinned down for ten hours in the open, where any movement meant a bullet in the head, exposed to the burning African sun, without water and with not a sight of a Boer; the Highlanders in their kilts suffered even more.

At about 10.00 am, three hours since they had come under fire, Bulfin was with the KOYLI when they advanced to within a few hundred yards of a farmhouse and *kraal* on the left flank, a short distance south of the river. This position and the rocky ground to its west were held strongly by the Boers; it was from here that most of the Boer crossfire was directed on to the brigade. Bulfin quickly realized that this stronghold must cover a ford across the river and, ordering the Lancashires on the left to get as near to the river bank as possible, he returned to Pole-Carew, needing little time to convince him.[29] It proved to be the turning point of the battle.

Pole-Carew noticed there was a *donga* (gully) that ran down to the river and ordered a company of Highlanders to dash forward and get closer to the river and between it and the farmhouse. Soon after, Methuen appeared, seeking to find out what was happening on the left flank and, 'most improperly' as he later confessed, decided to lead a reinforcing party down the same *donga*; he returned unscathed. Sometime after midday, helped by covering fire from the *donga*, the CO of the KOYLI with two companies succeeded in charging forward in small rushes and taking the farm and *kraal*, forcing Prinsloo's men back across the river to the buildings of Rosmead. Pole-Carew then gathered together a mixed bag of men, mostly Lancashires, and led an assault over the river, some across the drift, some over the dam downriver from the farmhouse and others through the deep of the river itself, struggling against the current on the slippery rocks. The Free Staters, finding their flank turned, pulled out of Rosmead, and the British now had a crucial foothold on the northern bank. It was about 1.00 pm.

There had been no time for Bulfin to join his commander in this breakthrough. Due to the heavy fire facing the Northumberland Fusiliers near the bridge, Pole-Carew had 'sent him to look after the right of the Line just before the assault on the Farm House took place, and it was impossible for him to rejoin me', as he wrote in his dispatch.[30] But Bulfin had already contributed more than any other staff officer in the division to swinging the pendulum of battle. He spent the remainder of the day assisting the Geordies, where 'the greater part of the Fifth was engaged in a hot fire fight with the front of the enemy's position. This fire, which began early, lasted until nearly dark.'[31]

Pole-Carew, after gathering together about 500 men of his brigade, pressed on through the buildings of Rosmead along the scrubby river bank towards Fraser's Farm and eastwards to the heart of the Boer position. De la Rey, furious at the irresolute Free Staters for letting go of Rosmead, as well as at Cronje's failure to act against the British threat, sent in his Lichtenburg Commando. Ably supported by Albrecht's clever use of his guns, they had the effect of arresting Pole-Carew's advance. Once again, de la Rey's influence was felt and the British momentum was lost. After two hours of scrappy fighting, its men exhausted and unable to communicate with the gunners properly, 9 Brigade was driven back into Rosmead. With the wisdom of hindsight, it might have been better for the brigade commander to keep Bulfin close by to coordinate this crucial period of the battle; if he had done so, the outcome of Modder River might have been different.

Even more critically – and unbeknown to Pole-Carew – Methuen, with the remainder of his division still pinned down and no reserve brigade close enough, sent off his chief of staff to make an appeal to Colvile for reinforcements; the latter could offer no assistance. On his way back on Methuen's horse he was mortally wounded and shortly after, at about 4.15 pm, Methuen himself became *hors de combat*, with a serious wound to the thigh. Colvile was ordered to take over, but this order took a while to reach him. By the time some semblance of command and control was restored, any chance of pressing home the advantage had passed and it was decided to wait for dawn to resume the attack. By then the Boers had slipped away, although de la Rey had to chase some Boers back to recover their guns. It was a tragic night for the resolute de la Rey; his young son Adriaan was hit next to him in the stomach by shrapnel and died the next morning in his father's arms.

Once again, Methuen had driven out the Boers but failed to achieve a decisive victory. That excellent historian of the Boer War, Baring Pemberton, wrote:

> Justly, then, has the Battle of the Modder River been likened to the 'Waterloo of the Victorian Age'. It was more than that: it was the farewell to the nineteenth century. Those who had fought at Talavera and the Alma would not have been altogether disconcerted at Belmont. At the Modder River they would have been bewildered.[32]

Methuen's summary of the battle as 'one of the hardest and most trying fights in the annals of the Army'[33] might be an exaggeration, but for many soldiers, who suffered more from the climate than the invisible enemy, it would have felt so.

In the next few days the 1st Division rested astride the railway line whilst the bridge was repaired. For the soldiers the Modder River soon lost its Henley charm: 'Water was scarce, and had to be boiled, and it was hard to get it cooled again. Always red dust and sand swirled through the tents. Enteric [typhoid] broke out.'[34] Disease in this war would claim far more casualties than any Boer bullet or shell.

Bulfin's part in the battle had not gone unnoticed. He was praised in his brigade commander's dispatch – 'My brigade-major – Captain Bulfin – also rendered me every possible assistance',[35] and Lord Methuen added in his own dispatch, 'Captain Bulfin did his duty admirably'.[36]

Magersfontein

Since crossing the Orange River on the 21st with the promise of reaching Kimberley within a week, Methuen's exhausted troops had now marched and fought three battles in six days. They were already days behind the optimistic schedule set them and still had the bulk of the Boer forces between them and beleaguered Kimberley. It must have been a daunting prospect, even for their resolute commander recovering from his wound. Some pressure was eased for Methuen when on 4 December Kekewich sent a message with the reassurance that he could hold out for forty days at least. At the same time, his reserve formation, the Highland Brigade led by the Black Watch General Andy Wauchope, arrived at the Modder River, including some much needed cavalry in the shape of the 12th Lancers. On the 7th the bridge was repaired, and Methuen was ready to move.

Since their withdrawal from the Modder River the Boers had not remained idle. Not only had they been strengthened by extra commandos arriving from Mafeking and Natal, but President Steyn had hurried over from Bloemfontein to inject some fire into the bellies of the shaken Free Staters. De la Rey also succeeded in convincing his fellow generals, notably Cronje, not to hold the *kopjes* of Spytfontein but to make the hills to the south at Magersfontein their line of defence. Most critically, he won the arguments he had deployed at the Modder River: to avoid the heights but to dig in at varying distances from the base of them. African labour was rapidly put to use in digging a series of mutually supporting trenches extending some 1,000yds long, of a sophistication unknown to the British Army and, equally importantly, not noticed by Methuen's scouts. Methuen knew the Boers were at Magersfontein, but was unsure of their numbers or disposition.

His battle plan was not subtle. He would bombard the Boer positions on 10 December and then use the Highland Brigade to approach the Magersfontein feature by a night march, making a dawn frontal attack on the southern ridge. Whilst 9 Brigade, 'which had done its share in the hard work of the past week',[37] would protect his left flank, with Rimington's Tigers to the north-west, the Lancers, mounted infantry and KOYLI would cover the right flank; the Guards were held in reserve. Given his experience at Modder River, Methuen was already playing a high risk game by only committing the Highlanders to the main effort. But he had seen them in action in the Ashanti and Egyptian wars and had complete confidence in the impact of the bayonet.

As all soldiers know, few plans survive contact with the enemy. The artillery bombardment on the Magersfontein feature merely alerted the enemy to the oncoming assault. The Highlanders had a miserable night march in hard cold rain – 'the darkest, inkiest night anyone could remember'[38] – bunched together in close column. Despite successfully reaching their destination before dawn, Wauchope thought they were not close enough to the hills to deploy into open order, insisting on advancing still further. But the Boer trenches were not at the foot of the hills. The grey dawn found the Highlanders trying to extend into open order about 400yds from the enemy when the Boers opened fire. Their brigade commander was killed almost immediately, followed by two COs being killed and one wounded. Inevitably, order was lost in the poor light, with many Jocks pinned down in the open for nine hours. Except for some isolated efforts to fight around the Boer flank, the attack stalled, and in the early afternoon muddled orders to fall back led to a chaotic withdrawal, in some cases in panic.

Methuen, unlike at Modder River where he was too closely involved in the front line, spent this battle on top of the aptly named Headquarter Hill. He seemed loath to influence the course of events, leaving it too late for the Guards Brigade to provide timely support and failing to use Pole-Carew's brigade to intervene on the left flank. By 7.15 pm all firing had ceased, but in the morning, unlike at the previous battle, it was found that the exhausted Boers had not pulled back. So, after a day's armistice to collect the dead and treat the wounded, it was Methuen who suffered the ignominy of defeat and retreat back to the Modder River.

Magersfontein was the second of three disasters that took place that 'Black Week', with Gatacre's defeat at Stormberg the day before and Buller's reverse at Colenso on the 15th. When news reached Britain of how their great Army had been repulsed by some Boer farmers, the country was stunned. The reaction was traditional – send for a hero, or in this case two: Field Marshal Lord Roberts of Kandahar, with Lord Kitchener of Khartoum as his chief of staff. Days before sailing for South Africa, Roberts heard that his only son had been killed trying to rescue the guns at Colenso. En route to Cape Town, where he landed on 10 January, he issued his first orders, one of which was to instruct Methuen to go on the defensive at the Modder River. Roberts, the leader of the 'Indian' ring, was not a supporter of the 'African' Buller and Methuen. Now he had even less confidence in them.[39]

Inevitably, recriminations followed about Methuen's tactics as well as his handling of the battle. Feelings ran especially high in the Highland Brigade. The Guards and 9 Brigade had, in many ways, been wasted assets. For Pole-Carew and his brigade-major it must have been a frustrating day, with a lost opportunity for their two battalions to exploit the Boer western flank. It would take months before Roberts regained confidence in GOC 1st Division and, in the meantime, his troops suffered the tedious job of securing the railway line, whilst newly arrived divisions had the honour of marching on Bloemfontein as well as relieving Kimberley. As the general's chief of staff wrote to his wife, 'The 1st Division – under Methuen – is under a cloud'.[40]

Bulfin would not have been aware that at the battle of Colenso in Natal a Major John MacBride, fighting for the Boers, had had his horse shot from under him; the incident would have been of little interest. This Irish nationalist was second-in-command of one of the two Transvaal Irish Brigades, filled by a few recruits from Ireland but mostly by their countrymen living in South Africa.[41] John MacBride would later be executed by a British firing squad for his part in the Easter Rising. His only son, Sean, later a senior figure in the IRA, would marry Bulfin's cousin's daughter, Catalina Bulfin.

Reorganization and Offensive

An unpleasantly hot Christmas and January were spent on the Modder River, as new divisions arrived in the area, including a cavalry one under Major General John French with his chief of staff, Douglas Haig. Amongst these troops were volunteers from the Dominions providing much needed mounted infantry. Roberts' decisive plans to reorganize his forces and regain the offensive were taking shape.

On New Year's Day the adventurous Jack Bulfin was mortally wounded at Colesberg, reputedly shot seven times, the last through the head. The Tigers had moved south to form the scouting screen for Roberts' great advance, and Jack was hit while beating off a Boer counter-attack on a hill taken by the Berkshires. Family tradition relates that cousin Edward was with him when he died four days later, although Jack never regained consciousness.[42] Since 9 Brigade had remained at the Modder River camp, some 150 miles away, he may have been able to make the journey. Losing Jack must have been a blow to him.

Back in Kent, Fanny was attending her brother Eustace's marriage to Augustus Pugin's granddaughter at Ramsgate. It was a high Catholic ceremony, led by the Lord Abbot of St Augustine's Abbey,[43] and a world away from the sweltering, dusty, fly-blown Modder River camp. Later, the Bulfins would live for a number of years in this part of Kent.

It was a depressing time for Methuen and his division, with the Highland Brigade withdrawn from his command to join the newly created 9th Division, together with much of his artillery and transport. At least Bulfin had an opportunity to catch up with old regimental friends, when on 1 February the 1st Battalion joined Kelly-Kenny's 6th Division on the south side of the river. They had landed at Cape Town on 15 December, and a month later had been 'blooded' in a small action at Slingersfontein, suffering their first casualties.

On 8 February 1900 Roberts arrived at the Modder River. Although his inspection of the troops drew huge cheers from the ranks, the meeting with Methuen was less warm. Despite receiving a reprimand for mishandling the Highlanders, Methuen retained his command.[44]

The second phase of the Boer War now commenced,[45] once sufficient forces had gathered from the corners of the Empire to take on the Boers in set-piece battles. Inevitably, the tide began to turn. But the emasculated 1st Division was not included in Roberts' ambitious flanking march to relieve Kimberley. Whilst French's Cavalry Division made its historic dash there, covering 100 miles in four days but ruining its horses, the main force, which included the Green Howards, attacked Cronje's men at Paardeberg on 18 February. Eventually, after a battle of unnecessarily high casualties, the stubborn Boer general surrendered on the 27th. The fact that Kitchener, with a large force at his disposal, made such heavy weather of defeating Cronje at Paardeberg is often forgotten. This was certainly not lost on the 1st Division, though: 'Talk of Methuen! He never committed half such a blunder as that', wrote Colonel Belfield.[46]

In mid-February Bulfin received his fourth brigade commander in three months. After Methuen had lost his friend Colonel Northcott, killed at the Battle of Modder River, he had appointed Colonel Charles Douglas of the Gordon Highlanders as his chief of staff, given the difficult task of acting as a go-between to the Highland Brigade and his general at Magersfontein. When Pole-Carew was promoted in February to command the newly formed 11th Division, taking with him the KOYLI from 9 Brigade as well as the Guards Brigade, Douglas was moved to replace him. Bulfin's new master had enjoyed an active career, accompanying Roberts from Kabul to Kandahar, as well as taking part in the First Boer War, although without fighting with his regiment at Majuba Hill. He had originally come out to South Africa in the autumn on Buller's staff. 'Naturally shy and reserved, Douglas gave the impression of being "a hard man" who could be abrupt and overbearing to subordinates.'[47] After the Boer War he rose to be Chief of the Imperial General Staff on the outbreak of the First World War, a 'widely acclaimed' appointment.[48] He died in office at the height of the First Battle of Ypres, from a combination of stress and long hours whilst suffering from bronchitis. Douglas would have been a demanding but instructive mentor to Bulfin (unfortunately he left no private papers or letters).

On 18 March 9 Brigade moved by rail to Kimberley. By then, the military situation had changed beyond recognition. In the west, Kimberley had been relieved, Cronje's army defeated, Bloemfontein occupied and Cape Colony almost cleared of the enemy. In Natal Ladysmith had been relieved and Botha had fallen back.

However, before the 1st Division had taken over Kimberley, Methuen had already been given the task of protecting Roberts' left flank on his advance to Pretoria, by taking control of the north-west area of the Orange Free State in what was now turning into a guerrilla war.

'The English swarm over our country'

These months were best remembered for long marches and short sharp engagements, as Bulfin's brigade fought its way up to the Vaal across the flat featureless veldt, with the elusive Christiaan de Wet and de la Rey always slipping frustratingly through the net.

> In 15 days, Methuen and his men had marched 168 miles through deep sands and over worn roads … By late May, they had earned the nickname the Mobile Marvels … A popular rhyme, later hummed, went: 'always somethin' up and doin', Major-General Lord Methuen' … The General always marched alongside his men on foot in the company of his staff officers, and would only call for his horse when trouble started.[49]

The infantry battalions travelled light:

> The kit allowed on the transport included two blankets and a greatcoat for each man; a jersey and canvas shoes were carried rolled in a waterproof sheet on the back of the waistbelt, while washing kit, sleeping cap, etc., were carried in a haversack on the back. Officers' kits were limited strictly to thirty-five pounds, including valise and blankets [carried on regimental mule wagons].[50]

As the Northumberlands' regimental history put it: 'Methuen's "Salvation Army" was hurried from point to point where danger was threatened … while Methuen turned the 9th into a flying column.'[51] Christiaan de Wet, in his campaign chronicle *Three Years War*, aptly titled this period 'The English Swarm over our Country'.[52]

A famous incident occurred at the end of May, the same time as Johannesburg fell to Roberts, when elements of 9 Brigade with the Imperial Yeomanry, led personally by Methuen, dashed from Kroonstad to Lindley. News had reached them that the 13th Battalion of the Imperial Yeomanry had been overpowered by de Wet's brother Piet outside Lindley and urgently needed help. Leaving Douglas and Bulfin to follow up with the infantry, Methuen went ahead with the three Yeomanry battalions and a battery of guns. The 13th, better known as the 'Irish Yeomanry', described by Thomas Pakenham as 'the political and social show-piece of the new volunteer army',[53] could not have been more different from Major John MacBride's Irish Brigade. One company, known as the Irish Hunt Contingent, consisted of a number of Masters of Foxhounds, including Pakenham's grandfather, the 5th Earl of Longford; two other companies numbered amongst their ranks eminent Protestant Unionists, including a future Prime Minister of Northern Ireland, James Craig. After riding 44 miles in twenty-four hours, Methuen's force arrived at Lindley in the early hours of 2 June. A five-hour fight followed as the British forced their way past de Wet and his 3,000-man commando, but the horses were too tired for a pursuit. But the 13th's dithering CO, Colonel Spragge, had been surrounded, and he and over 500 of his men were taken prisoner.[54]

By July, narrowly escaping capture by Bulfin's brigade at Rhenoster River the month before, de Wet had moved further north into the Transvaal. Meanwhile, 9 Brigade was transferred by rail to Krugersdorp, near Johannesburg, to continue the pursuit, pushing on the North Lancashires and a battery of guns to hold Olifants Nek, the crucial pass through the Magaliesberg hills. It was a welcome change of scene:

> Instead of the deadly flat plains of the Free State, we are now in a well-treed, rolling country. Around us are grand mountains, the climate is beautiful, the air quite mild, oranges hanging from the trees.[55]

August would prove to be the most testing month. Now they were drawn into the first large-scale hunt for de Wet, with a number of divisions brought to bear under the eye of Kitchener. Methuen's overstretched force fought many skirmishes, constantly pressing against de Wet's rearguards until the opportunity arose to trap him as the Boers headed for Olifants Pass and the cover of the Magaliesberg Range – 'After him [Methuen] pounded the columns … footsore, and with bloodshot eyes, choked with dust, and thirsty in a waterless land.'[56] Kitchener considered 9 Brigade's marching 'surpassed that of any other infantry brigade'.[57] As Colonel Belfield, Methuen's chief of staff, wrote:

> We were some nine miles from Olifants Nek and feeling pretty confident … Reports came in that he [de Wet] had crossed the mountains by Olifants Nek but these were absurd … We held the Nek. Further reports came in to the same effect and gradually the awful truth dawned on us that this was actually true. Someone had blundered sadly.

Poor Methuen was quite overcome … It was a sad termination of our efforts.[58]

Unbeknown to Methuen, General Baden-Powell had withdrawn the Lancashires from the Nek. General Hamilton's column, the other critical part of the intended pincer movement, was lagging behind schedule and had taken the wrong route to the Pass. Methuen's troops had marched 150 miles in six days with almost daily encounters with the enemy, and 'when it became apparent that the pass to which they had hunted their quarry was undefended, the rage and vexation of officers and men was unrestrained, loud and long'.[59]

When the pursuit ceased, 9 Brigade marched to Pretoria. 'Many of the men were in rags, with boots hanging to their feet. They had far outdistanced their baggage, and had been often without food or water. One of them wrote: "We are like greyhounds … our coats no longer fit us … but flap idly against our sides like a sail against a mast. As hardbitten and tatterdemalion a crew as ever … marched into Pretoria".'[60]

Throughout these months, according to Amery, an earlier critic:

Methuen was indomitable … Of the generals, Methuen was certainly the soul of the pursuit; often disappointed, he made few mistakes, and never for a moment would he let his quarry go. What little success was achieved was solely due to his dogged tenacity.[61]

In early September, with the Transvaal annexed and President Kruger fleeing to Portuguese Lourenço Marques, the 1st Division was ordered to take control of Western Transvaal, a strategic backwater. Based in Mafeking, at least its soldiers had a few days to recharge their batteries before 9 Brigade was ordered off to clear the country around Lichtenburg. By October the brigade was pushing de la Rey, now the chief target, towards Methuen's column at Boschoek Nek, near Rustenburg, but the wily Boer was in no mood to confront the British.

Good fortune greeted Bulfin when on 31 October 1900 he handed over as brigade-major, on the news that he was to be appointed as Deputy Assistant Adjutant General (DAAG) the following day. The *Green Howards Gazette*, with typical regimental indifference towards the staff, commented briefly:

'Captain Bulfin has, we see, got another Staff appointment.'[62] Appointment to brevet-major followed on 29 November.

After a short period acting as DAAG to 9 Brigade, which had by now been reconstituted into a mobile column, Bulfin was posted to Brigadier General Gilbert Hamilton's 4 Cavalry Brigade, where the commander took him as his brigade-major. The remainder of 1901 was spent on operations in eastern Transvaal and then the autumn on the Zululand frontier of Natal, a time to gain an understanding of the *arme blanche*, invaluable in the next war.

Column Commander

On 12 December 1901 Bulfin was given his first substantial independent command, a moment to gladden the heart and quicken the pulse of any self-respecting soldier. Since leaving his regiment five years before, he had been employed in various positions on the staff, albeit very much on front line duty. He was now to be the commander of a mobile column under Colonel Alexander Rochfort, a well regarded Gunner, in charge of 410 mounted infantry and two field guns.

Since the start of the African summer, Kitchener had been undertaking a series of drives by mounted columns against stop-lines of blockhouses, with the aim of cornering the elusive 'bitter-enders', Boers who continued to resist. This had met with little success, but in a letter to Roberts, 'K' wrote, 'I think about April we shall have pretty well exhausted the Boers, and so enclosed them in areas that they find it very hard to keep up much form of resistance.'[63] Kitchener's forecast proved to be close to the mark. With winter looming, he planned his last momentous drives.

Bulfin's column was to play a central role in this final effort. In March, thousands of mounted troops started descending on the little town of Klerksdorp, many from far corners of the British Empire with colourful titles such as the Australian Bushmen, the Canadian Mounted Rifles and Damant's Horse. Many of the British Mounted Infantry were drawn from county infantry regiments as well as yeomanry regiments. In Bulfin's case, his major unit was 16th Battalion M.I. consisting of squadrons from Yorkshire to Wiltshire and from Suffolk to Cheshire. For these volunteer soldiers, chasing the Boers across the veldt was a good deal more exciting than the tedium and discomfort of guarding metal-roofed blockhouses and railway lines. Kipling summed it up in a famous ditty:

I wish my mother could see me now, with a fence-post under my arm,
And a knife and spoon in my putties that I found on a Boer farm
Atop of a sore-backed Argentine, with a thirst that you couldn't buy,
I used to be in the Yorkshires once …
But now I am M.I.

Earlier in the year, Rochfort's column had been operating in the southern and western Free State, but now they crossed the Vaal and established themselves downstream from Klerksdorp at Commando Drift, well-known to Bulfin from his time chasing de Wet in the summer of 1900. It was a suitable jumping-off point for the forthcoming operation. But this major sweep was to be on a quite different scale. Some 16,000 troops were being brought to bear, distributed into four divisions, each about 4,000 strong. In Rochfort's division his six columns were largely commanded by lieutenant colonels, with Bulfin the only major leading a mounted infantry column.[64]

Only two weeks previously, Methuen had been ambushed by his old adversary de la Rey at Tweebosch and forced to surrender, the first and last general to be captured in the war. Kitchener locked himself in his bedroom for two days, so appalled was he by the disaster. A strong response was required.

It was one achievement to concentrate such a formidable force with such efficiency, quite another challenge to use them effectively. As the *Times History* commented, 'Hence came to be planned one of the most remarkable of the many remarkable movements of the guerrilla war.'[65]

Intelligence, now far more effective than at the start of the war, indicated that large numbers of Boers were some 30 miles west of Schoon Spruit, the river to the north of Klerksdorp. Kitchener's orders were ambitious: 11,000 troops would make a night march of 40 miles to the west of the enemy commandos, turn about, deploy into a 90-mile long cordon and sweep back in a single day's march to the Schoon Spruit blockhouse line, a distance of some 80 miles. Rochfort's force, in the extreme south, moving out from Commando Drift, would have a less taxing distance to cover. And so, 'On the night of the 23rd, riding in close order, without guns or transport, the columns shot out into the veldt.'[66]

Although this huge night manoeuvre was well performed, gaps inevitably appeared in the cordon by dawn, one of which was between Rochfort's troops and those in the column to the north. Although the Boers had been thrown into confusion by the sudden presence of so many of the enemy, nevertheless de la Rey, Steyn and other leaders succeeded in slipping through the net. The final 'bag' amounted to a mere 165 prisoners, three guns and two pompoms. Rochfort's force returned south of the Vaal, the rest to Klerksdorp.

Despite this lack of material success, increasing pressure was being exerted on the Boer political leadership. The final campaigning for Bulfin came two months later in early May, days before the peace conference at Vereeniging, when an even larger gathering of 17,000 troops was used in another methodical but unproductive drive north against the blockhouse line of the Vryburg–Mafeking railway. When the peace agreement was reached, Kitchener displayed a magnanimity in sharp contrast to his ruthless military leadership of the past year.

For Edward Bulfin, now an experienced thirty-nine-year-old major, it was the end of three and a half years' service in South Africa. As ADC and military secretary in the rarefied corridors of Cape Town, he had developed a political antenna and some useful staff skills, before quickly moving on to the more testing forge of wartime responsibility.

Whilst campaigning with the 1st Division he gained above all a close understanding of those qualities of leadership required to hold men together in war. It had been a period of intense, prolonged fighting and marching, burdened with considerable responsibility, not least in providing much needed continuity to his ever changing brigade commanders. His insight as a DAAG into the logistic challenges of conducting a mobile campaign, as well as serving in a cavalry brigade, would also serve him in great stead in the future. In addition, he had been at the forefront of the British Army's often painful transition from the tactics of colonial fighting to the beginnings of modern warfare and technology. And, most significantly, under the leadership of Methuen, the ability to steel himself in the face of setbacks and disappointments had been well and truly forged. As Rayne Kruger wrote in *Good-bye Dolly Gray*, 'Methuen occupied that special place in English minds reserved for men who did not give way to adversity.'[67]

Bulfin's war ended with him in command of a half battalion-sized force, having won four mentions in dispatches, plus the Queen's Medal with four clasps and the King's Medal with two clasps, to show for his active service. Two brevet promotions, 'a reward that fell to few officers',[68] were a further indication of his promise. He had also qualified formally for staff employment, as a result of the appointments he held during the war.

Ian Beckett, that expert on the Victorian army, wrote:

> What mattered most about the impact of the South African War upon the army was the general sense of the need for reform. The Army was undoubtedly better for the experience and, in August 1914, the fact that the BEF was such a finely honed military instrument owed much to the South African War.[69]

On Milner, the architect of the war, Africa had her revenge. On a visit there in 1924 he was bitten by a tsetse fly, contracted sleeping sickness and died.

Chapter 3

1902–1914
Inter-War Years

Bulfin's return to England, to be reunited with Fanny and his young son Eddie after nearly three years' separation, also brought good news for his career; in June 1902 he received the brevet of lieutenant colonel, albeit he was still only a substantive captain.[1] Such disparity between acting rank and seniority was a curious but normal feature of climbing the military ladder in the overblown post-Boer War Army.

That October he was serving again under his old brigade commander Charles Douglas in Aldershot, the nerve centre of the British Army. His appointment was as DAAG of Douglas's 2nd Division, on paper a similar administrative role to the one he had held in South Africa. However, the combination of serving in the prime location of Aldershot and the tutelage of the highly professional Douglas, at a time when the Army was just starting to grapple with the much needed Esher and Elgin reforms, would have provided Bulfin with a very different experience. It offered a golden opportunity to be noticed by such figures as the Corps Commander, Sir John French, amongst others, as well as to benefit from this impetus for change. Douglas's next job was to be Adjutant General in the War Office where, after the Liberals' election victory in 1906, he would be brought into close working contact with the incoming Secretary of State for War, that great mastermind Richard Haldane. Douglas, despite differences of opinion, worked hard to implement Haldane's reforms, especially in converting the auxiliaries and yeomanry into the newly formed Territorial Force. In the Edwardian army of the time it was difficult to further one's career without some degree of patronage. General Douglas, appointed CIGS in 1914, might well have been the man to offer that to Bulfin. A rare chance of settled family life for Edward and Fanny was also a blessing beyond measure.

When he received his substantive majority in the autumn, there were no vacancies in his own regiment, so Bulfin transferred to the Manchester

Regiment for the duration of his tour on the staff, not an unusual practice at the time. On 15 October 1904 he returned to regimental duty, after a gap of some eight years. But it was not to his own regiment, now titled Alexandra, Princess of Wales's Own Yorkshire Regiment; it was as second-in-command to the 1st Battalion The Royal Welch Fusiliers, moving the month before from Lichfield to South Camp in Aldershot.[2] Although almost forty-two, he was still too junior for battalion command.[3] Nevertheless, it was a convenient base for the Bulfin family, and garrison life in Aldershot would have been sociable and its duties relatively undemanding. His commanding officer was Randall Beresford-Ash, a fellow Irishman from Co. Londonderry, who had also entered the Army through the Irish militia.[4] The battalion was part of 3 Brigade in his old division, now commanded by Major General Sir Bruce Hamilton. Besides a week's Army Corps manoeuvres each September, RWF regimental records of the time paint a picture of royal visits, military tattoos and sporting competitions.[5] During this period the Bulfins lived in Wimbledon, probably an easier drive to his work than it would be nowadays.

The birth of a daughter, Eileen Mary Frances, the next spring must have been a joy, but tragedy followed in the summer of 1906, when a second daughter, Kathleen Maud, was born but died a mere month later at home of acute hydrocephalus – fluid on the brain.[6] The couple had no further children.

Return to South Africa

Bulfin stayed with the Royal Welch until the autumn of that year, when he was appointed brevet colonel and posted to Cape Town as AA&QMG to the wonderfully named Cape of Good Hope District (substantive promotion came two years later on 4 July 1908); this was a senior logistic and personnel staff appointment, to which he was able to bring considerable experience. Like many sensible officers, he sailed ahead of his young family on 17 November in the Union Castle *Goorkha* for Cape Town, to be joined by Fanny and Eileen the following spring. Nine-year-old Eddie, accompanied by his twenty-six-year-old nurse, followed in November, quite an adventure for both of them.

Bulfin remained in Cape Town for four years until 7 December 1910. For most of this time his immediate senior was Major General Reginald Hart, a

Royal Engineer from County Clare, who had won the Victoria Cross in the Second Afghan War rescuing a wounded Bengal Lancer *sowar* (cavalryman) under fire. His Commander-in-Chief in Pretoria for his final two years was none other than General Lord Methuen; the latter would have been pivotal in recommending him for brigade command.

An insight into Cape Town army life at this time is given by Richard Meinertzhagen in his diary. Meinertzhagen was an unorthodox and outspoken officer, with scant respect for 'good order and military discipline'. In his early life he had gained notoriety in Africa for assassinating a tribal chief, and he was later to be a talented intelligence officer under Allenby in Palestine. But in 1907, on more menial duties, he was posted to his regiment in South Africa and, on arrival in Cape Town, was put in command of a draft of soldiers to move up-country by train. His orders came from a certain senior staff officer in a manner that did not appeal to the young Meinertzhagen, who thought the process was being badly handled, and there was an inevitable falling-out – 'His name was Colonel Bulfin and I thought him stupid and unhelpful.'[7] They were to meet again in Palestine a decade later.

Cape Town, with its dramatic setting and comfortable climate, was a convivial posting. The Bulfin family had the benefit of being close to old friends in his regiment. The 2nd Battalion was stationed at Wynberg, a suburb of Cape Town under Table Mountain, a beautiful location near the vineyards of Constantia with sweeping views out to False Bay. The commanding officer was Lieutenant Colonel Arthur Hadow, who had recently taken command. Many of the Elgin reforms from the Boer War had not yet percolated down to battalion level, especially to such a far-flung corner of the Empire, and Hadow was not atypical of officers of his age in never looking beyond the regimental horizon. Outward ambition was frequently frowned upon in the officers' mess, and serious study of one's profession could be treated with a degree of suspicion. A subaltern at the time, who went on to become a full general in the Second World War, in old age drew a sharp portrait of his CO:

> For the first two years of his command the 2nd Battalion went steadily downhill and a climax was reached when it was reported as unfit for active service. This naturally stung Hadow in a tender spot and in a blundering and rather desperate way he tried to improve matters. One

remembers him waving a copy of 'Infantry Training' in front of his assembled officers and shouting, 'Here is a little red book which some of you read but most of you don't.' This was perfectly true, but it was equally true that he only just begun to read it himself.[8]

Bulfin, as a senior member of the staff responsible for judging unit performance, would have found himself in an awkward position, despite still being gazetted as a Royal Welch Fusilier.[9] Happily, the 2nd Battalion had recovered by the end of Hadow's command and went on to be considered amongst the most steadfast of BEF battalions during the German onslaught at First Ypres.[10]

One of the last tasks to land in Bulfin's in-tray was the organization of the royal visit in 1910 to South Africa of HRH Prince Arthur the Duke of Connaught, brother to the King. For this he was created Commander of the Royal Victorian Order and presented with the Union Medal.[11]

Promotion to Brigadier General

On return to England, Bulfin enjoyed some well earned leave on half-pay, living in South Kensington, and was able to turn his attention to domestic affairs. He launched his son into the Benedictine Downside School in Somerset, less austere than the Jesuit Stonyhurst of his own experience in Lancashire. The start of the year was marked by the death of his mother Teresa in February 1911. Then, in June, his career took a major step forward: promotion to general officer. He was to be a brigadier general in command of the Essex Infantry Brigade for the next two years, based in Brentwood, initially under the divisional command of Major General Julian Byng, then under Charles Townshend, who later gained infamy at Kut. It consisted of four volunteer battalions of the Essex Regiment, part of the newly created Territorial Force, a key component of Haldane's galvanizing reforms of the Army. It is likely that Sir Charles Douglas, now a full general and Inspector-General of Home Forces, would have had a hand in Bulfin's selection for this post. It was a time when the Army's eyes were very much on whether the militia could make a credible transition to providing a reserve for the regulars. Bulfin's experience of commanding volunteers in his mounted column in South Africa qualified him well for 'gingering' them up in their new role. Within a month, Bulfin had gathered his brigade at summer camp at Thetford with the rest of the East Anglia Division; of the division's enrolled strength of about 15,000 men, two thirds mustered for camp – more would have appeared but for an early harvest.[12] Bulfin's appointment as Commander of the Order of the Bath, in the 1913 King's Birthday Honours List, was proof that he was well established.

An indication of how the continental threat was beginning to concentrate minds at the higher levels of the War Office and the military became evident in September of the following year, when the largest peacetime manoeuvres ever held by the Army took place in East Anglia. The CIGS, Sir John French, directed the exercise, with 'Red Force' commanded by Sir Douglas Haig and the opposing 'Blue Force' by Lieutenant General Sir James Grierson, Bulfin's master in Eastern Command. Haig had the 1st and 2nd Divisions from his Aldershot command and a cavalry division, whilst Grierson led a similarly sized force but with fewer cavalry; the latter had the added disadvantage of a scattered command and an ad hoc staff. Bulfin's brigade did not take part – the only Territorial formation participating came from Liverpool;[13] but he may well have been an umpire and, in any case, would have followed the exercise closely.

Haig's troops took the role of an enemy force landing on the Norfolk coast and advancing south on London, with Grierson's force centred round Cambridge and protecting the capital. Both sides had a Royal Flying Corps detachment of some planes and a balloon. The climax of the exercise was Grierson's concealment of the 4th Division around Saffron Walden – 'I told them to look as like toadstools as they could and to make noises like oysters';[14] this took Haig by surprise, and his force was repelled. As the exercise ended, Haig was judged to have come off worse. But more seriously, in the ensuing final conference held in the Great Hall of Trinity College Cambridge, attended by the King and the senior hierarchy of the Army, Haig decided to dispose of his written notes, summarizing his force's actions, and speaking off the cuff. It was a disaster. Often awkward with the spoken word, as Charteris, one of Haig's closest staff officers and confidants, reported, he became:

> totally unintelligible and unbearably dull. The university dignitaries
> soon fell asleep. Haig's friends became more and more uncomfortable,

only himself seemed totally unconscious of his failure. A listener, without other and deeper knowledge of the Aldershot Commander-in-Chief, could not but have left the conference with the impression that Haig had neither ability nor military learning.[15]

Grierson's polished response only underlined Haig's inept performance. Nevertheless, Haig's career did not seem to suffer from this potential setback. Grierson's fate would be very different. A popular and able Gunner with strong Scottish roots, he had held high hopes of the Aldershot Command in place of Haig, but although young at fifty-five, he was nevertheless appointed to command II Corps on mobilization. A large and overweight man, he died of a heart attack on the train in France, en route to the front on 14 August 1914.

Command of 2 Infantry Brigade

June 1913 could be judged the turning point of Bulfin's career; he was given command of 2 Infantry Brigade in Aldershot, under the overall command of Sir Douglas Haig.[16] This regular brigade was part of a corps of two infantry divisions and one cavalry brigade, earmarked as the Army's major deployable force in the event of war, the core of the British Expeditionary Force. It was generally considered throughout the Army to be the best infantry brigade; the 1st was always a Guards brigade and could only be commanded by a guardsman. For someone who had not attended Staff College, commanded a battalion, or held a general staff appointment since being a brigade-major twelve years earlier, it was a rare achievement to gain such a keenly contested command. One can only conclude that it was a clear indication of Bulfin's ability as well as evidence that this Edwardian Army, becoming a more professional and less 'cliquey' organization than in the Victorian era, was better able to promote and appoint on merit. He was now among an elite band of senior officers.

Nevertheless, a closer look at the senior commanders of the 1st Division does raise some interesting observations for the modern soldier. In today's Army, the premier deployable division would be led by the rising stars of the service, carefully groomed for the role by having gained experience in key staff and regimental appointments during their career, ideally on active duty; all would have attended Staff College. In contrast, officer selection for the 1st Division's command appointments in the run-up to the Great War seemed to a degree haphazard. Patronage, which had exerted such a powerful and corrosive influence during the Victorian years, had become less pervasive after the Boer War, but was still evident. In 1914 the divisional commander was the fifty-nine-year-old Major General Samuel Lomax, in the saddle since 1910 and due for retirement in July, but who nevertheless took his division to France. The last time he had seen action, thirty-six years before, was at the climactic battle of Ulundi in the Zulu War. In an Army rich with recent operational experience from the Boer War, his appointment does seem strange. Nevertheless, he was to be judged 'the best divisional commander of those early days of the war',[17] only to be mortally wounded at the height of the First Battle of Ypres; the official historian, Edmonds, considered his death a 'brain wound' to the Army. Two of the brigade commanders, Bulfin and Herman Landon (3 Brigade), had distinctly unlikely career paths. Landon's last appointment had been as Inspector of Gymnasia in India, although he had commanded a battalion in the Boer War and again later. Not a young man, he would be invalided home in late November on grounds of exhaustion. The third brigade commander, Ivor Maxse, a Coldstreamer in command of 1 Brigade, had had a more conventional career. He had seen active service at Omdurman and commanded a battalion, but spent the Boer War as a transport staff officer, not exactly an eye-catching appointment; he would be removed from command by Haig for mishandling his brigade during the Retreat from Mons (this fine trainer's career would later recover, and he went on to command a division and a corps). None of these four officers had been to Staff College. Frustratingly, the Military Secretary's records of the time, which would give a fascinating insight into how they were selected, were largely destroyed during a Second World War air raid, then later deleted by the Public Records Office, to make space. What is clear is that Haig, who was determined to train his Aldershot command to a more professional level in the pre-war years, would not have tolerated such subordinates unless they met his high standards.

This could not have been a more stimulating time for Bulfin to be at Aldershot, and very different from his last posting there. Haig had been in command since the previous March and his impact had been immediate and far-reaching – 'The training of both officers and soldiers became much more strenuous.'[18] As Director of Military Training and then Director of Staff Duties in the War Office a few years earlier, he had worked hand in hand with Haldane to reform and modernize the Army. It involved carrying out vital but unglamorous hard graft, striving to introduce a common tactical doctrine and sound organizational structure to an Army historically wedded to regimental individualism and improvization. Haig's contribution to victory by the end of the Great War germinated in the seedbeds of this seminal period. Whilst most of the pre-War Army, and indeed most Government ministers, were more concerned with events in Ireland and the arguments over Home Rule, Haig, along with officers such as Wilson, Robertson and Grierson, understood the growing threat Germany posed to Britain and were determined to prepare her Army for war:

> Over the next two years Haig imposed his personality on his command, entertaining at his home and letting his guests see an informal side to his character. This was a crucial period in forging team spirit. Many of the officers who served under Haig at Aldershot were to be part of the 1 Corps team that went to France in August 1914.[19]

The fifty-year-old Bulfin was an integral member of this 'band of brothers', which would become the 'Contemptible Little Army'.

Before taking over his new brigade, Bulfin had returned to Ireland in January 1913 to check on the family house at Rathfarnham.[20] It would be his last visit until after the war.

That summer of 1913, a series of exercises was held within the Aldershot Command, commencing with a divisional exercise for 1st Division south of Farnham in July. During this, 2 Brigade drew criticism for being unnecessarily exposed to enemy artillery fire on Hankley Common; the next exercise, in mid-September, was a Command river crossing on the Thames, at which point Bulfin won praise from Haig:

> The value of feints in the crossing of a river cannot be exaggerated. The skilful use made of this form of stratagem by the GOC of the 2nd Infantry Brigade succeeded in drawing away a whole battalion from the vicinity of the crossing.

In the last phase of the exercise, in the Chilterns, Bulfin was again praised for his brigade's counter-attack: an omen of events to come.[21]

In September 1913 another large-scale annual exercise was held, this time in the quiet rural lanes and villages of Northamptonshire and Buckinghamshire.[22] Sir John French, who the previous year had umpired the exercise, this year commanded the main force. Compared to the more free-running exercise of 1912, this one was more tightly controlled to a timetable, with the purpose of testing General and Army HQs in a war setting. An exercise of this type, with hordes of soldiers, horses and vehicles pouring over private land and blocking the roads, would be familiar to soldiers serving in West Germany in the 1950s–1980s, but would be beyond British civilians' comprehension – or tolerance – today.

Bulfin's brigade was part of French's 'Brown Force', which had the task of pursuing a smaller 'White Force' engaged in a fighting retreat – very much a portent of future events at Mons. Three months after taking command, he now had the opportunity to exercise his leadership skills in an Army-sized exercise. His troops were drawn from famous infantry regiments, namely the Royal Sussex, the Loyal North Lancashire and the King's Royal Rifle Corps (the 60th), all of whom he would take to France the next year. He also had the 2nd Battalion of his own regiment, stationed near his brigade in Blackdown, for the duration of the exercise. 2 Brigade was very much in the forefront of the initial 'Brown Force' advance with a river crossing over the Ouse, the finale of the manoeuvres being Haig's coordinated corps attack on Sharman's Hill, north-west of Towcester, with Bulfin's brigade deployed on the west flank.[23] This time Haig was judged to have performed more confidently.

The Curragh 'Incident'

An event that went to the core of Bulfin's Irish roots occurred the following March, and nearly tore apart the officer corps of the Army. Since the 1910 general election, Prime Minister Asquith had been reliant on the support of the nationalist Irish Parliamentary Party, who demanded in return constitutional Home Rule for Ireland. This inevitably aroused the opposition of largely Protestant Ulster, which created a paramilitary arm, the Ulster Volunteer Force, numbering some 100,000 men by 1914. Irish

Nationalists had also formed the Irish Volunteers, to counter the Loyalists. The very real threat of civil war in Ireland stalked the political corridors of London and Dublin. The concern for the Army was the possibility of being sent to put down any violence in Ulster, a particular dilemma for officers of Irish descent. 'For the first time since the Glorious Revolution of 1688 there was a serious question-mark over the willingness of the leadership of the British army to obey their Sovereign's government', wrote Gary Sheffield in his biography of Haig.[24]

As tension mounted in early 1914, urgent meetings were held in the War Office on 18 and 19 March, attended by the GOC Ireland, General Sir Arthur Paget, and chaired by the Secretary of State for War, Jack Seely. On Paget's return to Ireland he met with his senior officers and, in a poorly judged briefing, gave them the impression that active operations against Ulster were imminent, when in fact all that was planned was the occupation of key armouries and bases. In doing so, he issued an ultimatum stating that, with the exception of those officers domiciled in Ulster, who could 'disappear', any officer who refused to take part would be dismissed without pension. This only served to inflame matters, with units amongst the large garrison stationed throughout Ireland feeling a strong sense of injustice at being placed in such a dilemma. On the 21st Paget made matters worse by addressing the officers of 3 Cavalry Brigade based at the Curragh, outside Dublin, who reacted strongly under the leadership of their hot-headed 'Anglo-Irish' commander, Brigadier General Hubert Gough; here sixty of the seventy-two officers offered their resignations. What became known as the Curragh 'Incident' had started.

The first news to reach Aldershot was Gough's telegram to his brother the day before, on the 20th:

> Have been offered dismissal service or undertake operations against Ulster. Two hours to decide. First means ruin of army as others will follow. This only consideration that counts. Am taking first contingency. Do you think if am right reply.[25]

Brother Johnnie was Haig's chief of staff and, after replying that he would resign immediately if ordered to 'serve against Ulster', he lost no time in contacting his master, who was enjoying a golfing weekend at Littlehampton.

On hearing what the Gough brothers proposed, Haig noted in his diary: 'Bad day. We play [golf] after lunch. I wire Gen. Gough to be calm! and arrange to return Aldershot next day.'[26] Haig had been aware of the implications of the Ulster situation for the Army since the previous September, but had been keeping his powder dry. Now, with the worrying prospect of the Curragh resignations spreading to his command and to key elements of the Army as a whole, he needed to take a grip on events, and headed up to London on the Monday morning. He told the CIGS that if Hubert Gough was removed from post, 'all the officers of the Aldershot Command would resign', news which came as a shock to Sir John French. On 25 March Haig gathered together his divisional and brigade commanders at Aldershot, noting in his diary:

> About 14 present. Pointed out danger of Disruption in Army to Empire and begged them to induce regt officers to give up dabbling in politics. We were all united to do anything required short of coercing our fellow citizens who have done no wrong.[27]

Eventually, the crisis was overcome, with the Gough brothers satisfied, but it brought down Seely and French.

The outbreak of war that summer not only put the issue of Home Rule in abeyance but concentrated the Army's mind on more serious and urgent matters. However, the Curragh Incident did irreparable damage to many relationships within the Army which festered throughout the war. As far as Haig was concerned, he had achieved a careful balance, not making enemies while retaining moral authority over his command. There is no reference in any contemporary diary or letters to Bulfin's response to this crisis (he would have attended Haig's briefing to his senior officers on the 25th). Given his Irish Catholic roots, he would have been in a difficult position, but in a less acute dilemma than his 'Anglo-Irish' colleagues.

It is difficult to comprehend today the degree of suspicion that existed against Catholics at this time. Haig, a Presbyterian Lowland Scot, displayed deep distrust in his diary at the time of Passchendaele about the Jesuit-educated Director of Military Intelligence in the War Office, Brigadier General George MacDonogh. He complained about the latter's gloomy assessment of affairs 'except that [he] is a Roman Catholic and is influenced by information which doubtless reaches him from tainted sources'.[28] Hubert Gough, however, who was to take against Bulfin at Loos, made no mention of the latter's Irish Catholic origins in his two books.[29] It was not that Bulfin had lost his Irishness. The eminent historian of the Great War, Cyril Falls, also born in Dublin, who served as a staff captain in the war, in describing him as 'almost a stage Irishman', made the point that he was also 'a loyal and patriotic soldier'.[30] It can only be assumed that Bulfin's absolute loyalty to the Army and the Empire was readily recognized by his brother officers.

Chapter 4

1914
'A Tower of Strength' – The Retreat from
Mons and the Battles of the Marne and Aisne

John Charteris, serving at the time on Haig's staff, recalled:

> Aldershot, in June 1914, was just recovering from the excitement of
> the Ulster crisis and settling comfortably down to normal times of
> peace. The annual training was about to culminate in manoeuvres. A
> new mobilisation scheme had come from the War Office. Some exciting
> polo matches were impending. Probably nowhere in the Empire was
> there less thought of the immediate possibility of a great war.[1]

When, on 28 June, a teenage terrorist shot the portly Archduke Franz
Ferdinand in Sarajevo, such an event in the distant and troublesome Balkans
did little to ruffle the hot summer air in southern England. Not until the
end of July, and Austria's declaration of war on Serbia, did the British public
wake up to the reality of 'Europe Drifting to Disaster', as the *Daily Mail*
headline shouted.

For the Army, the groundwork had started as far back as 1910, when Major
General Henry Wilson, then Director of Military Operations, commenced
discreet staff talks with the French to discuss plans for cooperation on the
continent. The aim was to deploy on the French left flank in the event of a
German invasion of France. Detailed mobilization plans had been drawn
up in the intervening years, to the extent that an Expeditionary Force was
organized and ready to move to the continent, something that had not
happened since Wellington's time. Unlike the armies of the other nations
involved, Britain's was a small professional body not based on universal
conscription – what Wilson termed 'our funny little army'; it was the Royal
Navy to whom the nation turned and devoted its wealth. Nevertheless, as
the official historian accurately pronounced, 'it was incomparably the best

organized, best trained and best equipped British Army that ever went to war'.[2] Some politicians and military men, such as Churchill and Haig, with a prescience that the war would not be over before Christmas, had argued for such a force to be held back until it could be properly enlarged with reinforcements from our imperial garrisons and the Territorials, and only then deployed as a potent strategic reserve. However, political imperatives – and Wilson's 'fait accompli' of coordinating plans with the French – demanded an immediate response in the form of concentrating at Maubeuge near the Belgian border. Allan Mallinson, in *Too Important for the Generals*,[3] has argued that, had the British Cabinet and War Office been properly constituted and capable of managing the war at the strategic level, an enlarged BEF could have been used as a war-winning counter-stroke force against the weak German right flank in September. It was not to be.

The day Austria bombarded Belgrade, 29 July, precautionary orders reached Aldershot and started to filter down to the divisions and brigades. This involved sending out warning telegrams to some 98,000 reservists as well as to the Territorial Force. At Bulfin's headquarters at Blackdown Camp, life for the staff would have been hectic. Events then took on an even greater urgency as Germany ordered mobilization on 1 August, prior to invading Belgium two days later, at the same time declaring war on France.

Just before midnight on the 4th, at his Aldershot residence of Government House, Haig received a phone call from his duty officer to say that war had broken out with Germany. The War Office, expecting the inevitable, had that afternoon ordered full mobilization, with a telegram consisting of one word, 'Mobilise', ordered by 'Trooper', the code name for the Secretary of State for War. Haig noted in his diary, 'Everything had been so well thought out and foreseen that I, as C. in C. Aldershot, was never called upon for a decision'.[4] But for the staff down the chain of command there was an immense amount to do, in particular bringing battalions up to war establishment, with the necessary weapons, stores and equipment, as well as assimilating the reservists into their units.

The BEF consisted of two corps and a cavalry division, some 80,000 strong, commanded by Sir John French, with I Corps led by Sir Douglas Haig and II Corps by Sir Horace Smith-Dorrien (in place of Jimmy Grierson). The cavalry was commanded by Major General Edmund Allenby. Bulfin's 2 Brigade remained in the 1st Division under General Lomax.

By 11 August Bulfin's brigade was as ready to go to war as time allowed. He had under his command high quality infantry regiments: the 2nd Royal Sussex, 1st Loyal North Lancashires (the Loyals), 1st Northamptons and 2nd King's Royal Rifle Corps (KRRC, the 60th). As he noted in his diary that day, 'Brigade Route march (full War strength) past Jolly Farmer, back by Frimley Green. Reservists very soft … many of the Loyal North Lancashire Regt. fell out, not much time to correct this.'[5] The same day, King George and Queen Mary paid a farewell visit to them at Blackdown Camp. The brigade embarked the next day at Farnborough station for Southampton, arriving in Le Havre on the 13th – 'ship very crowded only standing room' – where they were billeted two miles from the quay – 'much enthusiasm among inhabitants'. The following day, they moved by train up to Rouen – 'Men working splendidly and most orderly and quiet' – then on to Amiens and Arras, finally detraining at midnight on the 15th at Le Nouvion. An early morning march in heavy rain brought them to the BEF concentration area, centred on Maubeuge. In 2 Brigade's case, the battalions were billeted in the village of Esquéhéries to the south of the huge Mormal Forest. For the next three days Bulfin sent his battalions out on ever longer route marches, which would pay dividends in the weeks to come. There was time for some relaxation, albeit with a reprimand to follow: 'Brigade Drums played on the green … Drum Major Loyal North Lancs did not play retreat as ordered.' Sir Douglas Haig also paid them a visit on the 19th.

Britain's entry into the war on the continent has often been seen at home through a myopic lens. Heroic tales of the Old Contemptibles facing the German hordes at Mons shield the fact that the numerically superior French army had already been fighting hard for three weeks. The German general staff's strategy for winning the war in the west was based on the Schlieffen Plan, with a huge right hook through Belgium designed to encircle Paris. The French had their own pre-arranged offensive, Plan XVII, with two of their armies attacking in Lorraine, as well as two further ones being launched a week later into the Ardennes to hit the German southern flank as they moved through Belgium. General Joffre saw the British contribution as being to protect the left flank of Lanrezac's Fifth Army along the Sambre, itself on the left flank of the French. By 20 August the Germans had taken Brussels, destroyed the French offensive in Lorraine and were shortly to do the same in the Ardennes. Nevertheless, Joffre was determined to maintain

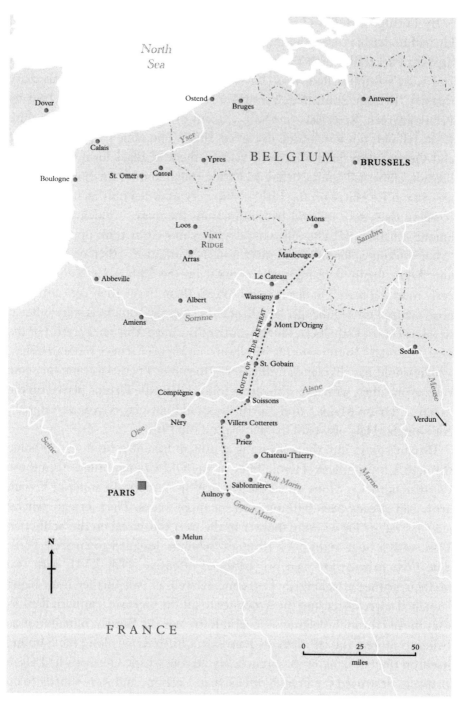

Map 3. France and Belgium 1914.

the offensive, ordering Lanrezac to make a limited advance towards Namur, in spite of his being keenly aware of the threat to the French left flank. The BEF were required to conform with this plan, and hence orders were issued for a general advance, unaware that this would mean heading directly into the powerful right hook of Von Kluck's First Army.

On the 21st, therefore, 2 Brigade set off from Esquéhéries (or 'Esqueries' as Bulfin spelt it) as part of Haig's I Corps, placed on the right flank of the BEF's advance. On the way up the troops sang as they 'marched through MAUBEUGE, inhabitants cheering *Vive* [*sic*] *les Anglais*'. But the soldiering soon got serious. Two day later, tired after marching in sweltering heat, the first sounds of war reached them. Bulfin recorded in his diary:

Orders out at 3 a.m. moved off at 4 a.m. Raining. Very narrow winding streets. Heavy firing north of us about 12 noon. Ordered to move to GIVRY at 8 p.m. German aeroplanes hovering about during afternoon.

The Great Retreat

I Corps remained relatively unscathed during II Corps' famous clash with the leading elements of the German First Army at Mons on the 23rd. Haig, lacking confidence in Sir John French's grip on events and keenly aware of the German military doctrine of encirclement, was anxious about the vulnerability of his right flank – as indeed he should have been, given that Lanrezac was pulling back. The next day, the 24th, the BEF, in order to conform with the French, was ordered to retire. The Retreat from Mons had started. In his first experience of commanding a brigade in action, Bulfin was faced with a fighting retreat, the most difficult phase of war and a challenge some of his fellow commanders would fail to meet. In a gruelling test of stamina and nerves, his priority was to keep his brigade intact and to steady his troops when fear and uncertainty could easily descend into panic. Fortunately, I Corps were less molested by the advancing Germans than its neighbours.

His diary for the 24th recorded:

A good deal of firing going on between the Cavalry and the enemy about 5 miles North and North East. Roads all blocked with crowds of

Country folk all fleeing from Germans – Ladies and Gentlemen and poor people all racing along pell mell in any sort of conveyance and on foot, children and women the largest proportion.

The entry for the 26th showed that Bulfin had not lost his regimental touch: 'Very sorry for men, sweating all day … now wet through'. Indeed, his diary for the retreat is striking in its concern for his troops' welfare and the physical demands placed on them; almost every day's entry refers to their fatigue after long marches and the efforts to feed and rest them. The day's diary finished with a notable understatement: 'Gather there was a bit of a mix up at LE CATEAU.' This 'mix-up' was Smith-Dorrien's controversial decision to make a stand there and hence, in many historians' view, save the BEF from envelopment. Haig's reluctance to come to his aid, more concerned as he was at the perceived danger his own corps faced, added to the dysfunctional state of high command. For most of the retreat the two corps acted as independent commands, and they remained out of contact with each other until 1 September. Bulfin's vague comment about Le Cateau underlines the lack of communication between the two formations.

The strain of command soon began to tell on many senior officers. At GHQ, the chief of general staff, Lieutenant General Sir Archibald Murray, was close to collapse, and some orders of his deputy, Henry Wilson, to pull back were ignored as being an over-reaction to events.[6] In II Corps, Smith-Dorrien admitted that 'some of the staffs of brigades and divisions are quite worn out and almost unequal to working out orders'.[7] During the next few days, the chiefs of staff of the Cavalry Division and the 4th Division collapsed, whilst Colonel Boileau of the 3rd Division had a total breakdown and shot himself in the head in a staff car. Admittedly, II Corps had a much tougher time for the first few days. In I Corps, Haig was very fortunate in having Johnnie Gough, still recovering from an operation a few months earlier. This calm, cheerful and competent staff officer was a major influence in the relative good order of I Corps's retreat. Gough's deputy, Colonel Jeudwine, added to a strong general staff team. At divisional level, Haig was concerned at how Major General Charles Monro, GOC 2nd Division, and his chief of staff were coping,[8] whilst within 1st Division, although the GOC, Major General Lomax, was responding to the pressure robustly, doubts were being raised about the performance of Brigadier General Ivor Maxse of 1 Guards

Brigade.[9] Bulfin seemed to be coping with the physical and mental strain better than most.

At regimental level, Lieutenant E.S. Needham, a platoon commander in the Loyals, encapsulated the ordeals of 2 Brigade's retreat:

> This continued marching in the wrong direction was beginning to get on everybody's nerves, and it was getting increasingly difficult to keep the men cheerful. They could not understand it, and neither could we for that matter. But otherwise they were simply splendid. No one who did not go through that retreat can possibly imagine what it was like. Up and away at dawn every day, marching all day in tropical sun and amidst clouds of dust, generally on the terrible rough pavé roads, or pushed down into the equally rough and very stony gutter by other columns of troops on the same road, or by staff cars rushing past and making the dust worse than ever. Never any proper meals, never a wash or a shave, never out of one's clothes, carrying a terrific weight of arms and equipment, and, as regards the 2nd Brigade, never getting a chance of a shot at the enemy except one day at Wassigny to cheer one up a bit.

He sympathized with the plight of the French refugees – 'very corruptible to the morale of the troops'; some of them cursed and spat at the troops, but 'the majority plodded painfully, thankful for any little help we could give them'.[10]

The 'chance of a shot' at Wassigny referred to a sharp encounter on the 27th, the first time Bulfin's troops experienced a close skirmish with the enemy. The brigade was acting as left flank guard to the corps on a day of constant rain. He had just bought a cartload of bread for his men, the rations having got lost, when German infantry coming up in lorries bumped into the Northamptons, with the enemy taking casualties and a Uhlan cavalryman captured. Bulfin pulled back the Northamptons through the 60th, and the latter then 'knocked out about 60 of the enemy'. More significantly, over to Bulfin's right, he observed a mile away heavy attacks being launched on 1 Guards Brigade's rear guard near Etreux. This was the 2nd Royal Munster Fusiliers being overwhelmed after a staunch fighting withdrawal. Bulfin was very aware of the dangers of being cut off. That very day he wrote: 'We had a big German force all round our rear today but they did not come on … Men wet through and very done. A very long march.' They got to their billets at Hautville on the Oise at about 9.00 pm.

The next day, the 28th, was probably their most nerve-wracking so far. Receiving orders at 2.00 am to cover the retirement of the corps, supported by a brigade of guns and some reinforcements of the Royal Warwicks, the brigade held on to the high ground on the northern edge of Mont d'Origny. At 7.00 am large numbers of German cavalry approached, followed by two brigades of infantry. By 10.00 am a real battle was raging, despite the main body of the corps not yet being clear of the town. The situation became serious when the Northamptons, placed in reserve a mile to the rear, reported that they were being attacked from their rear and urgently needed reinforcements – 'Sent message he (CO) must do without them as both Sussex and Loyal North Lancs were bearing the brunt of attack and K.R.R. were also engaged.'

By midday the whole of the plateau was being shelled by 'fully 100 German Guns and rear of Corps was still only three miles away.' Fortunately, a French division came up from their right and Bulfin managed to 'induce the General to lend a hand'. Two dismounted cavalry regiments were put in the line and Bulfin succeeded in pulling back his leading battalions and got the brigade away by 1.00 pm – 'Long march, arrived at FRESANCOUR at 11 p.m. Men dog tired. Heard the French troops that relieved us were almost blotted out.' As the brigade-major wrote in the war diary, 'Marched a total of 26 miles … men very exhausted, but marching well. Rations have been none too plentiful. Very little sleep.'[11]

Needham described that march:

I shall never forget the last halt we were to have that night. As usual, everybody – officers and men – threw themselves down just at the edge of the road. When the whistle blew for 'Fall in' many of the men lay where they were, not in any mutinous spirit but just because they were physically incapable of getting up. [With a fellow officer] I went round actually kicking the men till they got up and threatening, with our revolvers drawn, to shoot any man who did not fall in at once. We were reeling about like drunken men ourselves, past hoping for any rest, but knowing we had to go on.[12]

The following day, a Sunday and a 'hot fine day', the brigade was ordered to halt and rest – 'Badly needed. Men done to a turn.' But for the commander and his brigade-major, who had had the advantage of being mounted during the retreat, there was work to be done, and they set off in a borrowed car to reconnoitre positions along the River Oise. The importance of knowing one's ground and planning ahead was deeply rooted in Bulfin.

The march south continued the next day, as recorded by the official history:

Since crossing the Somme, the British had passed into a rugged country of deep woodlands, steep hills, narrow valleys and dusty roads. Severe gradients and crowds of refugees multiplied checks on the way.[13]

The 30th was intensely hot and the air was stifling in the Forest of St Gobain, through which they marched most of the day. The march had to be stopped early due to the men's exhaustion. Bulfin noted that day, 'Men felt heat very much but most got baths in the canal, which they needed.'

By 31 August the corps had completed the crossing of the Aisne, but the next day, hoping that they had shaken off the enemy, the march was again called off early, due to the extreme heat. However, 4 Guards Brigade and 6 Infantry Brigade, in the neighbouring 2nd Division to Bulfin's left, had to fight off a strong attack north of Villers Cotterets. About 460 casualties were sustained that day by I Corps, the heaviest toll for the corps during the entire retreat. Among the dead was the promising commanding officer of the Irish Guards, Lieutenant Colonel the Hon. George Morris, a fellow Irish Catholic of Bulfin's from Galway. The same day, II Corps had an equally tough time, with L Battery of the Royal Horse Artillery winning three VCs at Néry in the valley of the Oise.

But 1 September was more significant as the day when Lord Kitchener, Secretary of State for War, arrived in Paris in full field marshal's uniform. There he ordered Sir John French to remain alongside the French, and not to withdraw the BEF out of the line and retire to the Channel ports as he had intended. The next day, the French government fled Paris for Bordeaux and the BEF was ordered to deploy east of the capital, with I Corps pulling back to the Seine. Despite the prevailing sense of doom, the stubborn and resolute Joffre realized that the Germans were becoming over-extended and split – the Schlieffen Plan was falling apart. It had envisaged von Kluck's

First Army swinging west of Paris, enveloping it, but his troops had now become separated from von Bülow's Second Army, resulting in von Kluck being forced to turn east. This critical information came largely from Royal Flying Corps reconnaissance. The German right flank was now exposed to an Allied counter-stroke – and it was the 'swinging' right wing of von Kluck's army, designed to be the strongest in the Schlieffen Plan, which had been weakened, mostly at the hands of the British. Joffre saw his chance and, notwithstanding the deep exhaustion of his own troops, ordered an immediate general advance. It would cover a front of some 150 miles from Verdun to Paris, and Joffre urgently needed the BEF to support the French Fifth Army in the centre. As Allan Mallinson put it:

> The proverbial boot was now on the other foot, but it was a boot worn thin by a fortnight's fighting and marching – and in the case of some of the French troops, three weeks' fighting and marching.[14]

When Joffre drove to Sir John French's headquarters outside Paris at Melun on the afternoon of the 5th, there was an emotional meeting between the two. Joffre set out his bold plan:

> The time for retreating was over … turning full to Sir John, with an appeal so intense as to be irresistible, clasping both his hands so as to hurt them, General Joffre said, '*Monsieur le Maréchal, c'est la France qui vous supplie*' [it is France that begs you]. His hands fell to his sides wearily. The effort he had made had exhausted him.

Edward Spears, the British liaison officer to the French Fifth Army ('the most important subaltern in the British Army'), who was present at the meeting, continued to describe the scene:

> Sir John, with tears in his eyes, feeling unable to respond properly in French, turned to an officer besides him and exclaimed, 'Damn it, I can't explain. Tell him that all that men can do our fellows will do.'[15]

Whilst high strategy was being decided, the soldiers of 2 Brigade tramped on in the continuing scorching weather, crossing the Rivers Marne and Petit

Morin. Charteris commented that during 'the last few days of the retreat they [the men] were very glum, they marched silently, doggedly, never a whistle or a song, or even a ribald jest, to help weary feet along the road'.[16] The official history recorded:

> An inhabitant of the district put on record the appearance of the British during this period of the retreat: 'The soldiers, phlegmatic and stolid, march without appearing to hurry themselves; their calm is in striking contrast to the confusion of the refugees. They pass the night in the villages of the Ourcq … and depart at daybreak, silently like ghosts, on the whistle of the officer in charge.'[17]

Not surprisingly, morale and fighting spirit were variable across the BEF. Lieutenant Hyndson of the Loyals, marching alongside his platoon, portrayed a less weary picture. His observation was that by the 3rd improvements in physical condition and morale had become noticeable:

> The men have quite recovered from the awful first days of the campaign, and are in splendid fighting trim. The combination of sun, rain and wind has given them a bronzed appearance, and they are extraordinarily cheerful.[18]

On the 4th, 2 Brigade rallied at Aulnoy near the Seine, about 40 miles east of Paris near the Forest of Crécy, with German cavalry still pursuing. They were not aware that the retreat from Mons was over. I Corps had marched 160 miles in thirteen days, suffering some 2,261 casualties along the way, not all from enemy action – indeed, some were stragglers who would catch up with their units in the following days. There was now only meagre respite: in two days they joined the French in turning the tide in the 'Miracle of the Marne'.

The Miracle of the Marne – *'En Avant!'*

Gary Sheffield has described the Battle of the Marne as 'one of the decisive phases of the First World War',[19] a moment when the Allies had the opportunity to inflict a crushing defeat on the Germans in the West.

The BEF, although small in relative numbers, was still in good order and, importantly, well located to hit von Kluck's flank in concert with the French Fifth Army on its right. This was now commanded by General Franchet d'Esperey – inevitably nicknamed 'Desperate Frankie' by the Tommies – a determined commander, who established much better relations with his British neighbours than the sacked Lanrezac. Miraculous efforts had been made by the French to rush fresh troops out of Paris and elsewhere, transported in the city's taxis and omnibuses, to form a new Army, the Sixth, under General Gallieni. The situation had improved for the BEF as well with the arrival of a third corps, under Lieutenant General William ('Putty') Pulteney, including batches of reinforcements for the other two corps.

The fact that the Allies failed to achieve a decisive victory at the Marne has been put down, in part, to the caution and timidity displayed by senior officers in the BEF, led by a badly shaken commander-in-chief. Haig, amongst others, has been criticized for being too wary about the Germans striking at his flanks and not taking sufficient risks in pushing his divisions forward. Indeed, J. P. Harris, in his study of Haig, considered him not only to have been 'a nervous and distinctly battle-shy commander' during the retreat,[20] but also to have been sceptical about Joffre's plans for the Marne offensive. He observed that 'In later years Haig used to say that he never knew there had been a Battle of the Marne.'[21] This may be construed as a lack of commitment to the battle, but it was an understandable remark. Many other participants had a similar memory of the battle as a series of disconnected skirmishes against retreating German rearguards; indeed, the major 'contacts' did not take place on the Marne but near the Ourcq. Nevertheless, Charteris defended his master's command:

> Even a highly trained army does not easily adapt itself to the transition from retreat to advance; it is apt to be over-cautious … Even in his own Corps Haig noticed that Commanders who had previously been the strongest advocates of bold action now tended to hold back.[22]

The exhausted BEF had the added challenge of advancing across five deep river valleys, with all the attendant problems of river crossings. On the second day of the advance Haig showed his frustration at the lack of urgency, with Charteris, now his intelligence officer, noting:

Actually, our own troops, although the men were very keen, moved absurdly slowly, and D.H. spent the day going from one Divisional H.Q. to another to try to urge them forward. The cavalry were the worst of all, for they were right behind the infantry.[23]

Bulfin's diary for the first day of the advance partly reflects this hesitancy, although there seemed no reluctance to push on when instructed. His brigade was ordered to make 'a long halt from 11.00 until 4 p.m.' but, despite this, his men, still footsore and tired, marched almost 20 miles that morale-lifting 6 September – 'First day our retreat had changed to an advance. Men started whistling.' Matters seemed to improve the next day, when they covered a similar distance, hot on the heels of the enemy rearguard, including a unit of the Imperial Guard, reaching the banks of the Grand Morin. On 8 September, a wet and cloudy day, 2 Brigade, after acting as advanced guard, was pulled back to be rear guard of the division. At Sablonnières, on the north bank of the Petit Morin River, the cavalry were ambushed and, when Bulfin passed, 'they were burying my old friend John Norwood V.C.'.[24] Captain Norwood of the 5th Dragoon Guards had won his VC as a young subaltern at Ladysmith, rescuing a wounded trooper under fire; he had later served as staff officer to Bulfin in his mounted column in 1902, being mentioned in dispatches by him. By nightfall the BEF had reached the Marne, with I and II Corps offered a golden opportunity to press forward into the gap between the two German armies. But what momentum had existed seemed to be fading.

On 10 September the enervating hot weather finally broke, to be replaced by cold heavy rain, and this reduced mobility, complicated by the need for the BEF to swing north-east towards the Aisne to conform with the French Fifth Army. Here Franchet d'Esperey had von Bülow's Second Army in full retreat. But for the BEF it was a day of hard lessons. One of the tactical failures of the advance to the Marne was the poor communication and coordination between the artillery and advancing units, resulting in a number of 'friendly fire' tragedies in both leading corps. 2 Brigade was not to escape this. Back as advanced guard to the division, the brigade moved off at 5.00 am with a squadron from the 15th Hussars well out in front. By 9.00 am the squadron commander reported that the enemy were in force north of Courchamps. Bulfin rode forward with his brigade-major, Major Cooke, and saw that the Germans were pulling back over a ridge above Priez, with mounted troops hovering on both flanks. Having sent back a report to Lomax, Bulfin asked his fellow advanced guard brigade commander in 2nd Division, Brigadier General Davis, to support him on to the ridge. Bulfin then gave orders for a brigade advance to contact, backed up by three batteries of guns and howitzers, with the Royal Sussex and the Loyals in the lead. Although the Sussex got held up, 'Colonel Knight [CO the Loyals] handled his battalion splendidly.' Moving the Northamptons, in reserve, up to help the Sussex, Bulfin rode forward with Major Cooke and another staff officer to push them on – 'Meanwhile kept urging Davis to press on and bear a hand, but he never budged from his first position … enemy shells falling all over the place, most unhealthy.'

About noon, the senior gunner of the 1st Division, Brigadier General Findlay, was killed, and shortly afterwards, 'Cooke, my Brigade Major, [was] shot through chest. He was close by me at the time.' Bulfin's account carries all the immediacy of battle:

> Ordered all guns to bombard PRIEZ and then lift onto ridge. After 5 minutes bombardment, Sussex rushed PRIEZ and streamed up hill. Loyal North Lancs carried wood on the right, and enemy started streaming away. General Briggs with his Horse Artillery Guns, mistook Sussex with their waterproof sheets for Germans and opened on them. Very critical situation until we got Briggs to stop firing. Our Guns galloped up to ridge all among our infantry and opened fire on the Germans running away and fairly plastered them in column of fours, crossing the Marne north of NEUILLY.

2 Brigade maintained its momentum, taking Neuilly and seizing a bridge over the Marne by Rassy. Then bad news reached Bulfin:

> Heard that Colonel Knight had been hit in the stomach. He died next morning. The Army lost a very gallant and brilliant officer and a fine gentleman. From rough returns we lost today 4, wounded 21 (officers), Rank and file 21 killed and 136 wounded. Raining heavily.

The next day, he was forced to miss Knight's funeral, 'not having a Brigade Major', but in the evening 'wrote to Mrs Knight before turning in'. It was

Bulfin's first major brigade attack, and he must have been angered at the needless loss of life. The 12th found them marching through torrents of rain, the Brigade HQ being billeted that night in a chateau in Paars. The retreating Germans, ill-disciplined and angered at being forced back, left a trail of wanton destruction: 'Germans here last night. Have smashed and destroyed everything.'

The next day, they reached the Aisne at Bourg. Although I Corps had covered 70 miles in a week, taken some 1,000 prisoners and helped to throw the Germans on to the defensive, the BEF's failure to cross the rivers and take the high ground beyond the Aisne, before the Germans could reinforce it, was a serious lost opportunity. A greater degree of urgency would have forced the Germans to continue their retreat, possibly broken their brittle morale and perhaps even avoided the long stalemate of the trenches. But the Battle of the Marne was nevertheless a victory, in that it marked the German General Staff's failure to defeat France as envisaged in the Schlieffen Plan. As the broken von Moltke reported to the Kaiser, 'Your Majesty, we have lost the war.' But from whatever angle the battle is seen, it was essentially a French victory, given the scale of their contribution – and their huge sacrifice: their losses amounted to about 18,000 killed, 112,000 wounded and 80,000 missing.[25]

As for Brigadier General Edward Bulfin, during the past three weeks of campaigning he had started to be noticed as a commander imbued with a fighting spirit, one who could be relied upon to keep his nerve. What lay ahead was to test him much further.

The Aisne and the start of trench warfare

On 13 September the month-long bloody Battle of the Aisne commenced. It was evident the Germans had broken clear and intended to make a stand on the north bank of that wide and deep river. The Aisne was a formidable obstacle, more of its bridges having been destroyed by the French in their earlier retreat than by the Germans. To the north a series of spurs and re-entrants, interspersed with thick woods, rose over 3 miles to a pronounced ridgeline, running east-west, along which ran the Chemin des Dames, a road originally named by Louis XV for his daughters. The ridge was a daunting feature, with all the advantages needed by a defender. Edward Spears commented:

> I am deeply thankful that none of those who gazed across the Aisne
> ... had the faintest glimmering of what was awaiting them. They were
> untroubled by visions of mud and soaking trenches ... years of misery
> ahead.[26]

What Haig did not know at the time was that the sector in front of his corps
was very weakly held until about 2.00 pm on the 13th, when a corps of
German reservists arrived, after force-marching an extraordinary 40 miles
in twenty four hours from Maubeuge.

Bulfin's brigade was positioned on the right flank of the BEF, and by the
evening of 13 September had crossed the Aisne at Bourg by way of an intact
aqueduct. Although very tired, the brigade was given the task of attacking
the high ground above Cerny before daybreak, as part of a corps attack.

> Haig had little definite knowledge of the strength, positions or intentions
> of the enemy in front of him. He seems to have been by no means clear
> that he was sending I Corps into its first serious battle of the war. All
> he and his staff had done was to give the divisions their objectives and
> axes of advance.[27]

In addition, Sir John French can rightly be criticized for allowing the
opening of the Battle of the Aisne to dissolve into a series of uncoordinated
and often chaotic brigade attacks.

With little time to plan such a major undertaking, and disliking the prospect
of attacking uphill across difficult ground without a reconnaissance, Bulfin
sent out a KRRC patrol. This was led by a subaltern[28] and returned at 2.30
am, having bumped into enemy outposts but not reaching the key ground of
what became known as the Sugar Factory. Nevertheless, the brigade attack
started as planned, but the desperate uphill assault that followed, against
fixed German machine guns and heavy artillery support, degenerated into
a confused soldiers' battle. The 2nd KRRC with the 2nd Royal Sussex led
the advance in heavy rain and dense mist, the poor visibility hampering any
effective artillery support until about 9.00 am. But Bulfin, well up with the
leading troops, did his best to exert some grip on the fluid battle, detaching
the Northamptons to give support and ordering the 1st Loyals to push
forward to the Sugar Factory. Accompanying the Loyals, he witnessed 'lots

of shells and bullets flying about'. One of their soldiers, Private Frederick Bolwell, recalled his brigade commander urging his battalion on with the words 'That ridge has to be taken by nightfall – otherwise we shall be annihilated.'[29] An officer of the Loyals remembered 'cold rain on their faces and an uphill approach across the clay fields deep in beet plants, for a quarter of a mile over open ground under fire from front and flanks'.[30] Although the Sugar Factory was eventually taken, a German counter-attack pushed them out of it at 2.00 pm. Confused and close-quarter fighting continued throughout the afternoon, with the gunners firing at 500yds range. When darkness came, the men dug in just under the lip of the crest, fighting off two heavy counter-attacks. Bulfin was very much in touch with events: 'My headquarters in sunken road 150 yards in rear of first line … my horse shot. Got biscuits and bully beef and some tea for men. Ammunition, which had been running out, came up.' Trench-digging that night achieved little more than 3ft in the hard rocky ground – a portent of things to come.

It had been a punishing day, Bulfin reporting some 41 officer and 926 other rank casualties from the brigade, including the deaths of Ernest Montresor, CO of the Royal Sussex, and his adjutant, as well as the new CO of the Loyals, Walter Lloyd. The Loyals' losses in particular were very heavy indeed; their regimental memorial of the Great War stands a few hundred yards from the Sugar Factory. I Corps' casualties for 14 September were 3,500, similar to those suffered by the corps on the opening day of the Somme. Particularly worrying was the loss of so many valuable regular officers. At 11.00 pm Sir John French ordered the BEF to entrench. 'Although no one would know it, this marked the end of genuinely open warfare for the British Army on the Western Front. The stalemate would last until March 1918', wrote Gary Sheffield.[31] Nevertheless, in the BEF's first major offensive battle of the war, Bulfin's fighting spirit and determined leadership very nearly succeeded in getting the corps a firm foothold on the Chemin des Dames.

The next few days of hard fighting, in dreadfully wet weather, dug in between the Aisne and the high ground of the Chemin des Dames, saw many counter-attacks being beaten off. Bulfin's stubborn defence won the admiration of his divisional commander, General Lomax: 'Genl. Bulfin commanding 2nd Brigade … was always cheerful and cool … From the 15th the success of the Division in maintaining its ground is chiefly due to Brigadier General Bulfin and his brigade.'[32] Holding this contested sector meant quickly adapting to the new trench warfare, with wire laid out and trenches deepened. It was also the time when Sir John French, alarmed at the high officer casualty rate, issued an order to the BEF for officers to 'avoid undue exposure and take cover whenever possible'; on I Corps's copy there is a handwritten note: 'Seen by GOC [Haig] no action to be taken.'[33] When 2 Brigade was relieved on the 19th, Bulfin was recorded by Charteris as being 'really almost peevish when he was told that his brigade was being pulled out for a short rest and [he] replied: "We never asked to be taken out – we can hang on here quite well"'.[34] Bulfin's own diary admits he was 'very glad as my splendid Brigade is worn out'. The estimated casualties from 14 to 19 September for the brigade were 1,271 killed, wounded and missing.

General Haig arrived the following morning to visit Bulfin's HQ at 9.30 am – 'We were all very sleepy but Sir D said many nice things.' Haig confided in his diary that evening:

In spite of the wet, hunger and fatigue suffered, the troops seemed in excellent spirits. In fact I felt that a fine cheerful fighting spirit existed among the men: all I spoke to made light of their hardships and said: 'Everything is all right Sir.' I attribute this splendid result to the fine soldierly qualities of the Brigadier (General Bulfin), who has been a tower of strength to the Divisional commander (Lomax) and myself during the retreat and subsequent fighting.[35]

Two days later Sir John French visited the brigade and praised their work, speaking to assembled groups of soldiers.

The brigade returned to the front line on 25 September for a tough time of trench work, patrolling and suffering heavy bombardments; its commander was knocked to the ground by a shell as well as having his HQ blown in. He was increasingly aware of the lack of grenades in this close-quarter fighting, and the disadvantage this gave his infantrymen. On the 29th his diary entry commented:

About three weeks ago I wrote in asking for rifle grenades I had seen described in Army and Navy Gazette last year. G.H.Q. promised to find out. Today two boxes turned up. [The men continued working hard] All busy before daylight making communication trenches up to the first line. Making them 6 feet deep when possible.

The Northamptons' regimental history observed:

> The next days were spent in improving the hastily contrived trenches, which were as different from the system of the later stages of the war as a child's digging on a beach is from the underground railway system of London.[36]

The mud-spattered brigade war diary for these days has frequent mention of Bulfin and his brigade-major touring the fire trenches, day and night, and encouraging his officers and men during this testing time. On 10 October:

> Both General Haig and Field Marshal French sent messages saying how well the Brigade had done. Sent box of Three Castles Cigarettes to Loyal North Lancs for bagging sniper. Heavy shelling in afternoon.

At last a French brigade arrived, albeit late, to relieve them during the night of 15/16 October. The previous morning, the French colonel, on his reconnaissance, was offered a breakfast of bully beef and tea – what he made of this English fare is not recorded! Bulfin, seeing the last party out of their positions, wrote 'Thank God!' in his diary. On the Chemin des Dames the BEF had discovered the new nature of warfare: battles going on for weeks with no respite, barrages continuing for hours, the men encased in mud, and baths a distant memory. Field Marshal Sir John French was not alone in realizing that 'It was in the fighting on that river that the eyes of us all began to be opened.'

Looking back, it is easy to forget that in little over two months since arriving in France, Edward Bulfin, like most other brigade commanders, had experienced an extraordinarily wide gamut of command responsibility in a very short space of time. He had fought through four phases of war: the retreat from Mons, the advance-to-contact at the Marne, a brigade attack at Cerny and then defence on the Chemin des Dames.

The next day, 2 Brigade entrained and headed north for Belgium, not the most comfortable of journeys: 'Arrangements for feeding men en route, providing hot water, water for horses and latrine accommodation very bad and evidently not thought out at all.'[37] When they arrived at Cassel, Bulfin had the luxury of sleeping in 'pyjambers' for the first time in weeks. The Colonel of his regiment, Lieutenant General Sir William Franklyn, who had come over from England to visit the Front, called on him as well;[38] it would be the last time Bulfin saw him.

2 Brigade was one of the last brigades to leave the Aisne and had lost about a quarter of its fighting strength, a much higher casualty rate than most other formations. But the Battle of the Aisne forged Bulfin's reputation as Haig's 'tower of strength'. Senior commanders, such as Haig and French, 'showed a clear preference for individuals who displayed bravery under fire and a stoic acceptance of losses suffered by their formations … No British infantry commander in 1914 exhibited these qualities to a greater extent than Edward Bulfin',[39] commented Nikolas Gardner in his book *Trial by Fire*. But that did not mean Bulfin had no feeling for the losses his brigade suffered; his diary made frequent mention of concern for his men.

In the next campaign at Ypres – the British Army's 'most intense and sustained experience of combat so far in its history'[40] – Bulfin was to show more than courage and stoicism; indeed, rather more is required of any brigade commander. The qualities of leadership and command he was to display were a cool and astute tactical eye, skilled handling of an all-arms battle and the ability to seize the initiative when all seemed lost. That is why Haig picked him so often for the critical task of reserve force commander, one of his key 'fire fighters'.

Chapter 5

1914
First Ypres – 'Clinging on by our eyelids'

The British Expeditionary Force's move to Belgium was an integral element of the 'Race to the Sea', a move by both sides for the last open flank and hence the re-establishment of mobile warfare. As the fighting on the Aisne descended into a stalemate, with small gain for the casualties suffered by an already depleted BEF, Sir John French did not wish to be tied down to a subordinate role, squeezed between French forces on a static defensive line. He saw the northern flank of Flanders as an opportunity for the BEF to retain some independence and mobility. An additional benefit was that the British would shorten their lines of communication and be better able to secure the Channel ports.

On 13 October Sir John established his GHQ at St Omer, where the BEF came under the overall direction of the newly formed Northern Army Group. The commander was General Ferdinand Foch, responsible for coordinating the armies of France, Britain and Belgium in Flanders. Foch and French enjoyed cordial relations, and although the former had no direct command over the BEF, Sir John was soon caught up in Foch's enthusiasm for the offensive and the chance to return to more mobile operations, egged on by Major General Henry Wilson. These comrades-in-arms deceived themselves that the Germans, after the battle of the Marne and the sacking of von Moltke, were in disarray and incapable of mounting a serious assault. Now was the chance, they believed, for a general advance into Belgium, on the optimistic assumption that the Allies were facing only light opposition.

In reality, von Falkenhayn, von Moltke's successor, was set on enveloping the Allies' left flank in Flanders. On the move was Crown Prince Rupprecht's Sixth Army, strengthened on its right by a newly constituted Army, the Fourth under Duke Albrecht. Two armies were now gathering in the path of the Allies, with the corresponding aim of a general advance into France. Among the professional German regular corps were units of lesser quality,

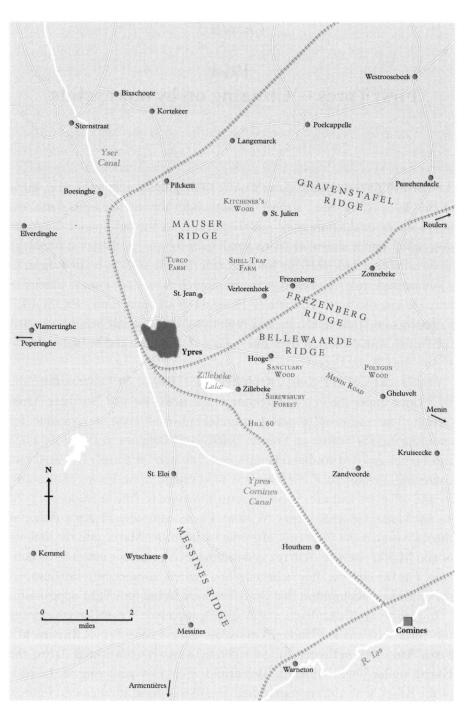

Map 4. The Ypres Salient 1914–1915.

composed of poorly trained and equipped reservists commanded by over-age officers. Nevertheless, the effect of numbers and courage, supported by superior artillery, would take its toll on the BEF over the remaining months of 1914. It would lead to the death of the old Regular Army in its famous stand outside Ypres; it was here that Edward Bulfin would meet the greatest test of his leadership so far.

Even before Haig's I Corps had left the Aisne, the first clashes of the new campaign were already taking place. South of Ypres, in the area of La Bassée, a tired II Corps came to a halt in the face of the advancing German Sixth Army. Further to the north of II Corps, III Corps with Allenby's Cavalry Corps were making better progress, taking the Messines ridge and occupying Armentières by 17 October. Some days earlier, the BEF had been augmented by the arrival of a new, albeit small formation, IV Corps under Lieutenant General Sir Henry Rawlinson, consisting of the 7th Division (Major General Thompson Capper) and the 3rd Cavalry Division (Major General Julian Byng); they reached the Ypres area on a circuitous route via Ghent, after an abortive effort trying to support the Belgian Army at Antwerp. Despite evidence from front line commanders and his own intelligence staff about the increasing strength of the Germans facing them, Sir John French felt encouraged enough to push on with his offensive and issued orders on 18 October for Rawlinson's corps to 'move on Menin', the small town to the east of Ypres. In their way was the advancing German Fourth Army. When French was confronted with this disturbing news by Colonel George MacDonogh, his GSO1 Intelligence, the Commander-in-Chief exploded: 'How the Hell do you expect me to carry out my plan of campaign when you keep bringing up these blasted divisions?'[1] Sir John's optimism lasted through much of 20 October, when he ordered Haig's corps to advance north-east from Ypres towards Bruges. However, the next day, it soon became apparent that the pendulum of battle was swinging. Among the infantry of Capper's 7th Division, holding forward slopes from Zonnebeke to Zandvoorde, exposed to enemy artillery and bearing the brunt of the onslaught, was the 2nd battalion of Bulfin's old regiment, commanded by his friend Cecil King. French reluctantly accepted turning to the defensive and ordered 'entrenchment', deploying Haig's troops to cover IV Corps' left flank and bolster the over-extended and shaken line. What became known as the First Battle of Ypres was under way.

Bulfin's 2 Brigade had arrived in Cassel at the same time as French ordered IV Corps forward; here he met Haig on the 19th, for orders to move the following day. By the night of the 20th, after a steady march, his battalions were billeted in Elverdinghe, to the west of Ypres. The brigade was to act as corps reserve, moving on the 21st to Ypres itself, as part of I Corps' deployment on the BEF's left flank. Throughout the 22nd, I Corps held a long front against repeated German assaults by massed infantry formations attacking in close order. These brave attempts were broken up by disciplined, accurate rapid rifle fire by scattered infantry groups in rudimentary shell scrapes. But some German companies succeeded, in the evening gloom, in infiltrating around the trenches of the 1st Cameron Highlanders (of 1 Guards Brigade). Here the enemy seized the crossroads hamlet of Kortekeer, north of Ypres, where a prominent inn (*cabaret*) was identified. This had created a 'big gap in the line' and a dangerous threat to the integrity of I Corps' left flank. As Charteris put it, 'It looked very serious and D.H. ordered the inn to be retaken, and the inevitable Bulfin had to do the job.'[2] It was only a short week since 2 Brigade had left its trenches on the Aisne. This was the first of two particular actions during First Ypres when Bulfin's leadership and initiative would have a critical impact on the course of the battle.

The counter-attack on the Kortekeer Cabaret

Bulfin's brigade HQ was west of the Yser Canal at Boesinghe, and its commander had spent the 22nd fruitfully reconnoitring the surrounding area. Haig's orders to counter-attack arrived at 11.00 pm and six battalions were placed at his disposal, four from his own brigade – with concentrated artillery support. 'All guns with 1st and 2nd Brigades were placed under my Command', wrote Bulfin, 'and I was to be in Command of the whole operation'[3] – the largest in his career to date. Three battalions (2nd KRRC, 1st Queen's and 1st Northamptons) were sent forward before dawn to prevent the enemy from exploiting the Kortekeer breakthrough, whilst the remaining three (2nd Royal Sussex, 1st Loyal North Lancashires and 2nd South Staffords) marched through the night from Pilckem. Bulfin then met the commanding officers further forward at 4.00 am and confirmed their orders. To mount such a large and complex operation at short notice – particularly at night – required impressively slick battle procedure.

Bulfin's plan of attack was to create a diversion on the right and concentrate his main effort on the left. Whilst the Northamptons would hold the enemy's attention, the Queen's and the Loyals would make a converging attack on the Cabaret. The South Staffords would be held in reserve close behind and the 2nd KRRC would stay in touch between the Loyals and adjoining Guards Brigade on the left flank. Bulfin, with the wisdom of 'recceing' the ground the day beforehand and with his 'remarkably astute eye for terrain',[4] realized that his left battalion, the Loyals, could advance 'more or less under cover', concealed by a wood to within about 150yds of the German positions at the Cabaret. Meanwhile, the 1st Queen's would have some 1,000yds of open country to cross, but this would draw the enemy's attention. The country here was exposed and flat compared to the more wooded and undulating land to the east of Ypres. Timing of the battalions' approaches and the supporting artillery would be crucial.

Captain Needham of the Northamptons recalled, as they set off from Pilckem that night:

> We could see the brigade commander, General Bulfin, and his brigade-major in conversation with the colonel. Presently the colonel rode back to us and told us we had to return immediately and take back the trenches lost by the Camerons. C Company was to lead the way, and I was told, not at all to my satisfaction, that I was to go ahead with the 'point' of the advance guard, taking every possible precaution, as nobody knew just where the line was, just where the Camerons were, or the enemy.[5]

After feeling their way forward through both French and British positions, the battalions got to their allotted destinations before dawn. Needham continues:

> Very shortly afterwards we heard loud shouting, cheering and singing in front of us, which we gathered was the merry Hun disporting himself after his victory of the afternoon.[6]

For the attacking troops, with ground new to them, start positions had to be found in the dark and the morning approach conducted in heavy mist. Bulfin's diary recorded:

Units got into position by noon. Heavy fire kept up. Germans in much greater strength than expected. Final advance delivered at 4 pm [although the 1st Queen's report stated they had captured the inn at 1.30 pm]; very good timing. Queens and Loyal North Lancs almost simultaneous, latter carried farm buildings.

Lieutenant Hyndson, a platoon commander with the Loyals, was at the forefront of the attack:

At ten-forty-five, having explained all we knew to the men, we deploy and advance. My company is on the right, and we almost immediately come under long distance rifle fire, so I order the men in my platoon to open up to four paces interval, and on we go.[7]

Private Bolwell of the same battalion takes up the story:

We went up in short rushes, and a word of praise is due to the men who took part in it. I never even on the barrack square or drill-ground saw a better advance: the men went up absolutely in line, each man keeping his correct distance.[8]

Hyndson continues:

Soon we work up to within two hundred and fifty yards of the enemy trenches, where we find the survivors of the Cameron Highlanders … we are now close to the 'Bosche' trenches, and must pause to wear down his nerves until he dare not show a hair, before we can complete the attack. We commence to fire for all we are worth at selected portions of their position … About this time, Miller [his company commander] made a gallant attempt to gain ground, but unfortunately both he and the men who followed him were shot down, and the command of the company descends on me again. I notice the Germans dodging past a gap in the hedge some two hundred and fifty yards to my front, and order a section to fire at them as they slip past. Remembering their snap shooting in peace-time on the range, the men enter into this task with zest, and many of the flitting figures are seen to fall. We afterwards found twenty to thirty dead Germans in this area. A red house in front also gives us considerable trouble … and so the fight goes on until about one o'clock, when the firing from the enemy trenches almost dies down. The time has come to put the finishing touches to the battle, and we work forward in small groups.[9]

With the 1st Queen's alongside, the two battalions dashed in on the enemy trenches, past the occupied buildings and, taking advantage of the enemy confusion, headed for the reserve trenches beyond:

[We were expecting] to meet with a stout resistance, but the Germans have had enough, and suddenly the glorious sight of masses of grey-coated men standing up to surrender meets our gaze … Isolated bodies of Germans still continue to resist, and must be rounded up; one particularly brave man established on the top of the windmill continues to fire, and refuses to surrender, so we have to set fire to the building; but in spite of this he goes on firing until the building collapses and its brave defender perishes in the flames. I go past a house … when suddenly … from the rear a screaming noise, followed in rapid succession by others with resounding crashes, as one after another shell lands amongst us … Our guns have mistaken us for retreating Germans, as we are well ahead of the remainder of the battalion … I shout to the men to get back to the house with the Red Cross flag. Back we run, with the exception of a few unfortunate men who are knocked out, and we get out of the danger zone. On reaching the house, what a sight meets my gaze! The whole place is crammed with German dead, dying and wounded, all lying together on the floor, packed as tightly as sardines.[10]

The official history recorded:

But so well was the movement timed that the whole front of attack arrived almost simultaneously within a couple of hundred yards of the Germans … Many of the enemy were already making off when the North Lancashire charged, but the sudden advance appears to have taken the others by surprise … that they were able to cover the last hundred yards of open ground with astonishingly little loss.[11]

Bulfin was especially impressed by the Loyals:

> Major Carter handled the Loyal North Lancs admirably, getting them close up to the enemy's lines unperceived and then seizing the right moment for going in with the bayonet just as the Queen's rushed the inn.[12]

The two key assault battalions, the Queen's and the Loyals, had killed 490 and captured almost 800 enemy – some 'were mere boys'[13] – releasing 54 Camerons, who came skipping out of the inn, 'in great delight … shaking hands and banging everyone on the back. Like a party everyone laughing and talking.'[14] Bulfin 'sent a special order to the Brigade praising their good work done and especially the Loyal North Lancs'.[15]

Later that afternoon, a delighted Haig saw Bulfin back at Pilckem. Messages flooded in. From Lomax: 'Heartfelt congratulations on your skilfully conducted attack.' From General Haig: 'Please congratulate Genl. Bulfin & all the troops concerned in the capture of the INN on the determination and pluck they have all shown. Last night was an anxious time for us all & I fully realize how hard everyone has worked to attain success.' Sir John French was equally appreciative, with a prompt message: 'I congratulate General BULFIN and troops engaged in counter-attack. This is the third time I have had occasion to congratulate General BULFIN.'[16] French's chauffeur, Frederick Coleman, recorded in his diary, with some euphoria and a degree of exaggeration as to numbers:

> At Haig's headquarters Bulfin's 2nd Brigade success of the day previous was declared to have been splendid. Six-hundred German prisoners, a field strewn with 1,500 German dead, and relief of the Cameronians [*sic*] from an isolated position were among the fruits of the victory.[17]

Anthony Farrar-Hockley, in his fine book on Ypres, *Death of an Army*, picked out Bulfin's 'deliberately and methodically' prepared counter-attack as a 'glorious success',[18] although there were not enough troops available to exploit the local tactical gain.

Not only had the counter-attack on the Kortekeer Cabaret helped to restore I Corps' morale and self-confidence, given such a knock the previous two days, but it had succeeded in unsettling the German corps commander as well as HQ Fourth Army; initially, they reported it as an Allied breakthrough. Farrar-Hockley considered it 'significant that there was neither a heavy bombardment of the Bixschoote–Langemarck line nor a counter-attack during the remainder of the day or the following night'.[19] Pressure, for a period, was taken off this sector by the German Fourth Army; as the German official account recorded, 'For the time being, any further thought of a breakthrough was out of the question.'[20] Edmonds, in the official history, summed up the Kortekeer action in a curious fashion, damning it with faint praise:

> The British had greatly increased their confidence in themselves by their successful counter-attack and greatly alarmed the enemy, but otherwise the result of the operation had been a waste of energy and unnecessary loss of life. The casualties of the 1st Division on this day were: 1,344; those of the XXIII Reserve Corps which attacked it [the cabaret] must have been considerably greater.[21]

A key lesson of generalship for the BEF from this action was the need to create a local reserve in order to respond quickly to breakthroughs, often by necessity put together from ad hoc formations. This 'puttying up', as it was called, had its chief exponent in Haig, as complimented by Cyril Falls, the Great War historian, for his 'extraordinary skill and nerve in this patching process'.[22] Bulfin's tactical skill and cool head made him the favoured man to whom to turn. The Kortekeer Cabaret operation was a fine example of the professionalism of the 'Old Army', and not available to the 'New Army', which would take until 1917/18 to replicate.

Field promotion to major general and command of Bulfin Force

On 24 October 2 Brigade handed Kortekeer over to the French, and Bulfin got his last unit out by 11.00 pm, with all in billets in Ypres by 8.00 am the next morning. But before Bulfin could get to bed:

> [I was] ordered to Divisional Headquarters at 10.00. As I had not slept for three nights, felt very stupid. Informed I was to be promoted Major

General tomorrow. Received cigarettes and matches from Sir D. Haig, wrote and thanked him. Sent cigarettes to Sussex on outpost.[23]

Promotion in the field for distinguished service was not unusual when senior officer casualties were high, but this was early in the battle and was a widely recognized reflection of Bulfin's ability.

Another brigadier general promoted at the same time was Henry Horne, the senior gunner in I Corps, who wrote home to his wife:

Of course it is delightful because it is a special selection and the other brigadier of this corps who is promoted – name Bulfin – has done awfully well, so it is a compliment to be coupled with him.[24]

Horne went on to command First Army.

Next day, the brigade marched to Hooge, and on the way, in the morning, Bulfin 'found the 2nd Bn. P.W.O. Yorkshire Regt. with a brigade of the 7th Division just in front of us. Had interview with Sir Douglas Haig at HOOGE CHATEAU at 6.30 p.m.' On the 27th he encountered Cecil King, the much loved CO of the 2nd Battalion, who was to be killed three days later in the front line. They were not to know that Sir William Franklyn, the Colonel of their regiment, had died unexpectedly in England that evening, aged only forty-eight.[25] Bulfin also ran into the quartermaster of the Royal Welch Fusiliers, also from the 7th Division, his old battalion from 1906 Aldershot days, who 'told me C.O., Adjutant and three Subalterns left to run the Battalion'. In six days' fighting, 7th Division, the 'Immortals', had lost 44 per cent of its officers and 37 per cent of its men.[26] The old BEF, fighting for its life, was a close but increasingly depleted band of fighting men. Fortunately for I Corps, which had taken 7th Division under its command that day, it had an able and imperturbable commander and chief of staff; Haig's troops were relatively well balanced and positioned, with reserves held back, for the trials ahead.

Now 2 Brigade, with Bulfin still in command despite his field promotion, was initially concentrated as corps reserve near the Menin Road at Hooge and then behind Polygon Wood, close to Lord Cavan's brigade. This was at a critical time, when the thinly held front line was taking enormous casualties, highlighted by a timely counter-attack into Polygon Wood and a ferocious defence around the Kruiseecke crossroads south-east of Gheluvelt. Anticipating its future role as a 'fire brigade', Bulfin sensibly dispatched 'all mounted officers to reconnoitre roads south and north in case we are ordered to move at night'.

The storm broke on the foggy morning of the 29th, when the axis of the Menin Road was hit in a morning attack by massed infantry formations, as part of an all-out effort by the Germans to finally overcome the exhausted Allied salient east round Ypres. Heavy attacks were made on Gheluvelt, and Bulfin was ordered to retire to woods further west, near Hooge Chateau off the Menin Road. It was here that the Ypres story originated of Bulfin offering 'sanctuary here to stragglers until they could rejoin their units'; hence the place became known for the rest of the war as Sanctuary Wood.[27] He had been ordered to release some of his men to Landon's 3 Brigade to attempt a counter-attack, which met with limited success, but with a gap of some 500yds still open by nightfall:

> All ground very unhealthy shells bursting everywhere … Ordered to send two strong Battalions to reinforce 3rd Brigade. Ordered Loyal North Lancs and the K.R.R. to join 3rd Brigade. Very hard to give up my Battalions at such a time. Saw General Landon and asked him to let me have my two Battalions back as soon as he could spare them … Do not like the situation at all … got back to my Headquarters after midnight. Road being heavily shelled also Woods round Chateau.[28]

In the middle of the night he was told to move what was left of his brigade (Sussex and Northamptons) forward towards Zandvoorde to 'fill up gap on right of 7th Division'. He found that the departing cavalry had left a huge gap, 'which the Germans could have marched through'.[29] He got his men into good positions in the woods that became known as Shrewsbury Forest, with his headquarters about 200yds behind the Royal Sussex. His diary records on the 30th:

> Men working like bees went round first line (banks along margins of woods) … Heavy shelling all day, a few casualties. Made a big dug-out for self and Staff. Don't feel a bit happy, no sort of Reserve.

Bulfin did not mention that he had been appointed Colonel of his regiment that day, following the death of General Franklyn;[30] doubtless he had more immediate and onerous preoccupations. Haig had just issued orders to use his Bulfin Force, as the latter's command was now termed, as part of a joint counter-attack with a flanking French formation of five battalions at dawn the following day.

However, this order was overtaken by events. Next day, the 31st, turned out to be the critical day of the battle, some say of the entire war, when the Germans threw themselves again at the thin British line. In the famous words of the official history, 'The line that stood between the British Empire and ruin was composed of tired, haggard and unshaven men, unwashed, plastered with mud, many in little more than rags.'[31] To the south, Allenby's cavalry held the line at Messines and Wytschaete, but the most serious situation was at Gheluvelt, a tactically vital plateau as the last observation point on the ridge line east of Ypres. Here Landon's brigade, including some of Bulfin's men, was being driven back. Soon after, disaster struck I Corps' command structure, when at 1.15 pm three enemy shells hit the combined HQ of 1st and 2nd Divisions at Hooge Chateau; a German aircraft had spotted staff cars gathered outside the chateau. Amongst many key officer casualties, Lomax was mortally wounded, leaving HQ I Corps very much cut off from the front line brigades with little superior direction. Bulfin was immediately ordered to take command of 1st Division. The ever calm and competent Johnnie Gough sent a speedily scribbled message in pencil to Bulfin, remarkably clear given the circumstances:

> Regret things very bad. 1st Division knocked about and retiring down road passed [sic] Hooge. Come up line yourself at once leaving Lord Cavan to take over your command. General Lomax wounded & Kerr (GSO1 1st Division) killed & you must take over command but Sir D. Haig wants to see you first. Tell Cavan to hold on tight with right to canal and throw left back northwards towards Hooge. Keep French informed on your left.[32]

Curiously, Bulfin made no mention of this message in his diary. In any case he never took over 1st Division since, with his force also under intense pressure, he was soon embroiled in a crisis of his own.

Many of the participants, as well as historians, have commented that in the confusion of the fighting Ypres devolved into a soldiers' battle, as units became fractured and mixed, with high officer casualties. In some ways 'the work of divisional and brigade commanders resembled that of men trying to repair a dam which is undermined by continuous flood'.[33] Fortunately for Haig, as this flood threatened to drown his corps that fateful 31st, he had three outstanding brigade commanders with the tenacity and initiative to get a grip on the dire situation: Charles FitzClarence VC, Herman Landon and Edward Bulfin. The former's counter-attack at Gheluvelt that afternoon by 2nd Worcesters is the best known of a number of decisive actions which saved First Ypres. 'However', wrote LoCicero, 'Bulfin's exploits in the defence of I Corps' endangered right flank, during which an audacious psychological ruse was employed to turn the tide of battle, are largely forgotten today.'[34]

At his dug-out in Shrewsbury Forest, Bulfin had been waiting for the start of the provisional counter-attack when, at 6.00 am, a very heavy German artillery bombardment commenced, heralding an attack along the whole front from Messines to Gheluvelt. Large infantry masses from two German corps advanced against 7th Division on the ridge to his left and, with shelling increasing, Bulfin recorded bleakly, 'Several shells a minute broke all along the line and men going down everywhere. No cover. Simply Hell'.[35] It was on the 31st that Captain Patrick Butler, a 'galloper' – or ADC – to Major General Capper, visited Bulfin in his dug-out to pass messages from 7th Division and noticed the soldierly style of Bulfin's Force HQ. He commented in his delightful book *A Galloper at Ypres*:

It was dramatic meeting him in this way. Years before, in 1898, just prior to the outbreak of the South African War, my father had chosen him, then a young regimental officer, to accompany him to the Cape as his Military Secretary. This was General Bulfin's chance, and from that moment he never looked back … When I explained my mission, and showed him exactly our alternative position on the map, he said he hoped to heaven we were not contemplating any retirement. I said we were not, but this was a measure of precaution. He thanked me for my information, and I saluted and withdrew … Before long I had to go with another message to General Bulfin. This time I told him who I was, and his pleasure at hearing I was the son of his old chief was very great. It was worth going through a lot for, was that moment ... some days afterwards General Bulfin wrote to my mother that on meeting me all his troubles had seemed to vanish.[36]

At 2.00 pm news came that the Germans had broken through and 7th Division was retiring. Not realizing that a counter-attack had stabilized matters on his left, Bulfin had gathered his COs to plan a conforming withdrawal. But events took on a faster momentum as it became evident that his small force was in danger of being outflanked. Orders were quickly issued to carry out a coordinated withdrawal in contact, the most difficult phase of war. As Bulfin left his HQ:

Germans opened rifle and machine gun fire on myself and my Staff. My Orderly carrying my coat was killed ... Streams of Germans in unending numbers kept pouring over the ridge. As far as I could see to my North, there were endless glinting of spikes of German helmets. The roar of guns and rifles was incessant.[37]

As troops pulled back into the cover of Shrewsbury Forest, Bulfin moved around calmly reorganizing leaderless groups.

The counter-attack from Shrewsbury Forest – 'One single glorious sweep'

Sensing that the German onslaught was running out of steam under serious officer casualties, Bulfin now saw the opportunity for an immediate counter-attack and started gathering together what units he could muster. Fortunately for him, Colonel Hugh Jeudwine, the GSO1 of I Corps, who had ridden forward to obtain information, was with him when they came under fire and was tasked by Bulfin to get reinforcements from GHQ. Later, at about 3.00 pm, 'Jeudwine rode back, coming along between our lines and the Germans, his hat and clothing hit in several places',[38] having given all the messages and with news of reinforcements. Two dismounted squadrons of the 1st Royal Dragoons, followed later by a sapper company – 'full of fight'[39] – were mustered together with what was left of Bulfin's Force of Royal Sussex, Northamptons and Ox & Bucks Light Infantry.

Straightaway Bulfin then issued his concise order:

Big reinforcements are coming up behind you. When you hear the cheering, give the Germans a 'hellish minute' [rapid rifle fire]. Then boost [sic] them out, for the position on the other side of the road is better than this.[40]

The 'big reinforcements' consisted of a mere 84 men of the 2nd Gordon Highlanders, a number being cooks and clerks gathered together from the rear by their adjutant, the giant Captain Stansfeld. But Bulfin made an advantage of this:

I told the Gordons to form line and advance through the Wood cheering like mad. I ordered the front line to open a one-minute rapid fire when they heard the cheering and told all first line to go for the Germans when the cheering proclaimed the arrival of reinforcements.[41]

As things turned out:

On the appointed signal being made, Captain Stansfield [sic] and his handful of Gordon Highlanders advanced, in extended order … cheering loudly. The 'hellish minute' broke out, a crescendo of rapid rifle fire – each man doing about eighteen rounds to the minute, for musketry as well as entrenching had been the great feature in the training of the 2nd Brigade. Then, as the Gordons charged, to General Bulfin's surprise, every man in his exhausted, thinned firing line sprang to his feet and went for the Germans with the bayonet. The effect was beyond belief. The Germans were broken and hustled and driven back through the wood. In fact, their rout was so apparent, and it was so doubtful how far the handful of the 2nd Brigade might be tempted to push on, that General Bulfin issued orders at once that directly the old position was regained the line was to halt and make it good. The counter-attack succeeded in driving back the Germans the necessary half-mile and (almost) regaining the old position.[42]

Bulfin's 'one fear was that in the excitement of the moment his men would never stop',[43] and he noted, 'No prisoners were taken but hundreds of Germans were lying bayoneted all through the wood, or shot by our people.'[44] The Gordon Highlanders' regimental history recorded:

> The Germans, who had fought very hard all through the battle, turned and ran. They were chased, shot down and bayoneted in large numbers. The counter-attack pressed on for well nigh half a mile. It was stopped on the eastern fringe of Shrewsbury Forest within little more than stone's throw of the position lost in the morning. This was a grand achievement.[45]

Units from 7th Division on the left and 4 Brigade on the right picked up the mood and joined the advance.

The recaptured ground was not critical in itself, but the routing of the Germans was pivotal in saving the right of I Corps. It was also invaluable in terms of morale, steadying British nerves on such a critical day for Ypres. The historian J. P. Harris considered Bulfin's counter-attack 'one of the outstanding feats of the war so far'.[46] Indeed, Ian Beckett, in his study of the First Battle of Ypres, detailed how the divisional commanders of von Fabeck's newly constituted army group facing I Corps wanted the offensive called off after the heavy casualties of the 29th.[47] Falkenhayn, in overruling these protestations, staked a great deal on the renewed onslaught of the 31st. The fact that it was brought to a juddering halt by these resolute small groups of the BEF's I Corps, from Gheluvelt to Shrewsbury Forest, was crucial to the survival of Ypres. Falkenhayn appreciated that Ypres, the last Belgian city in Allied hands, had more than symbolic importance to the Allies; it was the transport hub to the Channel ports of Calais and Boulogne. By seizing Ypres he could place Britain, Germany's greatest enemy in his eyes, in such a vulnerable position that her fight for survival would lead, in Sir Michael Howard's words, to 'a war of Napoleonic duration'.

In the meantime, Haig mistook Bulfin Force's success for an opportunity to resume the attack next day, and Johnnie Gough issued orders to its commander to this effect. Bulfin recorded with a degree of irritation:

> At 12 midnight I received an order to move out at 4, and with Lord Cavan's Brigade, to cooperate with the French in an attack on the German position. As we were only clinging to the ground by our

eyelids, the order was a mad one. My men were lying a yard apart with no supports or reserves, and, if we lost, the whole line was gone. I saw companies and told them to hold on at all costs. Saw the rations and ammunition going up to the Battalions, and rode into G.H.Q. with Packenham [Pakenham, his brigade-major].

At Corps HQ he located Haig's chief-of-staff:

I found Johnny Gough in bed in the Chateau. I told him he must cancel the order, that if we were able to hold the line tomorrow it was as much as we could do, but to advance was madness and we would lose all the ground and YPRES into the bargain. He said all right, the order was cancelled, and I left him falling off to sleep at 1.30 a.m.

There was no rest for Bulfin, though:

I then went on to Brigadier-General Fanshawe, the gunner, and got him to give me two howitzers which I put to [use] and hid out some machine guns from some scattered houses. I got back at 4, saw companies and laid down under a tree for an hour.[48]

1 November – wounded

After a night of little respite, 1 November started as a fine warm day. As soon as the perennial morning mist had cleared, German artillery recommenced its bombardment. At 11.00 am a heavy attack developed against Bulfin Force, with three enemy battalions being cut down as they crossed the front of Shrewsbury Forest, some being enfiladed at only 200yds range. Of one enemy battalion 800 strong, Bulfin calculated that only 60 got away.

Bulfin was busy at his headquarters near Zillebeke, committing what meagre reserves he had to fill the gaps, when he was wounded three times:

I was walking with Frith [a brigade staff officer] and an orderly when a shell came and killed the orderly, smashed up Frith and I got hit in the head and side and so went down. I told Packenham [sic] to put the Brigade under Lord Cavan and got away into YPRES after I had been patched up.[49]

The official history is less prosaic: 'Towards noon, to the great loss of the BEF, that determined fighter, General Bulfin, was disabled by wounds.'[50] Captain Butler, who had visited him the day before in his dug-out, heard that he had been wounded 'and before long he passed us on foot, going slowly back to the dressing-station, with some other wounded men'.[51]

That evening, Douglas Haig wrote in his diary: 'Bulfin reported wounded. A great loss to me as he was a tower of strength at all times.'[52] He was missed equally by his soldiers; Private Bolwell remarked, 'Every man in the Brigade felt very keenly the loss of the Brigadier; it was he who took us from Aldershot, and not a better General or a braver and cooler soldier under fire, ever stepped on field of battle.'[53]

As Bulfin was sent back by train to Boulogne, at Ypres the hospital and station were being shelled and several wounded were killed. The next day, in a hotel converted into a hospital outside the town, 'they took out a lot of metal from my head'. His diary ended with a short entry for 3 November: 'Embarked on board the ST ANDREW at 6 p.m. and left for England.'[54]

Although some historians have remarked that these wounds held him back from getting higher command more promptly,[55] he must have counted himself very fortunate to have survived the cauldron of Ypres, albeit seriously wounded, and with his reputation so high. His fellow brigade commander, Charles FitzClarence VC, was killed by a stray bullet on 12 November, and his divisional commander, Lomax, succumbed to wounds the following April (Landon was sent home with exhaustion in November).

John Bourne's assessment, in the *Oxford Dictionary of National Biography*, is to the point:

> During 1914 Bulfin established a reputation amongst his peers as an outstanding fighting soldier. The desperate days round Ypres at the end of October 1914 displayed Bulfin's courage, steadfastness and powers of leadership at their best.[56]

It is no exaggeration to claim that Bulfin ended 1914 as one of a small handful of exceptional brigade commanders whose crucial influence at Ypres saved the Allies from defeat.

1915 was to treat him less kindly.

Chapter 6

1915
Command of the 28th Division –
'A most rotten arrangement'

1915 has been labelled the 'forgotten year' of the war,[1] wedged between the heroic stand at Ypres and the 1916 Somme offensive. But for Bulfin, now a major general, 1915 would have been seared on his memory, and not for comfortable reasons. Professionally, it was to be the unhappiest of times for him.

Soon after Bulfin was invalided home to Sussex, Fanny had written to her son's headmaster at Downside to ask for him to be allowed home to see his father:

> [He] arrived home wounded a few days ago. I am thankful he is going on very well & his wounds are healing … It has been such a terribly anxious time for all of us & my husband looked worn out when he first arrived – I am glad to say he has had some rest & he badly needed it. I fear before long he may have to return to the front, but I hope this may not be yet as he is not fit for active service again at present.[2]

A mere six weeks after he was badly wounded, the War Office considered him fit enough to take command of the newly formed 28th Division. The critically short recovery time given him was a measure of the pressure to find experienced commanders in the rapidly expanding Army. As Bulfin joined the advance party on the downs above Winchester just before Christmas, accompanied by his ADC, Captain Hugh Cumberbatch, he would have had little inkling that the year ahead, both on the Western Front and in Gallipoli, was to prove to be such a bleak one.

The BEF, having started in August 1914 with four infantry divisions and one of cavalry, by January 1915 had expanded to eleven of infantry and five of cavalry. Moreover, by the end of 1915 it had grown to three armies, nineteen corps and forty divisions. This unprecedented expansion placed obvious pressures on the Government and the high command. For senior officers the immediate challenges crowded in from all directions. The lack of experienced commanders and staff needed to prosecute such a profoundly new form of warfare, and on a scale beyond the mindset of a small pre-war army, became obvious. This was compounded by the absence of a common doctrine on how to fight at the operational level and the lack of any formation training system and facilities. The want of sufficient heavy artillery and effective ammunition, soon to become public in the 'Shell Scandal', was crippling any successes. This, combined with poor infantry/artillery cooperation, primitive communications and a shortage of trench weapons and equipment, would place field commanders such as Bulfin under the greatest of pressure. It was a learning curve on a trajectory unknown to the British Army, but at least Bulfin had the hard-won experience of commanding a brigade through the tumultuous first months of the war.

'The difficulties of mobilizing are very great'

The 28th was one of the three remaining regular divisions in the Army, hastily gathered from the outposts of Empire: of the other two, the 27th deployed to France a month ahead and the 29th landed at Cape Helles in Gallipoli in April. But for the twelve battalions – 'real good regular battalions'[3] – brought back from overseas to form the 28th, pre-war garrison life in India, Egypt and Singapore[4] was no preparation for trench warfare on the Western Front. They had no time to train together once in England or to establish an esprit de corps. An inexperienced staff was cobbled together and had no time to 'bed in'. The men, most of whom had only sailed into Southampton in late December, were not acclimatized to the wet and cold of a miserable winter in England, let alone the trench conditions of the Western Front; indeed, many were still suffering from tropical diseases. The issued equipment was of a poor standard, with a number of regimental histories lamenting the inadequate quality of the boots.[5] A majority of the division's horses were overcome by exposure, made worse by an outbreak of mange: some 180 had to be placed in isolation and replaced. Mobilization stores were short and, to cap it all, heavy rain starting with a storm on 28 December made their tented camps outside Winchester a misery. All this forced Bulfin to send a furious letter to the local corps commander, who came to see for himself on New Year's Day. Bulfin had written:

> The condition of the camps is deplorable … [it] is today quite impossible to allow troops to remain in [them]. Owing to the continuous rain the tent bottoms in some cases are afloat. I have ordered 50% of the men to go on three days furlo' at once and the remainder to move today into billets at Winchester. In the case of 85th Brigade the condition is not quite so bad, but it is still very bad indeed. Today there is not a man with a dry suit of clothes on him and the Camp is one huge quagmire with men and horses wading about. I am putting this Brigade into billets. I need not tell you the difficulties of mobilising are very great – blankets, clothes, saddlery – all are soaking wet.[6]

When the division deployed to France it had only field artillery and lacked howitzers and heavy guns, a common weakness in the Army at that time. Its sappers and divisional troops were drawn from the Territorial Force, as were five infantry battalions and a mounted squadron of yeomanry. But it was a large organization of just under 20,000 men, with three infantry brigades (83rd, 84th and 85th), in total seventeen battalions.

28th Division's sister formation, the 27th, had similar experiences. Its experienced commander, Major General Thomas D'Oyly Snow, had led the 4th Division throughout the retreat from Mons, but had broken his pelvis after being crushed by his horse during the battle of the Marne. When called to Kitchener's office and told to take command of the 27th, he protested that he was not sufficiently recovered but received a less than sympathetic response from 'K': 'In his usual manner he said it did not matter: I was to see what I could do and if I found that I could not carry on I should be relieved'.[7] In his diary, Bulfin's ADC mentioned his general heading up to London a number of times before embarkation, so one might assume he underwent the same treatment. Like the 28th, Snow's men were given no time to get organized or train, its commander constantly pestered by Kitchener demanding to know whether he was ready to leave for France. Snow recorded, with horror, the poor fitness of his regular soldiers on their way to embarkation:

We marched from Winchester to Southampton, a distance of twelve miles by an excellent road. How many men fell out I don't know but the road, after the division had passed, resembled very much … the retreat from Mons, men lying about at the sides of the road and equipment thrown away. It was a discouraging sight.[8]

On 12 January the King, accompanied by Lord Kitchener, inspected Bulfin's division on Farley Down. 'Review was a great success', recorded Bulfin's ADC,[9] and those inspecting agreed that 'no finer body of infantry had ever taken the field'.[10] Three days later, the division was on its way to France, suffering a rough crossing to Le Havre and reaching their concentration area east of Hazebrouck by 19 January.

'A Division in name but not in being'

At the end of 1914, the expansion of the BEF had required the establishment of a new Army, the Second, under Sir Horace Smith-Dorrien, with V Corps, commanded by Sir Herbert Plumer, holding most of the Ypres Salient. This Army, to which Bulfin's division had been posted, was attempting to hold an inherently untenable position. The Ypres Salient was a bulge in the line east of Ypres, 8 miles deep with its perimeter extending in a 17-mile curve from Steenstraat in the north to St Eloi in the south. Despite the battles of the previous autumn, the land was still under cultivation and relatively undamaged; much of it, however, was low-lying and wet. At first sight it seemed to be a rolling plain, dotted with small houses and farms, and without any outstanding feature, as the ground never rises more than 100ft. A military eye would reveal, however, that it actually comprises a series of long, very gentle slopes, dipping down to narrow drainage ditches and then rising slowly to the crests of low, straight, flat-topped ridges. The problem was that most of the Allied positions were under German observation from the ridges to the east, with their heavy artillery able to dominate the battlefield.

On arrival in France, one of the first visits Bulfin made was to his erstwhile corps commander, Sir Douglas Haig, for lunch on 20 January. Haig was not now his superior, but commanding First Army in the enlarged BEF; the invitation was a nice touch to mark the return of his 'tower of strength' to the Western Front. Bulfin also used the opportunity to celebrate a reunion with his old division nearby and, with his ADC, to seek out his 2nd Battalion regimental friends. During the next few days he met up with his new chain of command. On the 24th he saw General Vidal commanding the French 31st Division, whose trenches the 28th Division were taking over, and the next day his army and corps commander called on him. '[They] gave us news of the naval success in the North Sea with the sinking of the *Blücher* … General [Bulfin] and Duval (the French liaison officer) both show signs of going down with 'flue' [*sic*]', recorded Cumberbatch in his daily diary.[11] Plumer returned on the 27th, and Sir John French came for lunch later that day.

Once at the Front, however, it soon became obvious that the 28th was a division on paper but not an effective fighting formation. A mere five weeks since gathering near Winchester, the division took over, on the nights of 1–3 February, part of the hard-fought sector near St Eloi, south of Ypres. Here the infamous Hill 60 was located. The official history noted:

> January was a month of rain, snow and flood, and although shelling and incessant sniping continued all day, the maintenance and repair of the trenches absorbed most of the attention and energies of the opposing forces … The trenches were in an exceedingly poor state, both as regards protection and drainage.[12]

On 4 February, before their trenches had been made properly defensible, the 83rd Brigade had a trench blown in and lost; the poorly coordinated retaking went equally badly, leading to the commanding officer of the East Yorkshires being sacked by Smith-Dorrien, whilst Brigadier General Boyle, the brigade commander, suffered censure.[13] By mid-February the three brigades, struggling in the knee-deep water of the trenches in heavy rain and high winds, were becoming seriously depleted by sickness, trench foot not surprisingly being the major concern.[14]

On 17 February – a day of 'appalling weather, mud and rain. Trenches v bad'[15] – an increasingly exasperated army commander met Plumer and Bulfin and decided that 'the men are quite unequal to the strain & as they are holding a vital position of my line I have had to arrange to swap them for other troops – a very complicated proceeding'.[16]

Cumberbatch's diary entry for the next day summed it up: 'Found General fairly chirpy. I hear our Division is to be replaced by 9th, 13th & 16th Bdes but Divisional Staff remains the same.'[17] Bulfin was evidently putting on a brave face but must have found it galling that his own brigades were being replaced by more experienced ones and were not to return until they were considered competent and fit enough for trench fighting.

The official correspondence between V Corps, Second Army and GHQ at the time reveals the long-standing poor relationship between French and Smith-Dorrien. In a paper concerning 27th Division's difficulties, Smith-Dorrien had added, in pencil, the following observation:

An example of the unreasonableness of the C-in-C – The Division was sent out by his orders & only handed over to me when actually marching up. Any shortcomings in arrangements were due to him and his staff's want of foresight. N.B. The next division the 28th were dry-nursed into the trenches a month later – every precaution being taken based on the experiences of the 27th Divn. & yet they suffered even more than the 27th – proving it was due to the want of fitness of the men from hot climates. The C-in-C however held me entirely to blame in the 28th Divn case.[18]

Notwithstanding the suffering imposed on Bulfin's troops, it was a calamitous start for him in a gossipy BEF where senior officers were frequently watching their backs. General Rawlinson, in command of nearby IV Corps, wrote to Kitchener: 'You may or may not have heard that there has been trouble over the 28th Division. They don't seem to be able to tumble to this trench warfare business and Sir John is much displeased with them.'[19] During this nervous period in the Salient, when the BEF was expanding its line, there was an extraordinarily close supervision by the chain of command of every action taking place on the front, to the extent that the commander-in-chief as well as the army commander were breathing down the necks of Plumer and his new divisions, the 27th and 28th. Smith-Dorrien, in letters to his wife, confided he was feeling ill with muscular pain and was restless to get home for some leave. Not surprisingly, he was irritated at being delayed by 28th Division's problems and anxious to fend off Sir John French's sniping, born of the ongoing antagonism between them.[20]

It is curious that the St Eloi sector, given its key location, was often used to introduce raw divisions to front-line trench routine. But senior officers would have expected a regular division to be more able to cope. Efforts were being made by Plumer, a general known for the care of his men, to provide more trench stores such as duckboards and revetting, as well as wellington boots and winter clothing. However, it would have been better use of the senior generals' time and energy to devote themselves less to fault-finding[21] and more to supporting the troops under their command.

Billy Congreve VC, serving on the staff of the experienced 3rd Division providing some of the replacement troops, hit the point:

> I hear the 28th Division lost a trench last night. The 28th Division has come in on the left of the 27th Division and is of about the same type – hurriedly put together Regular battalions, collected from all over the world, given staffs made up the same way and thrown out here. A most rotten arrangement.[22]

For the divisional commander it must have been a severe blow, to him personally and to his reputation. After dinner, when his master made a candid confession to his staff around him, Bulfin's chief of staff wrote despondently to his wife:

> General Bulfin said tonight that if he were in John French's place he would send him, Bulfin, home to train the army judging by results. Well, I am not sure he is not right. We all ought to go home judging by results. We were not much of a crowd to start with and we have been put into the most difficult place in the line and we have made a mess of it. There is no getting over the fact that up to the present we have done badly.[23]

When on 23 February V Corps demanded an explanation for what had gone wrong, Bulfin responded immediately with a robust memo, avoiding a litany of justifiable excuses but making a striking point:

> I attribute much of the difficulties and most of the embarrassments, which the 28th Division has had to combat, to the fact that the division

has not had any opportunity of any regular form of either Brigade or Divisional training … I am convinced that had this Division been got together for two months and trained as a Division when all might have got to know the others values and peculiarities, its striking power and its effectiveness would have been more than double and the casualties halved. A Division cannot be created by simply throwing Units together and calling them Brigades.[24]

In the early months of 1915 Bulfin was no better or worse served by his brigadiers and staff than the commander of any other formation hastily gathered together. One of his brigade commanders, Fitzgerald Wintour of 84 Brigade, would be told to 'go sick'[25] on 23 February, and another, R. C. Boyle of 83 Brigade, left exhausted and ill in mid-May. However, 85 Brigade had better fortune in its commander, Archibald Chapman, and his brigade-major, Cyril Deverell, the latter to become CIGS in the inter-war years. Although 27th Division did not suffer the ignominy of having its brigades pulled out of the line, it was faced with similar challenges, even to the extent that all its brigade commanders were replaced by the end of March, before the German offensive, for reasons of fitness or inexperience.

Bulfin's GSO1 (chief of staff) was Lieutenant Colonel Lord Loch, a Grenadier Guardsman and a graduate of the Staff College. He had fought in the same South African battles as Bulfin, from Belmont to Magersfontein in 1899, where he was badly wounded. Since the Boer War he had served largely on the staff, his previous appointment being as liaison officer between GHQ and Smith-Dorrien's II Corps throughout the 1914 fighting. He had also been an equerry to King George V and had the ear of the sovereign. His long daily letters to his wife, Mousie, have, up to now, been the principal insight into life in 28th Division during this period.[26] Although the correspondence is a revealing source of information, Loch held frustrated ambitions to gain promotion and his letters were a release valve for frequent criticism and complaint about his superiors generally. Once the German offensive opened at Second Ypres, Loch's criticism died down. Up to this time he seems to have led a sheltered life, as his unrealistic ideas about 28th Division's deployment were exposed in letters sent a few days before taking over its sector:

It is sad to think that we have to take these [trenches] over at all as it will take all the fight out of the Division and destroy what might be a good fighting force … It is perfectly idiotic to throw away about the only good and trained material there is left in the Army by putting them in the trenches.[27]

The division's chief administrative officer, the AA&QMG, had an unconventional past. Temporary Lieutenant Colonel Llewellyn Atcherley MVO was a reserve officer of the Army Service Corps, having been on Kitchener's staff in the Boer War, when his powers of organization were noted. He had left the Army in 1906 to become chief constable of Shropshire, and when the Great War started he was holding the same post in the West Riding of Yorkshire. During the King's inspection of the Division, before it left for France, his sovereign had awarded him the King's Police Medal, not a common occurrence on a military parade. He had undergone a torrid return to military duty, mobilizing the division for war, but was a strong support to his general. Plumer noticed his talent and promoted him out of the 28th Division to serve on his corps staff – on 22 April, the very day the German offensive hit the Salient.

Loch, loyal to his general and division, when writing a report for the King, laid out very clearly the reason for its setbacks, with a telling closing remark: 'It was therefore, a Division in name, but not in being.'[28] Sir Clive Wigram, the King's Private Secretary, replied:

The poor old division has had a rough time, but it did not have much of a chance at first … At one time, as you know, there was a tendency to belittle the work of the 27th and 28th Divisions, and it is accounts such as yours which put things in their true perspective, and dispel illusions.[29]

'He is not the man he was before he was wounded'

No general, even one in the best of health, would wish to start his command with so many cards stacked against him, even his sovereign being aware of his problems. But it does raise the question of how well Bulfin was responding to command of a division. The Canadian military historian George Cassar, in *Trial by Gas* (one of the best accounts of Second Ypres), offered this assessment:

> By experience and temperament he was not well suited for this new post. Nothing in his earlier career suggested that he possessed the tactical flexibility to cope with the frustration and challenge of trench warfare.[30]

A wider study of Bulfin's career would suggest, however, that his experience of trench warfare in 1914, as a brigade commander holding one of the hardest-pressed sectors above the Aisne, made him more qualified than most major generals of this period – without even considering the skill and tactical flexibility he displayed to such telling effect during First Ypres. Iris Oakey, to whose work Cassar referred, made an in-depth study of the problems facing 28th Division in 1915.[31] Her excellently researched dissertation is of great value to anyone wishing to understand the difficulties confronting the BEF in 1915, not an area well studied when she completed her MA in 2006. Her assessment of Bulfin's time in command drew a great deal on Loch's letters – 'The picture Lord Loch paints of Bulfin is of a courageous but debilitated man struggling to cope with responsibilities beyond his competence'[32] – but she readily agreed with the present author that her research on Bulfin did not extend in any detail outside 1915 and, in retrospect, she had seen him in too narrow a light.[33]

But whether he was fit, either physically or temperamentally, for divisional command remains a valid question. Loch felt:

> The Bullfinch [the GOC's nickname] is not well and I think his nerves are badly affected … he is not the man he was before he was wounded. He talks in a bombastic way and issues orders in an equally extravagant way expecting things to fall down before him. When talking to the brigadiers … he treats them apparently like dogs.[34]

Loch's wife's acerbic reply to an earlier 'grouse' showed little charity:

> Your reports on Bullfinch don't sound at all easy or pleasant. I expect a good bleeding would do him good, though he ought to have got that with his wound.[35]

Even allowing for Loch's frustrations, his letters reveal a general obviously not fully recovered from his wounds, still worn out from the previous year, and under considerable pressure in coping with the wider and more complex responsibilities of divisional command. One further challenge was the need to keep an eye on the training and welfare of his own brigades out of the line, all the while under the highly critical eye of his superiors. This was exacerbated by not fully trusting a staff which was 'new and nobody knew each other … we have therefore not pulled together', as Loch admitted.[36]

Early on, Loch wrote on another night to his wife:

> The Finch is a rum bird. I can't make him out quite yet. He has a sort of natural instinct for doing the right things when in actual command of men but he has not the brain to command a mass with all of which he cannot be in natural contact.[37]

At times, Bulfin's frustration in dealing with such a myriad of challenges exploded into temper, but Loch observed, 'His temper is quick though not bad.'[38]

The ADC's diary gave little indication of how his general was coping, only mentioning one incidence of bad temper, later on in the heat of battle. On 26 February he did offer a hint of the pressure facing him:

> General stepped out by himself to go round the Brigades … Horne [Bulfin's other ADC, from the Surrey Yeomanry] and I went out to hunt for General as he was so late. We got back at 1 am, having found he was alright. General returned at 4 am.[39]

He had been stranded in the trenches, in full moonlight. The next day, Cooke, his old brigade-major, wounded at the battle of the Marne and now a colonel, 'came in after lunch bringing 1 doz Whisky',[40] evidently aware that his old brigade commander needed cheering up.

The fact that Bulfin did manage to keep his sense of humour and fun during this testing time showed his considerable strength of character. Loch recorded:

The Bird is a great actor and tells stories really well … generally long winded but he tells them with plenty of expression and go, both in pace and voice. Some of the stories are very stupid but I can always get up a laugh at the way he tells them.[41]

The pressure was not only felt by Bulfin. Loch, who as chief of staff had the responsibility of translating his commander's intent into clear orders, a task needing an eye for detail, was finding his own job taxing. In mid-February, at a time when the division's staff work was under particular scrutiny, he admitted, 'I have never been good at working out the details of a plan but can generally say what ought to be done.'[42] The rest of the divisional staff were inevitably on a steep learning curve as well, not helped by their general's lack of confidence in them. A cavalry staff officer visiting Bulfin's HQ noted: 'Went on to HQ 28th Div. – things not right there; everyone looks very tired.'[43]

At least Smith-Dorrien, his army commander, appreciated what Bulfin was going through at this time:

Genl. E. Bulfin & his C.S.O.[chief staff officer] Lord Loch had a very bad time … & slept in their clothes 14 nights running & were quite worn looking, but are now (?) & smiling.[44]

All in all, Bulfin had his work cut out. For someone renowned throughout the Salient as a stout fighter and formidable leader, his start to 1915 had not been propitious. The forthcoming onslaught on the embattled Salient would test whether he had the stomach and ability to command at this level.

A fresh start

On 31 March better news reached them, the ADC noting:

We are going to get back our old Brigades pretty soon commencing with the 85th in about 2 days time. They all say our Brigades have been doing excellent work and one officer described our Brigades as the best in the Army.[45]

Billy Congreve VC, often critical about both the 27th (under 'that silly old man Snow') and 28th Division, had written in his diary on 23 March:

> I forgot to say that we have the 85th Brigade in exchange for the 9th, as the 28th Division – like the 27th – seem unable to manage their business properly. We have found the 85th Brigade to be first-class in every way.[46]

On a happier note, Loch seemed to be establishing a better relationship with his general. In his daily letter home on 11 April he wrote, 'We really get on well so forgive the grouse.'[47]

By early April the division was moved from its sector in the south and given a new one, north of the Menin Road, taking over from the French 39th Division, with the Canadian Division on its left and the 27th on its right, centred on Gravenstafel Ridge. Bulfin's battalions were allocated a sector from Polygon Wood to opposite Passchendaele (eight and a half battalions were in the front line, whilst a brigade reserve of two battalions were near Verlorenhoek and the remaining five and a half battalions formed the divisional reserve, around Ypres).

The historian George Cassar described the conditions eloquently:

> All three divisions of Plumer's V Corps had been warned of the poor condition of the French frontline trenches, but what they saw exceeded their worse expectations. The lengths of the trenches were unconnected and shallow, with breastworks of mud and sandbags that were only a few feet high and in most cases constructed too flimsily to stop a bullet. There was no parados [mound of earth at the back of the trench] in the rear to protect occupants from artillery shells bursting behind them and no traverses to prevent troops from enfilading fire. Wire entanglements were barely adequate in some places but almost nonexistent in others. On top of this, sanitation conditions were disgusting. Shell holes were used as latrines and the dead were buried in graves so shallow that often their limbs stuck out of the ground. It required a strong stomach to endure the putrid stench of decomposing bodies and excrement that hung permanently over the trenches.[48]

Initially, units not holding the front line were billeted in and around Ypres itself. But when a heavy bombardment of the city took place on 20 April, hitting the Cloth Hall near where Bulfin's HQ and two of his battalions were located, they had to be evacuated. He set up his new headquarters in Vlamertinghe Chateau, significantly, as events proved, to the west of Ypres.

Now Bulfin had the chance to get his brigades back together again and prove himself and his division. The fact that he had not been relieved of command, in a BEF usually ruthless towards failure at this level, indicated that he still retained the confidence of his superiors. There is no evidence in the official papers and letters between French, Smith-Dorrien and Plumer, or in Smith-Dorrien's diary or letters to his wife, to suggest any loss of confidence.[49] Sir John French, in a general order issued after the fight in April to retain the important feature of Hill 60, acknowledged the part Bulfin had played before he had handed over the sector: 'I fully recognize the skill and foresight of Major-General Bulfin, commanding Twenty-eighth Division, and his C.R.E., Colonel Jerome, who are responsible for the original conception and plan for the undertaking.'[50]

Plumer, new to the Western Front, would have valued Bulfin's knowledge of the Salient and experience from 1914. With his apprenticeship in another Yorkshire infantry regiment (he was a York and Lancaster), he had a similar grounding to Bulfin in looking after his soldiers' welfare. Known affectionately by his men as 'Old Plum and Apple' or 'Daddy' Plumer, his approach to command was based on three fundamentals: trust, training and thoroughness. Plumer and Bulfin were to form a strong partnership in the storm that lay ahead.

Chapter 7

1915
Second Ypres – 'Desperate fighting
in a desperate position'

On the warm spring afternoon of Thursday, 22 April 1915, an hour after a fierce artillery bombardment, the Germans released a dense cloud of poisonous chlorine gas, from pre-positioned canisters, towards the French trenches to the north-east of Ypres. The first major use of a deadly chemical weapon in modern warfare had joined the previous horrors of the Western Front. The French troops, from Territorial and North African units, many 'literally coughing their lungs out; glue was coming from their mouths',[1] fell back in panic-stricken retreat. This left a 4-mile gap in the front line, as well as opening up the Canadian flank to their right, in which direction the gas cloud was now rolling. The road to Ypres and the Channel lay wide open.

The Hague Declaration and Convention, to which Germany was a signatory, declared that poison gas was forbidden as a weapon of war. There had been a number of intelligence indications of its impending use, but the French and British high command chose to ignore them. Barely any thought was given to the use of gas masks, so the troops were totally unprotected and unprepared for the nightmare which was to come. Bulfin, when writing to Edmonds after the war, commented:

> I have no recollection of any Corps discussion on gas attacks but I have an impression that an Intelligence memo or summary reached us about the 16th April 15 stating that the Germans to the North in front of the French were believed to be preparing for a gas attack but I do not remember any indication being given as to what we should do to combat such an attack.[2]

It was a fortune of war that two quick-thinking Canadian medical officers were out walking behind their lines that afternoon. They promptly responded to the sight of the yellow-green smoke, sending word to the trenches for the soldiers to urinate into their handkerchief and make wet pads to press over the nose and mouth – the uric acid crystallized the chlorine and gave some degree of immediate protection. The gallant and steadfast Canadians poured rapid fire into the oncoming Germans, holding their positions long enough for more troops to be rushed forward to bolster the exposed left flank of V Corps.

Although the British and Canadian commanders were receiving a confusing picture of what was unfolding, by 7.30 pm Plumer was gripping events and rushing available troops into the area under threat. Indeed, Lieutenant General Alderson, commanding 1st Canadian Division, less than an hour after the first release of gas, had ordered his 3 Brigade to assist the French. The German advance continued into the gap during the evening, with the Canadians rallying and holding the thin line. There was little delay before elements of 28th Division entered the fray. 'From the roof of my Headquarters I had seen the French retiring',[3] Bulfin recorded, and without waiting for orders, together with Snow, he moved his immediate reserve units towards the threatened flank. The Buffs and the 3rd Middlesex, both from 85 Brigade and based at St Jean, marched north to the ridge line and deployed westwards as far as the Yser Canal. 83 Brigade's 1st York & Lancasters, in reserve west of Ypres, came forward to take over St Jean, with 5th King's Own held in reserve. Colonel 'Gussie' Geddes, a promising officer commanding 2nd Buffs, was in the process of moving from St Jean and was placed by Plumer under command of the Canadians; these four 28th Division battalions, in the early hours of the 23rd, formed 'Geddes Force' (sometimes referred to as 'Geddes Detachment').

The Buffs' war diary that afternoon reflected the incongruity of events before the battalion moved from St Jean:

Meanwhile French Zouaves and Turcos were [streaming] down the road towards YPRES. It was an astonishing sight to see British troops nonchalantly in the main street of St Jan [*sic*] and the Canadians marching calmly N & NE the direction from which the Frenchmen were retiring the latter exclaiming as they passed, *nous sommes trompés, tout est perdu* etc.[4]

In the confusion and urgency of that evening, it was understandable that Geddes, as one of the first COs moving up from the reserve area, should be put in command of what available units could be gathered together. But it was also unfortunate that 85 Brigade, now holding its sector of the front line with no reserves, should have its command structure disrupted so soon in the heat of battle. It was not that its brigade commander was found wanting (Brigadier General Archibald Chapman was later mentioned in dispatches), but it was an early indication of the way Second Ypres would develop. Local battles were often fought at battalion level and below, with units hastily cobbled together, and higher commanders struggled to impose themselves effectively. What Bulfin made of his division being denuded is not recorded.

The German troops were naturally reluctant to advance into their own cloud of gas and, fortunately for the Allies, the German High Command had been unable to find large reserves to exploit the initial success. The leading German division, the 52nd, did not advance beyond the southern slope of Pilckem Ridge, whilst other enemy troops moved forward to Kitchener's Wood and Mauser Ridge and dug in to face a counter-attack. Momentum was lost, and the chance of a sudden strategic breakthrough was thrown away. Nevertheless, the Germans had opened a substantial gap and had penetrated some 5,000yds into the already constricted and vulnerable Ypres Salient.

'The confusion of command'

For the next month, fierce see-saw attacks and counter-attacks took place, in what the Battle Nomenclature Committee tidily called the Battles of: Gravenstafel Ridge (22–23 April), Saint Julien (24 April–3 May), Frezenberg Ridge (7–13 May) and Bellewaarde Ridge (24–25 May). For Bulfin and the 28th Division, for whom this demarcation meant little, it was a time of unrelentingly hard and confused fighting.

The night of 22/23 April was one of appalling confusion. After midnight, enemy attacks were made against the fronts of 27th and 28th Divisions, failing with heavy casualties. This resulted in General Plumer hesitating to move all his reserves of these divisions to his threatened left flank. Soon after dawn, the leading elements of Geddes Force, moving up to the left of the Canadians and with no time for orders or reconnaissance, advanced on the dominating Mauser Ridge alongside 1 Canadian Brigade. With no artillery support, they were met by heavy machine gun fire and brought to a halt. By 9.30 am Geddes had five battalions under his command – but without even the staff of a brigade HQ. That morning, Sir John French had visited Foch's headquarters; on being assured that the French intended to retake their original line, he agreed to mount a counter-attack in cooperation with them later that day. Hence Second Army was duly given 50th (Northumbrian) Division to strengthen the depleted front.[5] The French did nothing. Smith-Dorrien and Plumer, concerned that any further delay would allow the Germans to consolidate their hold on the area, ordered V Corps to attack alone.

That afternoon, Geddes mounted another attack on Mauser Ridge, this time with 13 Canadian Brigade; it was carried out with great resolution, but as soon as the 'men rose from the ground, the enemy opened with heavy gun and rifle fire'. After some two and a half hours the advance came to a halt below Mauser Ridge, the survivors hanging on in hastily dug shell-scrapes; the attack was a 'magnificent display of discipline and courage ... but the price paid had been heavy',[6] the official history recorded. The CO of 3rd Middlesex was killed, whilst 1st York & Lancasters lost their CO, 13 officers and 411 men. The 2nd East Yorkshires suffered similarly, with 14 officers and 369 men hit. Plumer broke the news to his wife that their old friend, 'poor little Burt', CO of the York & Lancasters, had been killed with his adjutant, adding, 'You know how I feel about these losses.'[7] The gallant Geddes was killed by shellfire on 28 April.

The next day, the pressure continued, with more gas being released by the Germans, to the extent that General Snow had to commit Bulfin's reserve battalions, ready nearby, without time to consult the owner. Bulfin was not happy with this:

I still claim he had no right to touch my divisional reserve. I had meant to use them to gain Gravenstafel the loss of which I had heard at Alderson's Headquarters where I was when Snow snaffled them in his panic.[8]

These two strong-willed generals had not always seen eye to eye; back in mid-March, Plumer and Bulfin went to visit Snow, and Loch recorded: 'There seems to have been a row and he [Bulfin] went for General Snow – I am glad of it.'[9] Bulfin's chief of staff, once the hard fighting had started, seemed to have changed his opinion of his commander. In his daily letter home to his wife that night, Loch complained about his corps commander:

> There is no senior man here capable of taking command and running the show. General Plumer is a dear but he is too weak and not big enough to take command. Gen. Alderson commanding the Canadian Division is very much the same – he muddles. Gen. Bulfin is the best and the strongest man but he is the junior.[10]

Notwithstanding Loch's curious judgement on Plumer, who was to become one of the most trusted and effective Army commanders of the Great War, Bulfin was evidently regaining his confidence once battle was joined and he could make better use of his proven powers of leadership.

The lack of suitable anti-gas protection was a worry. On the 23rd Bulfin used his initiative and tasked his chief medical officer, Colonel Fergusson, to engage the services of the nuns of a convent at Poperinghe to make up lint bandages to tie over the mouth – 'We got 3000 of these sent up to the first line trenches by the night of the 24th April & others followed rapidly.'[11]

The Battle of St Julien

By 25 April, the day of the Gallipoli landings, which had taken so many men and artillery shells otherwise destined for the Western Front, Plumer realized some order needed to be brought to the command structure. As the official history put it, 'Both Divisional Commanders were directed to reorganise their commands, putting battalions under proper brigadiers if possible, or at any rate under a definite general.'[12] Battalion and company commanders had been forced to act independently in the face of such a fluid situation, in which the line was held very thinly by small, often isolated, groups of tired soldiers. Many brigades and battalions had been rushed into the front line and often broken up to be sent to where they were most needed. Now Bulfin was placed in clear command of those units in his sector. To his division was added 2 Canadian Brigade, 150 Brigade and 8th Durham Light Infantry from 151 Brigade, as well as the newly arrived 11 Brigade, a force amounting – on paper – to approximately two divisions.

The next day, whilst his troops struggled on in hard hand-to-hand fighting to restore the exposed left flank, the dilemma of where the GOC should best place himself came to the fore. Loch recorded:

Our men are getting very tired. They have fought wonderfully well but there is a limit to human endurance. The General ought to go up to the East of Ypres instead of which he has remained West. I know there are many arguments one way & the other but on the whole I think he ought to go.

He added in the following day's letter:

Really the General should have been forward living in a dug-out all this time himself. I am glad in a way he has not as we would have had a very bad time of it but feel in my bones that he should.[13]

For Bulfin, it was a choice between staying back at his HQ or going forward to the front and risking the loss of any control as a result of being engulfed in the immediate battle. To a man who had led his brigade at First Ypres from a dug-out at the front it must have gone against his nature to stay back. But that option allowed him to maintain a closer contact with his corps HQ as well as his flanking Canadian division, vital given the confusion of the battle. Bulfin, when writing to Edmonds in 1925, observed:

The Vth Corps Advanced HdQuarters was ... about 400 yards from mine at Chateau Vidal about 1 mile West of Ypres & Plumer was generally there even late into the night ... Plumer I saw daily, Snow only a few times & the last time to have a row with him – Alderson I saw daily naturally. But Snow was only on the fringe of the fighting in comparative safety so long as I held on – of course Snow grew big once the retirement of the 3rd May took place when he was splendid.[14]

In his war diaries Snow set out 'certain points' from the Second Battle of Ypres, the first one being the 'confusion of command'. He made a strong case for being based east of Ypres, where he had placed himself, at a time when 'all wires were down, and approaches, which practically only amounted to two, were swept by hostile fire'. Adding that 'unfortunately the 28th and Canadian Commanders, for lack of accommodation, had taken up their positions too far back',[15] he went on to argue:

> It would have been better if, as soon as the battle began, the G.O.C.'s 28th and Canadian Divisions had established their advanced Headquarters somewhere in the Salient as far forward as those of G.O.C. 27th Division. They could then have kept in touch with their Brigadiers all through the Battle and much confusion would have been avoided.[16]

Snow's argument for an advanced headquarters east of Ypres is convincing. Loch underlined the challenge of keeping in touch with the brigades:

> Our communications with the front have been our greatest difficulty during the last 8 days. We started with six lines. One day's shelling got the lot. Since then we have been struggling day and night to get wire through … However I have got one wireless set from the Cavalry and an extra detachment from the 2nd Army Signals, thanks to my knowing people privately.[17]

Over the next few days, the drama of Field Marshal French's sacking of Sir Horace Smith-Dorrien unfolded (heralding the famous remark from the ex-ranker General 'Wully' Robertson, "'Orace, you're for 'ome!'). There had been bad blood between the two for years, and French was looking for an excuse to get rid of him. He saw his chance when Smith-Dorrien sensibly recommended pulling back to a more tenable position within the Salient, a move which the C-in-C interpreted as defeatist. Plumer, appointed as his successor in Second Army, immediately started implementing his predecessor's plans, indeed with French's endorsement. Bulfin wrote an appreciative letter to Smith-Dorrien on his departure, as did many other subordinate commanders.[18]

During this time, 28th Division, at the apex of persistent German attacks and shelling at St Julien, had matters of life and death to confront. Heavy casualties, especially to 83 and 85 Brigades, continued to weaken the front, but it was held by stubborn and determined defence. The situation was made worse by Sir John French, encouraged by General Foch's unfulfilled promises of flanking support, delaying to agree to V Corps pulling back to Frezenberg Ridge. It was another demonstration of the commander-in-chief's failure to grasp the reality of what was happening to his front-line divisions. The two days' delay only served to punish the 28th Division with further needless casualties.

By 1 May, at last, orders were issued for the three front line divisions (4th, 27th and 28th – the Canadians having been pulled back in reserve on 25 April) to withdraw some 4,000yds to a rudimentary line of new trenches on Frezenberg Ridge, just east of what was called the 'GHQ Line', over the next two nights. All movement was to be regulated by 28th Division in the centre. This meant moving back to places made notorious in First Ypres, such as Hooge and Sanctuary Wood. The official history, not always given to praise, recounted:

> Although the 85th and 11th Brigades were in such close contact with the enemy that in places the opposing sides were within a few feet, they were able to draw off under cover of darkness, and the whole retirement was carried out as planned and without a hitch, favoured by the usual ground mist. When reports came in, it was found that only one soldier of the three divisions was missing, and he rejoined the next morning (he had fallen asleep in the front trench) … [These divisions] had successfully passed through the highest test of discipline of an army, and withstood the greatest strain on the nerves of individual soldiers – a retirement in close contact with the enemy. And this they had accomplished undetected after nearly a fortnight of fighting and, in the case of 28th Division, of desperate fighting in a desperate position at the point of the Salient.[19]

It was one of the few times the divisional commander was able to be proactive. It would have given Bulfin some satisfaction to achieve this feat of arms, after a taxing and frustrating period of command, during which he was often unable to exert any real influence on the confused fighting. As at Gallipoli, the withdrawal was the most successful part of the Battle of St Julien. Whatever the success of the operation, however, it could not disguise the fact that the BEF was being pushed back. 'It is a defeat and I hate it especially as I am not sure that our new position is going to be any easier to hold than our old one', wrote Loch on the 3rd.[20] How right he was about the new position.

The Pause – 'We felt we were simply cannon fodder'

The new defensive line was established in the form of a semicircle of 3 miles radius round Ypres, running from Turco Farm in the north, contouring around Frezenberg Ridge, then south to Hooge and along the eastern edge of Sanctuary Wood, to rejoin the old line near Hill 60. Bulfin's troops were given a sector from the Roulers railway line north to Shell Trap Farm, with 27th Division on its right and 4th Division on the left. The trenches allocated to the front line brigades were mostly dug on the easily enfiladed long forward slope of Frezenberg Ridge. They found the existing trenches narrow and only 3ft deep, with a high water table. There were few sandbags, little wire and practically no communication trenches; dug-outs had hardly been begun. It was not a strong position. In particular, there was a severe shortage of artillery and ammunition. Since about 24 April the daily ration of shells to Second Army had been pitiful: for each 13-pounder gun it was two, for 18-pounders, three, for 4-inch howitzers, ten, and for 6-inch howitzers, three.[21] Indeed, there were good tactical arguments for the British to withdraw from the Salient entirely and dig in behind the Yser Canal, in conformation with the French. But that would mean abandoning Ypres, with all its emotional and political significance.

With much work needing to be done, the tired troops of 28th Division were given no respite. At dawn on 4 May the Germans began shelling the now empty British front line; then, realizing what had happened, they moved forward and entrenched some 200–600yds in front of the new BEF trenches. Next day, heavier artillery preparation started against 28th Division's front, and those units on the forward slope of the ridge paid for their vulnerable positioning. 2nd East Yorkshires and 5th King's Own, gallantly supported by the 3rd Monmouths, bore the brunt of the incessant shelling. Miraculously, they held on, but for the next three days the torment continued, with the reduced Salient becoming little more than a concentrated artillery target for the superior German guns. Sadly, the under-resourced Royal Artillery was unable to offer an effective response. The official history called this period 'the Pause' (between the Battles of St Julien and Frezenberg Ridge); but for the soldiers being shelled unmercifully in their flimsy new trenches, there was no respite whatsoever. As a field officer of 1st Welsh in 84 Brigade remarked, 'We felt we were simply cannon fodder'.[22]

The Battle of Frezenberg Ridge

By 8 May General Duke Albrecht, the commander of the German Fourth Army, had assembled three corps and sufficient artillery astride the Zonncbckc–Yprcs road to attack 27th and 28th Divisions.

That day – in many ways the critical day of Second Ypres – Lieutenant General Edmund Allenby took over V Corps for the remainder of the battle. A cavalryman with a forceful and bullying personality, he had the unenviable task of holding this new line while pressured from above not to give any ground and needing to stiffen the resolve of his exhausted troops. Not an easy man to please – 'Everyone hates being in V Corps' was the opinion of Major General Haldane[23] – Allenby was determined not to lose Ypres. He wrote to his brother-in-law, 'I shall not go down in History as the Man Who Lost Ypres and with Ypres on my heart like Queen Mary and Calais.'[24] His task was made harder by Plumer's orders that the line should be held 'to the end' without seeking reinforcements from Haig's First Army (Haig was about to mount his own attack on Aubers Ridge to the south the following day). With hindsight, it was a curious balance of priorities, given the existential struggle taking place in the Salient.

At 5.30 am the German bombardment started, coupled with gas, and by 7.00 am the whole 28th Division line of shallow trenches had been 'pounded into mounds of earth'. The following day, the entire 84 Brigade of six battalions could muster only 1,400 men; the 1st Suffolks suffered the loss of their CO, with only one officer and twenty-nine men left to man their line, whilst the 12th Londons were only fifty-three strong, led by Sergeant Hornall. Brigadier General Louis Bols, who had taken over the brigade from Wintour and would later be selected by Allenby as his chief of staff for most of the war, proved to be a steadfast commander – 'his rare spirit did much to keep up the hearts of those who fought with him in the face of dreadful losses incurred'.[25]

83 Brigade, also on the exposed forward slope of Frezenberg Ridge, suffered similarly, many buried alive as their flimsy trenches collapsed under the weight of German artillery barrages. After three waves of enemy

infantry had been beaten back, Brigadier General Boyle ordered forward his reserve battalion, the 2nd East Yorkshires. At the same time Bulfin brought up his reserve brigade, Chapman's 85 Brigade held back at Vlamertinghe, to recover some of the lost ground. A counter-attack, bedevilled by confused orders between the brigades and units, met with disastrous casualties. The 1st York & Lancasters were reduced to 83 men under one sergeant, the 2nd East Yorkshires could only gather 3 officers and 200 men that night, whilst the 2nd East Surreys mustered 8 officers and 300 men. But the robust defence of Frezenberg Ridge by 28th Division and the 'great counter-attack', as the Germans described it, evidently dissuaded the enemy from following up their successes. 'Poor Bulfinch is very worried over our situation,' wrote Loch, 'and I am afraid does not sleep at all when there is trouble on, consequently he is a little bit upset and difficult on occasions. However we get on wonderfully well.'[26]

It was not until 13 May that the enemy launched a further strong attack on the ridge, but 28th Division enjoyed some respite as it had been relieved by the Cavalry division the day before. An indication of how much the Division had borne the brunt of the fighting was in the casualty figures: during the six-day battle of Frezenberg Ridge, of V Corps' 9,391 casualties, 3,889 were from Bulfin's hard pressed troops.[27]

The German commanders were certainly conscious of the impact of these losses. After Lieutenant Colonel Enderby, the CO of 84 Brigade's 2nd Northumberland Fusiliers, was captured on the 8th and expressed his distress at the destruction of his battalion, the German general replied, 'Maybe so. But you may reflect that had it not been for the resistance of that battalion I would not now be here. I should have been in Ypres tonight'.[28]

Whilst his men were given some rest, Bulfin took this opportunity for two days' home leave, departing on the 19th, unaware that his division was to be ordered back into the front line on the night of the 21st/22nd astride Bellewaarde Ridge, a continuation of the British line to the south of Frezenberg Ridge.

The final battle – Bellewaarde Ridge

Bulfin returned the day before the Germans launched their final push against the Ypres Salient, the two-day battle of Bellewaarde Ridge, when 28th Division in the centre was yet again in the thick of the fighting. Early on the morning of 24 May, the Germans began a heavy and prolonged artillery bombardment, of gas and high explosive, with the weight of their attack concentrated on 85 Brigade, in muddy trenches just north of the Ypres–Roulers railway line. The opposing lines being so close, there was little time to don respirators; with the German infantry attacking this time immediately behind the gas, and all telephone links severed, the British line was under intense pressure. After some two hours the Germans overwhelmed the 8th Middlesex and 2nd East Surreys of 85 Brigade. Its brigade commander, 'Pinto' Pereira, had only just taken over command on the 20th and had sustained a bullet wound to his head the following day.[29] He was desperately trying to cobble together a counter-attack when Bulfin stopped him and told him to go on the defensive; it would need two brigades to do the job. Although support from 84 Brigade and the neighbouring 80th was mustered later in the day, tragically the ill-coordinated counter-attacks that followed, with a force too weak and exhausted for the task, met with awful losses. But the line was held.

By the end of 25 May both sides were exhausted and anxious to bring it to an end, and 'so the battle slowly sputtered out', as John Terraine put it.[30]

Reflections on Second Ypres

Throughout the Great War the Germans mounted only four offensives on the Western Front: the opening invasion of France and Belgium, the gas attack at Ypres, Verdun and the Spring offensive of 1918. Second Ypres started as an experiment in the use of gas with the general idea of removing the Salient, whilst the Germans' main attention was focused on the Eastern Front. By the end of Second Ypres they had indeed bitten off some of the Salient but held no strategic advantage, whilst the British had retained Ypres but suffered appalling casualties in, 'for its size, one of the most murderous battles of the war'.[31] The enemy's superiority in artillery was a major factor, and the BEF's lack of an effective response would bring down Asquith's Liberal government.

Bulfin, when commenting to Edmonds on the draft of his coverage of the battle for the official history, offered a vivid insight:

It was a dreadful time, even now reading it brings back the nightmare feeling – getting the wounded back at night from the front lines where the poor fellows had to remain all day. Getting rations & water up – I never knew that the ASC [Army Service Corps] had so many gallant men among them and the Doctors were heroes to a man. It was a terrible time & with our poor gunners on their limited supply of ammunition … they did their very best but they were powerless against the weight of metal against them. Our artillery weakness as you truly point out accounts for the failure of our counter attacks to regain lost ground.[32]

A key criticism of Second Ypres, with its fearful casualties, was the mistaken emphasis on regaining lost ground. Desperate counter-attacks were often mounted at short notice with little preparation or artillery support, exacerbated by a severe breakdown in communications throughout the chain of command. Even the French, wedded to the doctrine of *offensive à l'outrance* (to the end), were perplexed by the British passion for counter-attacks at all costs. However much one might accuse Sir John French of such cruel and wasteful orders – and criticize the obedience of those down the chain of command, even divisional commanders such as Bulfin – once the decision was made to hold Ypres, there was often little option for them to do otherwise. The tragedy was that the only riposte for the British was to turn to their infantry.

The historian Tim Travers has suggested that generals at the time were more afraid of being sacked by their superiors than they were of the enemy.[33] Although there was always the threat of being 'Stellenbosched'[34] and its debilitating effect on initiative, Bulfin was a stubborn man and not easily bullied, as his next battle, at Loos, would prove.

The question remains, however, whether these counter-attacks could have been managed more effectively. The first requirement for divisional commanders, if they were to exert any proactive influence on such a chaotic battlefield, was accurate and timely information. At Second Ypres this was singularly lacking and compounded by poor communications for commanders and the artillery. John Terraine, quoting from a divisional GSO1 that it was 'the only war ever fought without voice control', then continues:

When you let that statement sink in, you know almost as much about World War 1 generalship as you need to know … Generals, in fact, became quite impotent at the very moment when they would expect and be expected to display their greatest proficiency.[35]

This problem would remain well beyond 1915. Thus counter-attacks were often left to the judgement and ability of company, battalion, and, in some cases brigade, commanders to organize and lead. The situation was further hampered by the paucity of artillery support and inexperience in providing such to the counter-attacking infantry. The BEF, at all levels, was on a learning curve never before experienced by the British Army – little surprise, therefore, that casualties were so horrendous.

Nevertheless, such a casualty rate was unsustainable. Of the eleven divisions that fought at Second Ypres, the 28th suffered by far the worst. Some 15,533 casualties were incurred in just over a month – more than the original fighting strength of the division – compared to the Canadian Division at 5,469 and its sister division, the 27th, at 7,263. These disproportionate figures can be partly explained by 28th Division's location, often at the apex of the attacks on the Salient and bearing the brunt of the German assaults. Artillery shelling, rather than gas or machine gun fire, caused most of the losses, as the rudimentary trenches were destroyed and their dogged occupants often buried alive. This was exacerbated by Sir John French's delay in ordering the withdrawal to the Frezenberg Ridge.

Robin Neillands' words are wise:

> Even with hindsight, there is no easy answer to the question of whether Ypres was worth defending. There is room for criticism and even guilt, but these must be shared, and the guilty include a government and nation which failed to provide a field army with the equipment and supplies necessary to fight a modern war. But then, who in Europe, nine months before Second Ypres, could have imagined such a battle and such slaughter?[36]

Although 28th Division was criticized for its earlier performance, its gallantry and tenacity during Second Ypres could not be denied. For its GOC, with a regimental officer's concern for his soldiers but also imbued with an offensive spirit, the experience of witnessing his division being so badly 'smashed up' must have been deeply affecting.

Bulfin's own performance, in a battle where divisional commanders struggled to impose effective command, is difficult to gauge in comparison with that of his divisional colleagues. John Dixon, who has made a deep study of Second Ypres in *Magnificent But Not War*,[37] concluded that 'he did not handle his troops any worse that any of the other commanders' and felt that 'the organization, and success, of the withdrawal to the Frezenberg line indicated a high level of control and discipline within his troops'.[38] Notwithstanding the success of that phase of the battle, Bulfin would undoubtedly have had a greater influence over the tactical handling of his division, and possibly its level of casualties, had he established an advanced headquarters east of Ypres, closer to his forward brigades. Nevertheless, Allenby must have been impressed with Bulfin, since he was to select him for corps command in Palestine two years later; the latter evidently enjoyed serving under Allenby, unlike many of his colleagues.

For a man who started the year not fully recovered from his wounds and endeavouring to surmount the many challenges facing his new command, the 'dreadful time' did not end at Ypres. It would be repeated at Loos within a mere four months – and with more serious consequences for his own career.

Chapter 8

1915
Loos – 'A horrid nightmare'

When you see millions of the mouthless dead
Across your dreams in pale battalions go[1]

After a mere fortnight's rest, Bulfin's battered division was back in the line by 14 June, this time in the St Eloi and Wytschaete sectors of the Ypres Salient. In contrast to the previous two months it was a relatively quiet time, despite a steady drain of casualties from German shelling. Bulfin used the period to emphasize to his men the need to dominate no-man's-land with sniping and raiding. Although the division was able to regain its strength in numbers as new drafts arrived to be trained and assimilated, the fresh troops were mostly recently recalled reservists who had never seen action. New faces also appeared amongst its senior commanders and staff: Lord Loch had been succeeded by Lieutenant Colonel Richard Hare as GSO1, and the new AA&QMG was another Gunner officer named Henvey. The exhausted Brigadier General Boyle of 83 Brigade had been replaced by Hurdis Ravenshaw, who had led 1st Connaught Rangers through the early months of the war. Brigadier General Louis Bols of 84 Brigade was shortly to leave to be the senior staff officer (BGGS) at XII Corps; his successor was Tom Finch Pearse, promoted after commanding 2nd Cheshires through Second Ypres. Brigadier General Cecil ('Pinto') Pereira, now recovered from his head wound, retained 85 Brigade. Although a relatively new team and raw division, the reputation it gained during the summer in this sector was sound.

By 22 September 28th Division was relieved by the Canadians and moved to the Bailleul area, south of Ypres, into Second Army's reserve. There it hoped to recuperate. Its next battle would be a great deal sooner than expected – in five days' time at Loos, some 20 miles away. Its commander was to remember it as 'a sort of horrid nightmare'.[2]

During the summer the Allies had been locked in arguments over strategy. Haig's First Army battles at Neuve Chapelle in March, in what was the British Army's first planned offensive, and Aubers Ridge in May, had met with heavy losses for little advantage. Second Army's hard struggle at Second Ypres had added to the exhaustion of the BEF, underlined by the severe shortage of artillery pieces, ammunition, grenades and essential entrenching stores. Nevertheless, by early June, Joffre, despite the French Army's even more critical losses, was drawing up an ambitious plan to launch a concerted Allied attack against the flanks of the German salient at Noyon, some 50 miles north-east of Paris. One attack with thirty-five French divisions would be north from Champagne, whilst the other with eighteen French and twelve British divisions of the First Army would drive east from Artois.

At the first Anglo-French conference of the war at Calais on 6 July, when Asquith observed that he had 'never heard so much bad French … in his life',[3] the tensions between the French and the British strategic priorities came into sharp relief. Kitchener, with his fluent French, dominated proceedings and argued against any offensive on the Western Front until the BEF was enlarged and strengthened with his New Army and better munitions. Added to this was his intention that the Dardanelles campaign be reinvigorated with landings at Suvla Bay. His view was that the BEF should pursue a policy of 'active defence'. The French, although keen to continue efforts to eject the Germans from their soil, seemed won over, and the British delegation left relieved. However, at the military conference which followed at Joffre's headquarters at Chantilly the following day, the French commander-in-chief declared himself intent on pursuing his 'powerful offensive at the earliest possible opportunity',[4] with which Sir John French, never a believer in a strategy of passive defence, concurred. Historians have argued that Kitchener, conscious of the need for coalition cohesion, came to a compromise with Joffre before the Calais conference and agreed that the British would pull their weight that summer. As 'K' put it in his typically brusque manner, 'Unfortunately we had to make war as we must, and not as we would like to.'[5]

The ground chosen by Joffre for the British part in the coming offensive would be between La Bassée Canal and Vimy Ridge, in what was the French coal-mining region of Loos. It was – and still is – a gloomy area of open country, dotted with large slag-heaps and pit-head towers (*fosses*), ideal for the entrenched defender. Haig reported back to French, in a document which was 'a model of clarity and sound military reasoning',[6] that the area was 'very difficult'[7] and quite unsuitable for an advance over open ground dominated by enemy artillery and machine gun fire. Sir John French, who now had seen the ground himself, felt similarly concerned by what the French were demanding of the BEF. Caught between the need to support the French and the desire not to pitch his army into a calamitous battle, he came up with a plan for First Army's guns to neutralize the German front, as a holding operation, but to avoid releasing its infantry in an attack across such open ground. This was rejected by his ally. Relations were becoming more strained by the day, as Sir John realized that Joffre saw the British effort rather as a subsidiary operation than as a critical part of the overall offensive proper. Kitchener, although under coalition pressure from the French, was more concerned about the vital need to bolster a wobbling Russia, following its reverses at Tannenberg and the Masurian Lakes that summer. The result was that the reluctance of French and Haig was overcome and, inexorably, there was no escape from what Liddell Hart described as the 'unwanted battle' of Loos.[8]

After Allied delays, it was not until late September that the armies were ready to launch their offensive, giving precious time to the Germans to strengthen their positions. Although Kitchener had instructed the BEF to support the French-led offensive, his orders allowed considerable operational scope to GHQ and First Army. French's orders to Haig were to 'support the French attack to the full extent of your available resources',[9] but Haig then went beyond what could have been a more limited subsidiary operation. He took these orders to mean an all-out infantry assault and thus planned for a major offensive aimed at a strategic breakthrough, something much more high-risk.

An intriguing feature of the run-up to Loos is the transformation that took place in Haig's attitude and thus his planning for the battle. From a position of grave doubt about the wisdom of such an offensive, he moved to one of optimism and ambition. What had changed his mind, as well as many of those within First Army's senior ranks? Partly it was the agreement by the Government to the use of chlorine gas to support the attacking infantry, only months after the British condemnation of the German use of this banned weapon. It was an opportunity enthusiastically seized upon

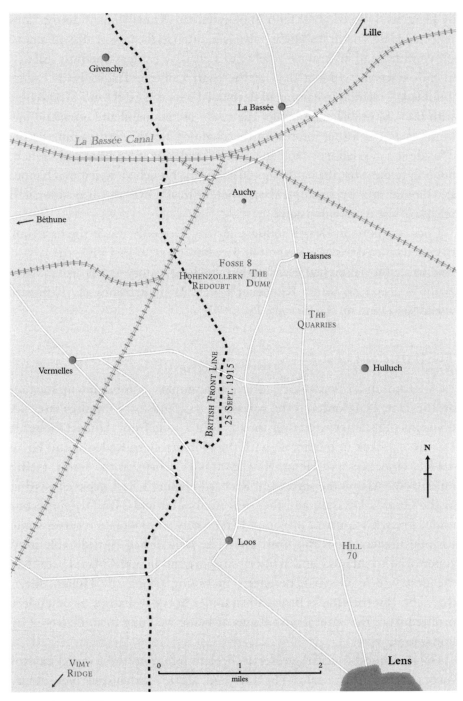

Map 5. Loos 1915.

by Haig, who placed great faith in its potential. Equally significantly, Loos reflected Haig's natural abiding optimism, often in the face of all evidence to the contrary, and his enduring belief in a decisive battle, something imbued in him since his student days at the Staff College. Tragically, as events unfolded, a vacuum in command developed between GHQ and First Army, with French, visibly ailing under the strain of command and often laid low in his quarters, losing interest in the planning for the forthcoming battle. This dissonance led inevitably to a lack of clarity between Haig and French, not only about what the battle should achieve – French viewed it much more as a limited step-by-step operation – but, critically, over the disposition and release of the reserve divisions.

Loos is unique in British military history. Not only was it the first time Britain had used gas as a weapon of war, but it was, at that time, the largest land battle the nation had ever fought in its long history. It was also the first major occasion on which Kitchener's New Army divisions of volunteers would see action on the Western Front.[10]

The Battle of Loos

At 5.50 am on 25 September, after a preliminary bombardment starting on the 21st, Haig ordered the release of gas, and forty minutes later six divisions of infantry went over the top on a 7-mile front. Hubert Gough's I Corps attacked in the north, with the Hohenzollern Redoubt and Fosse 8 a key objective, and Henry Rawlinson's IV Corps in the south, facing Hill 70 (see Map 6 on page 132). Richard Haking's XI Corps, consisting of the Guards Division and the New Army 21st and 24th Divisions, but under French's control, provided First Army's immediate reserve, some 13 miles distant from the front line. The British had considerable local superiority in infantry and artillery support and in many places breached the first line of German defences, including taking the Hohenzollern Redoubt. But the attacks broke down under heavy casualties, as defenders profited from the natural advantages of being well dug in and covered by undamaged wire.

Haig's request to use the reserve corps to follow up these initial tactical successes is a tragic tale. The raw and already exhausted New Army divisions, after a tiring march and no food, were thrown into battle on IV

Corps' front. Released too late and too far away by French to exploit Haig's initial gains, the 21st and 24th Divisions struggled to the front. Here, with muddled orders, they were launched against the now reinforced German second line, suffering appalling casualties. They should never have been given such a cruel baptism of fire. Bulfin's own regiment's 10th Battalion, in 21st Division, poorly briefed and with only one small-scale map of the confusing and broken area of Hill 70, suffered a similar fate to other units. His friend from South Africa days, Colonel Arthur Hadow, was killed urging his men forward in a futile charge over open ground.[11] When he fell, his second-in-command, Bulfin's best man, Wilfred Dent, took over and also lost his life, followed by two further senior officers. By the end of the day the battalion had lost almost 300 men. There is no mention of this in the ADC's diary, so news of this tragedy may not have reached Bulfin until much later.

Despite the calamitous failure of the attacks of 26 September, French and Haig were under considerable demands from Joffre, who was faced with the news that the French attacks elsewhere were bogged down, to maintain the pressure at Loos. If this was to be done, the dominating feature of Hill 70 needed to be taken. The only division available was the Guards, which was finally placed under Haig at 1.45 pm that day, arriving at about midnight after a long march. Their attacks next afternoon, gallantly made but lacking effective artillery support, were repulsed.[12] This, and the loss of Fosse 8 in the north, left First Army with the desperate challenge of stemming German counter-attacks and regaining lost ground.

As Nick Lloyd, in his pre-eminent study of the battle, *Loos 1915*, commented:

> The Battle of Loos is primarily remembered for the dramatic events of the first two days when almost all the British gains were made and when the vast majority of the casualties were incurred. That the battle continued for a further three weeks has been largely forgotten or ignored.[13]

Bulfin's division was to be at the fulcrum of this second phase of the Battle of Loos.

Bulfin and 28th Division enter the fray

28th Division had just arrived near Bailleul, hoping to get some rest, when on 23 September Bulfin had his first warning of involvement in the forthcoming battle. After a hasty lunch he was called to see Sir Douglas Haig; by late afternoon he was holding a divisional conference to address the possibility of moving at short notice. At the same time the divisional war diary recorded,[14] 'All troops ordered to route march and do PT to get fit', a sensible precaution after so many months in the trenches. Two days before the infantry assault was launched, it was becoming evident to French and Haig that more reserve troops, in addition to Haking's corps, should be made available for Loos. Indeed, the following day, the 24th, Sir John ordered Second Army to hold 28th Division 'in readiness to meet unexpected eventualities'.[15] The ADC's diary entry for the day ended: 'Gen[eral] not very well to-night – feverish – & so did not come in to dinner'[16] – not the most promising state of health for a commander about to start a major battle. At 5.20 pm on the 25th, the opening day of the battle, orders reached the division to be prepared to move at two hours' notice 'by train, bus and march route [*sic*] to an unknown destination'.[17] Throughout the evening further instructions followed: cancelling the transport, telling them to march at dawn and then 'saying we can use any roads we like, confirmed at 11.30 pm'.[18] The official history gloomily recorded:

> The original arrangements were for one brigade … to move by motor-bus, one by train and the third to march. At the last moment however, GHQ were unable to arrange this and the whole division marched. As a result of the delay, it was too late to save Fosse 8.[19]

The battalions covered 17 miles the next day, 26 September, in incessant rain, arriving in billets in and around Béthune that night, some 6 miles from the Loos front; after so long in the trenches, the day would have tested their stamina and march discipline. That day, 85 Brigade was told to relieve 9th Division troops in the Hohenzollern Redoubt, the 'remainder to move up in support'[20] with the division coming under the orders of I Corps 'forthwith'. The following day, the tired troops struggled on, 'down a road a foot deep in mud',[21] towards 9th Division's sector at the Hohenzollern Redoubt. It was only the start of a litany of errors in how not to commit a division to battle.

Bulfin's arrival on the 27th at Gough's HQ, south of Béthune, was inauspicious. Gough's observed in his book, *The Fifth Army*:

> [At 10.00 am] Bulfin came in to report to me. He was a bluff, red-faced man, and at once on entering the room commenced to explain that infantry were not cavalry – and it seemed to me that he was more intent on instructing me how to command a corps than he was to deal with the serious problem before his division and to help the troops already in great difficulties round Fosse 8.[22]

Undoubtedly, Bulfin would not have been in the best of moods, not helped by his fever. He must have been angered by GHQ's contradictory orders and poor staff work in moving his division to the front along congested and disorganized routes. His mood was probably worsened by an infantryman's frustration at cavalry commanders' historic inability to understand his soldiers' more pedestrian progress (French, Haig and Gough were all from the *arme blanche*, and the latter had the reputation of understanding little about any arm other than cavalry). Another infantry divisional commander in 1915, Major General Haldane, admitted to a similar irritation: 'I do not feel Cavalry officers should have command of Infantry for they expect everything to gallop and in consequence are the least patient of mortals.'[23] In any event, the meeting was to mark the start of an acrimonious relationship, and one in which the junior always came off worse. Whether it had anything to do with Gough's 'Anglo-Irish' roots, brought into relief during the Curragh 'incident', and his possible reaction to Bulfin's Irish Catholic ancestry, can only be conjecture. In addition, Bulfin may have harboured some jealousy of Gough's rapid promotion whilst he himself was recovering from wounds; Bulfin was some seven years older than his new corps commander. Gough was a notoriously difficult man to work for, with an impatient and adversarial style of command. A protégé of Haig, who admired him as 'a 'thruster', a man who plunged ahead and got the job done, Gough was, however, a 'thruster who attacked regardless of the situation and his troops suffered in consequence'. Such was the historian Robin Neillands' assessment.[24] After the death of Gough's younger brother

Johnnie, Haig had turned to the elder brother as a confidant and sounding board. Iris Oakey, who studied 28th Division's performance at Loos, made the wry observation that 'Gough was the kind of officer the Army thinks it needs, but dislikes when it gets.'[25]

Fosse 8 was a formidable objective, on rising ground, dominating the British front line in the north. Although marking a coal mine, it actually encompassed a wider area of strongly defended German positions, with a 30ft high slag heap ('the Dump'), a manager's house and adjacent miners' cottages. In front was the Hohenzollern Redoubt, an enemy strongpoint thrust out some 500yds from their front line and close to the British. This redoubt was connected by a number of trenches running back to the Dump and Fosse 8; 'Big Willie' and 'Little Willie' were two such trench systems, linking to Fosse and Dump trenches behind (see Map 6). The Redoubt

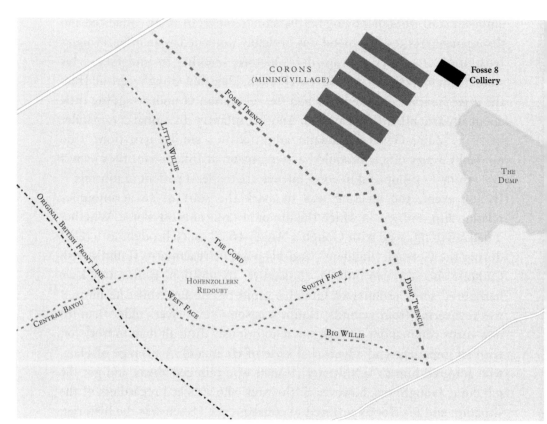

Map 6. Hohenzollern Redoubt and Fosse 8.

had been successfully taken on 25 September and, by the morning of the 27th, the eastern edge of Fosse 8 was held by three inexperienced New Army battalions of 73 Brigade, exhausted after forty-eight hours of fighting and with little food or water. Their elderly brigade commander had been removed the day before by Gough, allegedly for a lack of offensive spirit; his troops were now showing signs of wavering. At noon that day a powerful German attack had driven out these spent men from Fosse 8 back to the Hohenzollern Redoubt, held by Thesiger's 9th Scottish Division. Vicious close-quarter fighting took place as German bombing parties attempted to outflank the Scots by working along Little Willie trench. The Scots' courage had, however, stiffened the resolve of 73 Brigade's men, and the remnants of the Highlanders' 26 Brigade were now poised to try retaking the lost ground.[26]

The situation across Haig's whole front was now serious, not least at Fosse 8. At 2.15 pm he arrived at Gough's HQ, where he heard the news that 9th Division's commander, Major-General George Thesiger, who had gone forward to assess the situation at Fosse 8, had been killed. Haig, normally implacably calm, according to Gough was 'visibly worried … sharp' and 'cross'.[27] He told Gough to place Bulfin in command of the sector, with orders to retake Fosse 8.

Before his lead brigade had arrived, Bulfin set off to 9th Division's report centre at Chateau des Prés, just north-west of Vermelles, to take over command, assuring Haig that 'he would regain Fosse 8 by tonight'.[28] Congestion on the roads was appalling and it took almost an hour to cover 3 miles by car. This was the first time Bulfin had served under Haig since being wounded the previous November, and his army commander would have kept faith in the ability of his 'tower of strength' to restore desperate situations. Assuming Haig's record of Bulfin's promise was accurate – and even if Haig did not include any qualification Bulfin may have offered – it was a rash one to make. The day before, the 26th, the 'General went out to front in afternoon & watched attack proceeding'.[29] Hence Bulfin had seen something of the ground and the difficulties of tackling Fosse 8. On reaching his new command, the attack by the remnants of 26 Brigade, some 600 men, was launched. Despite great gallantry, the Highlanders were unable to advance any further than the eastern edge of Hohenzollern Redoubt. At least the Redoubt, if not Fosse 8, remained in British hands.

85 Brigade holds on to Hohenzollern Redoubt

By 1.00 pm that day 85 Brigade under Brigadier General 'Pinto' Pereira had arrived at Vermelles, a couple of miles from the Redoubt. The 85th was the division's best brigade and its commander was much admired by Bulfin – 'one of the very best soldiers out in France'.[30] They were about to pay a terrible price for being chosen to lead the attack.

Gathering together his COs and holding one map, Pereira began a chaotic afternoon of receiving frequently changing intelligence reports and orders, as the fluid battle in front continued – 'first that some of the captured trenches were lost, secondly all the captured trenches were lost, finally that the Hohenzollern Redoubt was still held; this meant three sets of orders'.[31] With only two officers from 9th Division to guide them, and a dozen incomplete maps of the German trenches, progress to the front was dreadful. The main access was along the Central Bayou, a single communication trench, and they were hampered by constant delays in getting past the troops they were meant to relieve. In Pereira's words, 'The trench was very deep and narrow, wounded men were trying to come down it, further on there were dead bodies and equipment blocking the way.'[32] All this time, continuous rain was making the infantrymen's life a misery as they struggled through the calf-deep mud. At 4.15 pm this confusion was compounded by General Gough, over Bulfin's head, directly 'ordering an immediate counter-attack across the open'[33] to retake Fosse 8, an impossible task. The brigade commander, with his brigade-major, accompanied the leading battalion – 'the communication trenches were so congested with troops that the 2nd Buffs quitted them and reached their appointed positions being shelled heavily on route'.[34] Soon afterwards Pereira and his brigade-major, Captain Flower, were wounded, the former hit by shrapnel in the foot.

What followed does little credit to the commander of I Corps – or to GOC 28th Division. With command of the brigade devolving on Lieutenant Colonel Roberts of the Royal Fusiliers, Lieutenant Colonel Hare (Bulfin's GSO1) had gone forward personally to order him to mount an attack to retake Fosse 8 at dawn. But at 6.00 am the battalions, struggling to reach the front through an unfamiliar labyrinth of trenches at night, were not in position. An hour later, the COs of the 2nd Buffs and 3rd Middlesex arrived and managed a scanty reconnaissance. Their assessment was that such an attack was impossible in daylight, and they requested that it be delayed until nightfall. Gough would not countenance it, and at 8.00 am Hare revisited Roberts and impressed on him that 'the attack must take place at once with the utmost resolution, there must be no cause for delay until the fosse is taken'.[35] Roberts wrote later that he had 'begged B. [Bulfin] to let me carry out the attack in my own way … but no, that word counter-attack was sent down the telephone every ¼ hour'.[36]

Bulfin's ability to influence Gough, during the division's less than smooth arrival at the front, would have been limited. But why he did not visit the front line trenches himself, but sent his chief of staff instead, is open to question. It is unlikely that Bulfin would have paid great attention to the high command's concern about senior officers exposing themselves to danger, which was already filtering down (on 3 October GHQ had issued an order to the BEF 'guarding against a tendency by senior officers such as Corps and Divisional Commanders to take up positions too far forward when fighting is in progress').[37] Three divisional commanders were killed in a week at Loos, Thesiger being the first. More likely it was that the challenge of getting to grips with taking over 9th Division's front, as well as supervising his own division's arrival, consumed his immediate attention. The divisional war diary that day made mention of Bulfin organizing artillery support for the brigade and then having to be available for a visit from the corps commander. But by seeing matters for himself Bulfin would have been able to obtain an accurate picture of the difficulties facing his leading brigade, and would have been better able to judge whether such an attack had any reasonable chance of success. Realistically, given his recent arrival at the front and to Gough's command, he could do little else but follow through his senior's orders. To be fair, Gough would have been under considerable pressure himself from French and Haig to maintain these attacks. In any case, Bulfin was in a weak position to protest, as he had apparently promised Haig he would retake Fosse 8 'by nightfall', and he was already late.

The night before, Gough, seeing that 85 Brigade would be late and appreciating that the slag heap of the Dump held the key to the Fosse 8 position, had ordered a nearby battalion, the 1st Royal Berkshires, to make a surprise night attack. Sustaining heavy losses, they were unable to hold the summit and were driven back to Dump Trench below. Among those killed was Second Lieutenant Alexander Turner, posthumously awarded the Victoria Cross, one of two brothers to be so recognized. The poor quality and paucity of hand grenades, a battle-winning weapon in such trench fighting, was starting to take its toll.

Next morning, the leading battalions of 85 Brigade attacked, with predictably disastrous results. 2nd Buffs, aiming for the summit of the Dump, faced delays getting to its jumping-off position and was only able to launch itself at 10.00 am, some time after the covering artillery bombardment had ceased. They were met by heavy machine gun fire as the men went over the top, in full view of the Germans on the slagheap, and an hour later were forced back to their trenches in the Redoubt. Two companies had at least crossed the summit of the Dump and reached the enemy trenches at its foot, but they were driven back by shellfire, leaving 100 men killed or wounded on the Dump; the battalion counted a minimum of eleven enemy MGs facing them. Their CO, Lieutenant Colonel Claude Worthington, lost his life in this endeavour. The 3rd Middlesex, tasked with bombing its way along South Face trench, made progress initially, until their soldiers ran out of bombs in this claustrophobic close-quarter fighting. Enfiladed by machine gun fire from both sides, they were forced to withdraw, the Germans following up close behind. Whilst leading his men up a communication trench, their CO, Lieutenant Colonel George Neale, was killed. Throughout the rest of the day and night, as the incessant rain continued, this bombing competition with the enemy was sustained by both battalions. The British came off far worse:

Our bomb throwers were nearly all killed or wounded and others were borrowed from neighbouring units. Owing to the rain the fuses were damp, matches gave out, and the only way to light the fuses was by means of keeping cigarettes alight. The organization of the enemy bombers was outstanding. He threw at least five bombs to our one and of much more powerful description. During the night every endeavour was made to get in the wounded. Neither rations nor water were obtainable. Attempts were made to dig in but the mud rendered it a slow and laborious task.[38]

The following day, the 29th, brought more relentless heavy rain, adding to the woes of the embattled men of 85 Brigade, as trenches became quagmires of mud, rifles jammed and bombs failed to ignite. An attempt was made that night to relieve 2nd Buffs with 1st York and Lancasters from 83 Brigade. Once again, congested trenches and poor guiding delayed its arrival and forced the handover to be attempted in daylight, under German observation. The Germans used the moment to launch a bombing raid, causing confusion in the busy trenches, but the Yorkshiremen responded with a charge over the top, driving the Germans back. So the day continued with fierce see-saw fighting. During this critical period, Private Samuel Harvey of the Y&L won the VC for crossing open ground under fire, again and again, to re-supply his fellows with an astonishing thirty boxes of bombs.

3rd Royal Fusiliers, given the task of holding the centre of the Redoubt, had an equally gruelling time. As the day lengthened, the hard-pressed battalion started to lose its hold, but was given some respite by an impromptu counter-attack from a company of the Y&L. When the Fusiliers were eventually forced to pull back, the 2nd East Surreys next door became unsteady. Second Lieutenant Fleming-Sandes climbed on to the parapet and, despite being wounded in the arm and face, continued to bomb the Germans in Little Willie trench and inspired his men to hold on; his was the second VC won by 28th Division.

During this anxious day Bulfin had gone down in the morning to visit 85 Brigade HQ and 'went on to the front line. They had a very lively time in the shelling line, & got back coated in mud at 3 p.m.'[39] On taking over from 9th Division on the 27th, he had established his divisional HQ's report centre there, at Chateau des Prés. In contrast to Second Ypres, Bulfin was much closer to the front and better able to stay in contact with his brigades, despite the problems of approaching the forward positions.

The following day – 'a glorious fine day for a change'[40] – 85 Brigade held on stubbornly but, by nightfall, had shot their bolt after four days of constant fighting. That night they were relieved by their comrades of 84 Brigade. The brigade-major reported their losses as 52 officers, including two COs killed, and 1,214 other ranks. But as Nick Lloyd commented, 'If anyone had expected that this failure would have shaken Gough out of his preoccupation with recapturing Fosse 8, they would have been disappointed.'[41]

Bulfin had spent the morning visiting 84 Brigade and then went on to 83 Brigade's HQ by the railway line just east of Vermelles. After lunch he continued to I Corps HQ, then returned to 84 Brigade to 'explain the plan'. The ADC added significantly, 'I Corps very troublesome in their attentions & have either got the wind up or don't trust this Division',[42] and again, 'Corps have been very persistent from 4 am.'[43] Bulfin was being chased about by Gough, given little leeway in how to fight his division.

Whilst 85 Brigade clung on at the Redoubt, the remainder of 83 Brigade who were not assisting them held the line to the east near the Quarries. Faced with constant shelling and bombing attacks, they nevertheless succeeded in making significant improvements to their trenches, and by 2 October were able to hand over a well constructed sector to the Guards.

84 Brigade lose the Redoubt

On the night of 30 September Brigadier General Pearse's 84 Brigade, until then held in reserve, faced the daunting task of taking over a thoroughly confusing and tenuous situation in the trenches around Hohenzollern Redoubt. In reality, the only trenches held by the British were now the western face of the Redoubt and Big Willie; the Germans held most of Little Willie and still dominated the area from the Dump and Fosse 8. The only obstacle to the enemy taking over all the Redoubt were a few barricades in some trenches leading back to Fosse 8, stubbornly defended by the brigade's bombers. It was not a stable platform from which to retake the Redoubt, the task set them by Bulfin.

In the morning of 1 October matters deteriorated swiftly. By 8.30 am reports were coming in to divisional HQ that the Germans had penetrated into Big Willie. Bulfin, who had planned to go down the trenches that day, had to return. Orders were issued to retake the trench, and throughout the day, although handicapped by a lack of sufficient bombs, efforts by the 2nd Northumberland Fusiliers, supported by the 2nd Cheshires, succeeded in retrieving part of it. But the real challenge, one that would stigmatize I Corps' view of 28th Division's performance at Loos, was now facing them. 84 Brigade was set the task of retaking Little Willie and a new trench, named the Chord, running north–south across the Redoubt, and thus securing the Redoubt that night. The idea was to undertake a silent night attack, with no artillery to alert the enemy. Although the 1st Welsh, led with great dash by their CO, succeeded in capturing a large part of Little Willie, they were almost cut off from their sister battalion, the 6th Welsh. All morning the next day, 2 October, the brigade struggled to hold on against repeated counter-attacks. But by the afternoon, their supply of grenades exhausted, they were forced to retreat. Little Willie had returned to German hands. An indication of how much the senior commanders across the BEF were monitoring 28th Division's efforts was reflected in a message sent in the morning by General Plumer, north in the Ypres Salient, with already outdated congratulations on the recapture of Little Willie.[44] In the afternoon Pearse ordered the 1st Suffolks to retake the trench that night. It was a forlorn effort and the precursor of an all-out assault by the Germans the following day to drive all of Pearse's troops from the Hohenzollern Redoubt, less a section of Big Willie clung on to by the Northumberland Fusiliers. The brigade could do no more. Pearse suffered the normal fate of failure and was relieved of command. 'Two of the Colonels of the 84th went off their rocker and have been sent home', reported Roberts of the Royal Fusiliers.[45]

83 Brigade's turn – Bulfin stands up to Gough

By the afternoon of the 3rd it was 83 Brigade's turn to bang their heads against the 'brick wall' of the Redoubt. 28th Division was now largely back to the British front line of 25 September, and the task set them by I Corps very much had the smell of reinforcing defeat. The ADC recorded: 'Gen. Ravenshaw was asked for plan to retake the redoubt. He said he preferred to attack at dawn & not by night owing to Brigade not being familiar with ground. This was sanctioned by I Corps.'[46]

The brigade had no time to rest after handing over their sector to the Guards. That night, they took over from the spent 84 Brigade, doing their best to prepare themselves in the hurried time available. Officers were given little opportunity to reconnoitre the ground or time to move their troops to their start lines. Two battalions were due to go over the top at 4.15 am to charge the Redoubt, hoping to surprise the Germans, whilst a third, 2nd King's Own, would retake the lost part of Big Willie. Such tactics had failed before, and there was little indication they would work this time. The ADC, who was at the divisional report centre that night, wrote:

> 83rd Bde counter attacked redoubt at 4.15 am. Extraordinary heavy rifle and M.G. fire. Our men were caught by M.G. fire getting over parapet. Attack made by 1/KOYLI & 2/East Yorks. Only 20 of former got within 30x of German trenches & then came back. Attack failed.[47]

The ADC's account of 4 October then took on an even more urgent note:

> At 7 am I spoke to Corps Commander, who was very angry, over telephone. He came over to see Gen. at 9 am & Gen *took a very decided attitude* [author's italics]. No further attempt was made to take redoubt.[48]

Evidently Bulfin had had enough of Gough's impossible demands and was standing his ground, bitter about the way he was unable to provide effective support to his troops. After the war, in a letter to the official historian about Loos, he wrote, most likely about this attack:

> I remember he [Gough] ordered me to attack a Fosse and late on the night before the attack, which started at dawn, he called me up and told me the guns which had registered and been given their targets were to come out, and I had to put in a new lot of artillery who knew nothing of the targets and had not registered. Of course the whole show was hopeless.[49]

Bulfin heads for home

Gough now decided Bulfin had to go, and went to see Haig, who recorded in his diary:

> He (Gough) considered the Staff work of the Division was bad, and that several operations had failed through ignorance and bad management on the part of the Brigadiers and Divisional Staff. The conclusion I arrived at was that it should be withdrawn for a period of training and discipline.[50]

Interestingly, there was no specific criticism of Bulfin, although he bore ultimate responsibility. In the First Army commander's eyes the division was not 'equal to the task',[51] and orders were issued that afternoon for the Guards Division to take over the following day, tellingly a task they only achieved after experiencing as much difficulty and delay as Bulfin's men.

On 5 October the ADC noted, 'Corps Commander came over in the morning and was fairly affable.' Gough may have seemed so, but his anger with 28th Division had not diminished. Its failure to retake Fosse 8 heralded a strongly worded rebuke from I Corps, with a twelve-point litany of criticism of poor staff work, brigade leadership, soldierly discipline, etc.,[52] in a tone often patronising and out of touch with reality at the front. Conversely, officers of 83 Brigade were furious at what had been asked of them. Lieutenant Colonel Blake, commanding 2nd East Yorkshires, was one of three commanding officers to submit blunt after-action reports; he complained of no artillery bombardment, a complete lack of surprise and the fact that 'Company officers had only very indistinct idea of the trenches they were occupying, and none of all the positions they were to attack.'[53] In spite of the outspoken criticisms from his COs, Bulfin's own report to his corps commander was surprisingly restrained.[54] Relations between Corps and Division had become strained and bitter. Gough even tested the loyalty of one of Bulfin's COs by pressing Roberts of the Royal Fusiliers as to what had gone wrong in the attacks on the Redoubt:

> It was damned awkward and one can't give away things and he was all out for pumping me, but I just laughed too. I told him I was no good applying a Cavalry brain to Infantry feet.

By this time, Roberts thought, '28th Division simply stinks in the nostrils of First Army'.[55]

On the 8th, Haig, more sympathetic than its corps commander, visited the division 'all very busy practising bombing. I thought the units in good heart, though they had suffered severely and had had a bad time about the Hohenzollern Redoubt.'[56] But on the 11th, following further criticism from Gough about the division, Haig wrote: 'Bulfin said his head (where he was wounded at Ypres) troubles him, and he could not sleep o'night. So he is to go home for a rest.'[57] The ADC corroborated this in his diary: 'Corps commander came in before lunch to see General, the outcome of which is that the General is to go home sick & have a rest.'[58] In the afternoon Haig visited Bulfin and 'was very nice about everything'.[59] Haig's 'tower of strength' of the previous year left his division the next day.

Bulfin must have been at a very low point. Normally at ease with his men, and someone who instinctively shouldered his responsibilities for them, he felt unable to go round his brigades and say goodbye in person:

> Gen[eral] spent morning finishing up the narrative. Gen Briggs [his successor] … arrived at noon and the Gen left by car for Wimereux at 2 pm. Alan [the other ADC] & I feel absolutely lost. In the afternoon we went round all Bdes, Yeomanry etc to say goodbye for the General.[60]

Bad news travels fast, and three days later Loch, now the BGGS at VI Corps in the Ypres Salient, wrote to his wife:

> I saw the Army Commander [Plumer] today who told me that poor Finch had been sent home – I am so very sorry though I own I expected it. He will be very sad and I must write to him. What I am to say I don't know.[61]

Army gossip was rife. Lieutenant General Sir William Pulteney, a Scots Guardsman commanding III Corps, wrote to Lady Londonderry the day after Bulfin was sent home: '28th Division lost the Hohenzollern redoubt from being completely bombed out by six Germans, simply because Bulfin did not believe in bombing and the men were ignorant.'[62] This was a poorly informed accusation, given the lack of effective bombs issued to 28th Division (the Guards Division was soon issued better ones) as well as Bulfin's interest in bombing since the Aisne.

On 20 October Bulfin called on Pereira, recovering from his own wounds. His old brigade commander recorded:

> General Bulfin came to see me; he has come home on two months sick leave; his eyesight gave out. Also he could not get on with General Gough who accused the Division of being slow and who was always

(*Right*) Patrick Bulfin, Edward's father, as Lord Mayor of Dublin in 1871. (Bulfin family collection)

(*Below*) Woodtown Park, where Edward Bulfin spent his childhood. (Peter Clarke)

(*Above*) Officers of 2nd Battalion the Yorkshire Regiment in Bangalore, India, 1890. 2/Lt Bulfin is seated on the ground front right. (Green Howards Museum)

(*Left*) A young Bulfin in amateur dramatics in India. (Green Howards Museum)

Butler and Bulfin families 'Off to the Paarl' in South Africa, 1899. (Sketch by Lady Butler)

British troops pinned down at the Modder River, South Africa, 28 November 1899. (Spencer Jones collection)

(*Above*) Bulfin's cousin John (Jack), standing second from left, in the British Army in India. (Bulfin family collection)

(*Left*) Fanny on her engagement to Edward, 1898. (Sara Richer)

(*Right*) Edward on his engagement to Fanny, 1898. (Sara Richer)

(*Below*) Regimental lunch party in Wynberg, Cape Colony, November 1907. Colonel Bulfin is seated back right, his wife second lady from the left. Lt Col Hadow is seated in front of Bulfin. (Green Howards Museum)

(*Left*) Bulfin as a brigade commander, 1914.

(*Below*) The Sugar Factory, 2 Brigade's objective above the Aisne, September 1914. (Yves Fohlen)

132. - CERNY-en-LAONNOIS (Aisne). - La Sucrerie

Kortekeer Cabaret, Ypres Salient, as it stands today. (Author's collection)

Mess gavel presented by Bulfin, made from a tree in Sanctuary Wood, 'In memory of Ypres October 1914'. (Green Howards Museum)

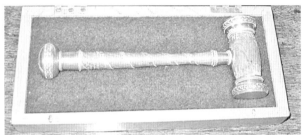

2nd Battalion the Yorkshire Regiment (Green Howards) at the Menin Crossroads, October 1914, by Fortunino Matania. (Green Howards Museum)

'Gassed' (the opening day at Second Ypres, April 1915) by Fortunino Matania. (*Illustrated London News*, Mary Evans Picture Library)

General Plumer (left) with Field Marshal Haig (right), 1918. (IWM Q23665)

Vlamertinghe Chateau, Bulfin's HQ during Second Ypres, as it stands today. (Author's collection)

British dead on German barbed wire at Loos, 28 September 1915. (IWM Q28975)

(*Above left*) Cecil 'Pinto' Pereira, Bulfin's favourite brigade commander, 1915. (Pereira family collection)

(*Above right*) General Sir Hubert Gough, GOC I Corps at Loos. (IWM Q35825D)

(*Left*) Eamon Bulfin, who raised the Irish Republican flag on Easter Sunday 1916. (Bulfin family collection)

Officers of the London
Regiment enjoying a
meal on the Macedonian
front, spring 1917.
(IWM Q111912)

(*Right*) 60th London
Division's 'Bee' badge.

(*Below*) British infantry
marching through Palestine,
December 1917. (IWM
Q24374)

(*Left*) 'The Bull' – General Sir Edmund Allenby, by James McBey. (IWM ART 1552)

(*Below*) Bulfin, third from right, with HRH Prince Arthur, Allenby (on left) and other generals on the Mount of Olives, Jerusalem, 19 March 1918. (AWM A02746A)

(*Above*) Bulfin receives
his knighthood from HRH
Prince Arthur in Jerusalem,
19 March 1918.
(IWM Q12546)

(*Right*) XXI Corps sign, with
its shamrock, acknowledging
its Irish commander.
(IWM FEQ 383)

2nd Bn Black Watch
(7th Indian Div) entering
Beirut 10 October 1918,
having marched 96 miles in
eight days. (IWM Q12407)

(*Left*) A tired Bulfin, painted in Beirut by James McBey, December 1918. (IWM ART 2472)

(*Below*) Bulfin, second from right besides Allenby (both with canes), Beirut, 1919. His son Eddie, as ADC, is fourth from left. (*Tatler*, Mary Evans Picture Library)

Armoured train arriving
at Tala just as Egyptian
saboteurs pull up the
track, March 1919.
(IWM Q111932)

(*Left*) 2/Lt Eddie Bulfin as ADC to his father, 1916. (IWM HU 114626)

(*Right*) An affectionate caricature of the General by Fred May. (Green Howards Museum)

(*Above left*) Eileen, Edward and Fanny's daughter, 1927.

(*Above right*) Edward Bulfin in retirement in Bournemouth. (Sara Richer)

(*Below*) Bulfin takes his last salute as Colonel of the Green Howards, Alma Day, Portland 1934. (Green Howards Museum)

pressing for attacks without what General Bulfin considered sufficient artillery preparation.[63]

'Pinto' Pereira, a Coldstream guardsman who would go on to command 2nd Division, was equally furious with the way Gough had treated 28th Division:

> The proof and absurdity of the accusation of slowness is the time it took the 2nd Guards Brigade to relieve the last Brigade of the 28th Division … The injustice and crassness of a Corps Commander who will not or cannot realize the above facts is beyond belief. It is true the 84th Brigade had the misfortune to lose the Hohenzollern Redoubt under an extremely violent attack; but there is no reason why the whole of the 28th Division should be under a cloud. General Bulfin told me that the 85th Brigade had done magnificent work and all that could be expected of them.

Pereira then added a revealing remark: 'Sir Douglas Haig pressed General Bulfin to remain with the division but he declined'[64] – indicating that, whilst Haig retained his confidence in Bulfin, the normally resolute Bulfin had had enough.

A month later, Cumberbatch, now on the staff of III Corps at Bailleul but in touch with his old master, received a letter from him – 'hopes to be out again next week'.[65] Bulfin, evidently feeling better, was keen to get back and find a post on the Western Front. By this time his old 28th Division was en route to Salonika, its reputation in tatters and destined to spend the remainder of the war in this backwater.

The battle of Loos dragged on into the autumn with further failed efforts, even by the Guards Division where 28th Division had been repulsed. One of the last throws of the dice at the Hohenzollern Redoubt – and at Loos – was a frontal attack, ordered by Haking and carried out by 46th (North Midlands) Division on 13 October, when the division suffered its heaviest losses of the whole war in one day: some 3,500 casualties, most in the first ten minutes, even more than on the Somme. Its commander, angered at being 'hurried into the trenches', faced almost identical problems to Bulfin.

Assessment of Loos

Whatever the 28th's shortcomings, they were not unique to the BEF at the time. But there was no shortage of courage, as witnessed by two out of the five VCs of the battle being awarded to the Division. For the worn-out 28th Division, during its long week in the front at Loos, the butcher's bill amounted to 146 officers and 3,230 men, almost 30 per cent of its infantry strength. Equally worrying was the high casualty rate amongst COs from the close-quarter fighting. Those historians who have studied 1915, and in particular the battle of Loos, have concluded that the condemnation of 28th Division was unfair and that no division could have achieved what was expected of it.[66]

28th Division's brave but wasted efforts, often in awful weather, epitomized many of the tactical weaknesses of the British at Loos. Congested and labyrinthine trenches limited commanders' ability to get their orders disseminated or troops into position in time. Piecemeal attacks were ordered at short notice, often by only a couple of companies, over ground dominated by the enemy. Insufficient and poorly planned artillery support was a major failing and compounded by a critical shortage of effective grenades. Soldiers did their valiant best, making stubborn efforts to hold the Redoubt, but what failed them above all was that senior commanders – all down the chain of command from French, Haig, Gough and, indeed, Bulfin – ordered assault after assault with what can only be described as bone-headed stubbornness. These generals were insufficiently aware of conditions in the front line trenches and held over-optimistic and unrealistic expectations of what their men could reasonably be asked to achieve.

There was a desperate need for more regimental officers, especially trained staff officers, able to plan, organize and lead such modern battles. Precious little was gained except for valuable experience, albeit bought at a very high price. Worse, the generals were slow to learn the right lessons. The BEF would still need to experience the Somme before it developed the skills necessary to attain eventual victory in 1918. The cruel irony was that the Germans learnt more from Loos than the British did, and – crucially – were far better and quicker at putting these lessons in place by the time of the Somme in 1916.

Bulfin was not the only general to be sent home from Loos. More significantly, Sir John French would join him by the end of the year. With the country shaken by the grievous losses of the New Army divisions, he no longer held the confidence of his political masters or that of his subordinate commanders. His replacement as Commander-in-Chief was the ambitious Sir Douglas Haig, with the willpower and optimism – often Panglossian – to lead the British Army on the Western Front until the end of the war. Although Haig's reputation had been enhanced by Loos, his plan of battle, and then his handling of it, were not without flaws. Gough, often starved of reserves, nevertheless let his naturally offensive spirit cloud his judgement of the possible. His careless handling of 28th Division was a case in point.

What of Bulfin's own performance at Loos? It goes without saying that a divisional general's first duty is to carry out the orders of his superiors, which required a degree of ruthlessness on the Western Front as on any battlefield; Bulfin did not lack this. But Loos, unlike Second Ypres, was an offensive battle, the first that Bulfin had fought at this level, and as with many of his colleagues very much new territory for him. Added to this, a divisional commander's ability to influence the battle in the conditions of Loos was limited. He had no choice over where to fight and little flexibility over when or how to carry out his orders. The success or failure of each phase of the battle depended more on the brigade commanders. Bulfin's main inputs were in the provision of artillery support, the generation and handling of what reserves he could muster and the sustaining of his troops with the necessary logistic help.

Notwithstanding his early rash promise to Haig that Fosse 8 would be retaken, in all of these inputs Bulfin performed as capably as most at Loos. That said, nobody came out of Loos well. In comparison with the professionalism of the BEF in 1917/1918, there was generally a low standard of competence across Haig's First Army. In Bulfin's case, his frustration was clear at the way the artillery was handled and his inability to apply lessons he had picked up from Ypres. It does seem he had taken on board another lesson from that battle by placing himself further forward at Loos, better able to influence events within the straightjacket allowed. Whilst a culture of fear of being sacked frequently pervaded the BEF at the time, Bulfin showed he had the moral courage to stand up to Gough. What is more difficult to explain is why it took until the third and last brigade's failed attack for Bulfin to stand his ground. It was evident that he was not back to full health, his head wound affecting his sleep and eyesight, and this must have inhibited his performance. Both Sir John French and Douglas Haig felt that 28th Division had not been up to the task in 1915 and that must, to a degree, have reflected on its commander. Nevertheless, in Sir John French's Dispatches of November 1915, Bulfin received a 'Mention' for services at Loos, a quite normal occurrence but a small indication that he was not completely out of favour. Bulfin was well aware that he had had difficulties at Loos; when commenting to Edmonds after the war about his official history's coverage of the battle, he admitted: 'I have no comment to make on your draft chapters – you have let me off easy.'[67]

In many ways, Loos is one of the saddest battles of the First World War, not only 'unwanted' but one that need not have been fought in the way it was. Arguments over the impact of Sir John French's failure to release the reserve divisions of Haking's XI Corps in time have been well aired. What has not been raised before is why 28th Division was not brought into the battle more effectively, given that it had been warned off as early as 23 September. The official historian thought the end of the battle a 'useless slaughter of infantry'.[68] The poet Robert Graves, who fought in it, heard a blunt description from fellow soldiers – a 'bloody balls-up'[69] – whilst Lloyd George, never slow to blame the 'red-tabs', called it 'futile carnage'.[70]

The last word must come from Edward Bulfin. When writing to the official historian in 1927, he said:

> I have a very confused memory of Loos – a sort of horrid nightmare. I was under Hugh [sic] Gough – and I never want to serve under him again … I wish I had been under Allenby at Loos.[71]

But 1915, a 'nightmare' year for Bulfin, ended with news that he was to raise a territorial division, the 60th (London) Division. Captain Cumberbatch, left behind in France, wrote on 20 December: 'Wrote to Gen. in the evening, but did not know whether to sympathise or congratulate him on his appointment'. In truth, this new post was very much a backward move for Bulfin at a time when, if he had not been in poor health or had clashed with Gough, he could have expected to be promoted to corps command. The only small compensation was that his new command gave him the opportunity, whilst regaining his health and strength, to build and train a fighting formation, something he had not been able to do with the 28th. Bulfin arrived at Bishop's Stortford in Hertfordshire on 22 December to take up his new challenge. He must have been keen to put 1915, the nadir of his professional career, behind him.

Chapter 9

1916–1917
The Making of a Territorial Division: the 60th (London) Division

By January 1916 the British Army had changed out of all recognition. Kitchener's call in August 1914 for 100,000 men had met with widespread enthusiasm; further appeals, five in total, eventually produced a 'New Army' of thirty divisions, to join the eleven regular divisions and twenty-eight of the Territorial Force (TF). All this time, the BEF had managed to keep its fighting units topped up, despite being severely weakened by the early battles of the war. This rapid expansion, on a scale never before experienced in our nation's history, meant that second-line TF units, such as the 60th Division, were last in the 'food chain' for men and equipment. The 47th (London) Division, a first-line TF division, had deployed to France in March 1915. The 60th was initially entitled the 2nd London (Reserve) Division and was based at White City. It had spent most of 1915 struggling to equip and establish itself as a new formation, its resources constantly being diverted to the 47th. When Kitchener inspected it at the start of the year, there were just enough drill weapons to arm the front rank. By March it had moved to Hertfordshire and spent the summer training with the prospect of overseas service, but 'disappointment after disappointment was our lot, and draft after draft was called for and dispatched'.[1]

As Christmas 1915 approached, with Bulfin arriving at his new command, the *Green Howards Gazette* loyally recorded: 'We congratulate General Bulfin in his restoration to health and strength and his appointment to the Command of the 60th (London) Division'.[2]

Command of a territorial division, after the regular 28th, would not have been seen as promotion. It is not difficult to imagine that Bulfin, after such a dispiriting year, would have had to summon all his determination and enthusiasm to face 1916, a year that the British Army and the nation would never forget.

But Bulfin was made of resolute material and 'at once made a close inspection of all the units in the Division … His first impression was not a very hopeful one.'[3] Its new commander wrote: 'The 60th had been bled white in officers, N.C.O.s, and men to furnish reinforcements for the 47th Division. The strongest Infantry unit was about three hundred of all ranks.'[4] His predecessor, the elderly Brigadier General Thomas Calley, had been removed as unfit to command a division in the field.[5] Bulfin wrote sympathetically to him: 'I know you have had all the hard work and drudgery in getting the Division together and it cannot be pleasant to hand over all your good work to me whose only claim is being a junior Major General without a command.'[6]

His first task was to win over the Territorials' loyalty; the next was to make a strong representation to the War Office on the state of his command. The response to the latter was a promise, provided the Division was brought up to standard, that it would be sent to France. Importantly, in the meantime, it would not be called upon to furnish further drafts.

'The rank and file were above my expectations'

Soon after Bulfin arrived to take command, at the end of January 1916, the division moved to Warminster on the edge of Salisbury Plain. At the same time it received its official title of 60th (London) Division.

Training now started in earnest. Bulfin had the influence and experience to obtain proper training facilities and instigated a progressive regime for his men. This was not the first time he had commanded Territorials, in peace and war, and he understood how to get the best out of them:

> The point that struck me most about the Division was the extraordinary quickness, intelligence, and alertness of the rank and file. They seemed to be capable of understanding what one was going to say before one had completed half a sentence. To one used to handling Regular troops, this higher plane of intelligence struck me most forcibly. The rank and file were above my expectations.

He was equally perceptive about the officers:

> The officers worked out their problems, and arrived at the same results as Regular officers, but taking totally different and much longer methods.

The training of the officers for war, I early recognized, required much more trouble, and much more care than it was had been possible to bestow on them before.[7]

Nevertheless, Bulfin realized he needed an injection of operationally tested officers and brought in Regular captains and majors from regiments with war experience.

In April he ordered a complete set of trenches to be dug on the Plain to replicate what the division would face on the Western Front, supposedly the first commander to do so in England; each battalion occupied these trenches for two days and nights. Emphasis was placed on improving battle procedure, officers being tested and timed on getting orders disseminated speedily from divisional headquarters down to units and the front line. He also concentrated on collective training, with his three brigades being exercised throughout April on an ever increasing scale of intensity, until the entire division was ready to turn out. Brigadier General Herbert Studd, newly arrived to take over 180 Brigade, found the 'regulated' training regime restricting but admitted, 'I quite agree with his ideas and could not better his programme … I think he is a man who knows his own mind and his ideas are sound.'[8]

During this busy period, many senior visitors cast a critical eye over the division's progress, including Field Marshal French as well as Lord Esher, Chairman of the London Territorial Force Association, who took a great interest in his soldiers. Bulfin was aware of the need to keep men's spirits up once they were in the line, and he introduced bands into each brigade and encouraged concert parties whilst they were in Warminster; the division being Londoners, 'the performers included many well-known people from the concert and theatrical world'.[9]

Conscious of the lack of divisional identity and *esprit de corps* in the early days of 28th Division, Bulfin introduced one of the more notable divisional signs of the war, the 'Bee' symbol of the 60th Division (see plate section). It was the one Bonaparte had used when he ascended the French throne to reflect the first letter of his name, and Bulfin copied it. The men quickly identified themselves with the 'Bee' and Bulfin.

The opportunity to train his new command properly, and implant so many lessons learnt in the unforgiving school of the Western Front, must have given him considerable satisfaction. Above all, he was able to avoid it being 'a division in name but not in being'. One of the few similarities with the early days of his previous division was the weather – incessant rain, not to be recommended on Salisbury Plain.

The Easter Rising

On Easter Day 1916 Bulfin was reminded forcibly of his Irish roots. Irish nationalists started what was initially considered an ineffective and generally unpopular 'rising' by occupying the General Post Office in Dublin.

One of the two men to raise a flag on its roof was Eamon Bulfin, the son of Bulfin's first cousin William, who had imbued into his son a strong sense of Irish history and political activism. A talented hurler and a student of University College Dublin, Eamon was one of the first to join the Irish Volunteers in 1913. On Easter Sunday, ignoring the orders to the Volunteers to stand down, he joined his Rathfarnham company and took up position on the roof of the General Post Office, where he raised the green flag of the Irish Republic on the Prince Street corner. After they had held the GPO until the Friday evening, orders reached them to lay down their arms, and they eventually surrendered to British forces at the Parnell Monument in Sackville Street (now O'Connell Street). For his part in the Rising Eamon was sentenced to death. But after Prime Minister Asquith personally confronted the British commander, Lieutenant General Sir John Maxwell, to stop the executions, Eamon was sent to prison instead. The fact that he had been born in Argentina also helped save him from the firing squad, their ambassador intervening on his behalf. Upon his release in December 1916, he returned home to Co. Offaly, where he rejoined the Irish Volunteers, eventually being re-arrested in July 1918. After gaol in Portlaoise Prison and in Somerset, in May 1919 he was deported to Argentina, where he was again arrested, supposedly for avoiding military service there. On his release, Eamon de Valera appointed him as the first representative of the Irish Republic to Argentina. Amongst a large and often wealthy Irish expatriate population in Argentina, he launched, together with Laurence Ginnell, the Irish Fund and negotiated shipments of ammunition for the IRA during the War of Independence. He returned to the family home in Derrinlough in

1922, and died on Christmas Eve 1968. He is remembered today by a street named after him near Portlaoise prison.

Eamon's sister Catalina ('Kid') also had a close connection with the Rising through her future father-in-law. Born with a fighting spirit and brought up with strong nationalist sympathies like her brother, in 1925 she married twenty-one-year-old Sean MacBride. His father, John, had sided with the Boer commandos in the South African War, serving in the Irish Transvaal Brigade against the British. His short marriage to Maud Gonne, W. B. Yeats's muse, produced Sean, who served as chief of staff to the IRA in the 1930s. Sean's later career followed a more peaceful path: he was a founding figure in Amnesty International, won the Nobel Peace Prize in 1974, held senior diplomatic posts in the UN and served as a government minister in the Dáil. Catalina's part in the history of Irish independence is less well known, but not insignificant. Before her marriage she was secretary to Austin Stack, a minister in the outlawed Republican parliament. When the War of Independence began, she had access to much intelligence, becoming a useful courier carrying messages as well as hiding weapons and ammunition for the volunteers. She was firmly against the 1921 Anglo-Irish Treaty, and continued to be politically active in the subsequent Irish Civil War, ending up spending six months in Kilmainham gaol in 1923.

After the South African War Major John MacBride had returned, eventually, to Dublin. Because he was well known to the authorities, he was excluded from the Volunteers' secret planning for the Easter Rising, and hence found himself on Easter Monday in Dublin, unexpectedly caught up in events as he walked to meet his brother. After offering his services to the Volunteers, he was arrested by the British and then sentenced to death. He was executed on 5 May in Kilmainham gaol, refusing to be blindfolded and uttering the words: 'I have looked down the muzzle of too many guns in the South African War to fear death, and now please carry out your sentence.'

Bulfin had only just, in February, sold the family home at Woodtown Park, on the outskirts of Dublin in Rathfarnham[10] to the brothers James and Eoin MacNeill. Eoin, a noted Gaelic scholar, was a founder member of the Irish Volunteers, and many of the key figures involved in the Easter Rising frequented Woodtown, among them Patrick Pearse. It was Eoin who took the curious step of placing an advertisement in the *Sunday Independent* warning the Volunteers not to turn out for the Easter Rising as the conditions were so unfavourable. On that Sunday, the MacNeill brothers stood on the roof of the house and watched Dublin burn.[11]

The British over-reaction to this act of rebellion, sentencing to death the republican volunteers, made them martyrs to their cause and only served to incense the Irish and add fuel to the flames of rebellion. Trouble spread to other parts of Ireland and large contingents of troops were speedily dispatched to the south.

One of those contingents was 179 Brigade of Bulfin's division, given three hours' notice on 28 April to move from their base outside Warminster to Ireland. After a night crossing dodging German submarines in the Irish Sea, two days after leaving Warminster they reached Queenstown (now Cobh, the port of Cork). The Sinn Fein rebellion, as it was then termed by the British Army, had spread to Cork and the south-west. The battalions were 'received by the inhabitants in quite a friendly manner',[12] although the Civil Service Rifles had a mixed reception, some women shrieking 'City clurrks!' at them, whilst a man mysteriously produced a box of cigars from under his arm for the troops.[13] From there they dispersed around the Cork, Tralee and Limerick countryside rounding up bands of Sinn Feiners. Faced with little resistance, the brigade was back in Warminster less than a month later. For some of the division it was their first taste, albeit a mild one, of active service.

It is inconceivable that Bulfin – or more significantly, the British establishment – can have been unaware of his relations' involvement in the Easter Rising and later events. This does not seem to have drawn any adverse comment at the time, and his career continued unaffected.

'None thought or cared whither that first march would lead them'

In the middle of May, Bulfin received the official news that his division was deemed fit for active service, and shortly afterwards they were ordered to be ready to move to France in mid-June. All the paraphernalia of war was issued – identity discs, field dressings and active service pay books – and they were granted four days' embarkation leave. On 31 May the King inspected the troops, drawn up in line of brigades on the high ground above Warminster, and delivered the invariably encouraging accolade that he was 'highly gratified with the turn out and bearing of the troops'.

Bulfin recorded his feelings as his division headed off to war.

> I well remember on a grey, wet morning in June 1916, as the 60th London Division filed past me at Sutton-Veny on their way to embark at Southampton for the front, I noted the young animated faces and admirable bearing of the men, and none thought or cared whither that first march would lead them.[14]

It would lead them to the Western Front, the Balkans, Egypt and Palestine.

The division's departure for France did mean that Bulfin would miss his son's graduation from Sandhurst. Eddie, just eighteen, had finished school at Downside in December the previous year and decided on a career in his father's regiment. Unlike his father, he was commissioned from Sandhurst on 16 August 1916 and he would later join him as his ADC in France; serving in such a position to one's father was a common practice in those days.

Under Vimy Ridge

Anyone visiting the striking Canadian Memorial atop Vimy Ridge today is inevitably drawn to look north-east, as does the memorial, over a sharp drop to the coalfields of Lens and Loos and the plain of Douai beyond. What is less obvious, with its shattered slopes now so heavily wooded, is how the chalky ridge, 450ft at its highest, also dominates the ground to the south-west and towards Arras. Vimy Ridge provided unparalleled observation of the Allied lines, better than anywhere else on the Western Front. In the precarious low-lying area below, the Allies fought to hold their front throughout 1916, from early summer drawing off as many German troops as possible from the Somme battlefield to the south. Since the spring of 1916 the British had taken over the sector from the French, hard-pressed at Verdun, but it would not be until the following spring that they were in a strong enough position to launch their major offensive at Arras, culminating in the Canadians' triumphant but costly seizure of Vimy Ridge. It was in this sector of the Western Front that the 60th Division would receive its baptism of war.

By 27 June the whole division had landed in France and moved by rail from Le Havre to St Pol. Here the brigades route-marched to their concentration areas to the north-west of Arras, and two days later closed up in rear of the

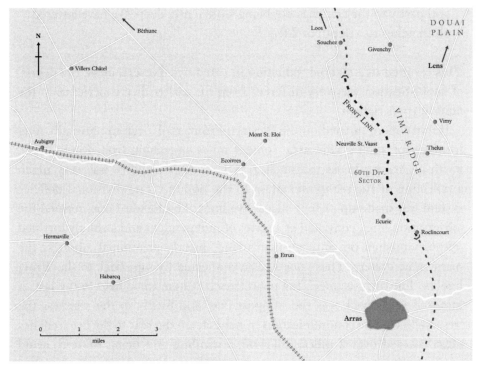

Map 7. Arras/Vimy Ridge, July–October 1916.

front line around the ruined villages of Ecoivres, Mont St Eloi and Etrun. Divisional headquarters established itself close by at Villers Châtel, only a few miles from where Bulfin's best man, Wilfred Dent, was buried. It was a busy time, as the period allotted to be tutored and to take over from the 51st Division was suddenly cut short. On the night of 13 July the brigades took over the Highlanders' trenches under intense artillery bombardment from an alerted enemy.

Faced with the considerable vulnerability of his entire divisional frontage, overlooked as it was from Vimy Ridge, Bulfin was not reassured even by the significant improvements made to the trenches in this chalky country since the French had left. Writing to the King's private secretary, following George V's visit to 60th Division on 9 August, he reported:

> During the first week of August in the trenches our casualties amounted to 44 Killed and 164 Wounded – a heavy toll, partly due to inexperience

and partly to the trenches not being sufficiently deep. We have lowered all trenches to a depth of 7 feet.[15]

This resulted in a marked reduction in casualties. Nevertheless, the degree of sophistication was very different from his earlier dire experience in the muddy Ypres Salient.

Bulfin's men, untried on the Western Front, took over an unusually long frontage for such a vital area, some 4 miles stretching from Roclincourt, north of Arras, almost to Souchez. Such a responsibility was very much a reflection of the manpower drain to the Somme. The divisional defence system was made up of four successive lines. The forward one, termed the 'observation line', consisted of a series of independent and strongly fortified outposts pushed out into no-man's-land, mostly positioned amongst the many mine craters. These posts were connected by saps back to the 'firing line' or 'line of resistance', the main trench system to be held to the last. A hundred yards back was the 'support line' and finally in the rear was the 'reserve line'. The communication trenches from the rear to the fire trenches often covered over 2 miles, following a winding and tiring route to avoid enemy artillery.

Each brigade spent a fortnight at a time at the front, with a week in the 'firing line', rotating to support and then reserve. Bulfin was determined to impose a strict form of discipline in the front line, akin to that aboard ship. An officer was always 'on watch', relieved every four hours. Sentries were double-posted to ensure alertness and security. Importantly, the smallest possible number of soldiers were kept in the front-line trenches, which were often under bombardment, and a system was put in place to reinforce the front line speedily when required. Being in the support trenches was often the least popular part of the rotation, long nights 'dragging sandbags full of damp chalk … the most awful heart-breaking work imaginable'.[16] The lessons of 1915 were rightly spreading throughout the BEF.

Mining and counter-mining, and in particular crater fighting, were the chief pre-occupations of the division from the end of July. The whole front taken over by Bulfin's troops was found to be honeycombed by mine galleries, old and new. No-man's-land was pitted with huge craters and mounds, the latter sometimes rising to 150ft. In one brigade frontage up to twenty of these mounds scarred the landscape. As soon as a mine went up, fierce fighting would take place to seize one or both lips of the crater and thus consolidate or, even better, improve one's front line.

At the same time, intensive night patrolling by the Division kept the troops sharp and aggressive. Often ten patrols would be out at the same time. By August, these had developed into systematic large-scale night raids, sometimes in parties of 50–60 strong, which carried on with no respite throughout September and into October. The aim was chiefly to gather intelligence on the enemy and keep him behind his own wire. With the battle of the Somme now raging to the south, it was vital to find out which German units had been moved away to counter Haig's offensive. These raids were well prepared with training and rehearsals, including the learning of some German phrases. A soldier from the Civil Service Rifles recalled:

> When one thinks of two men standing in a German trench, one at each entrance to a dugout, shouting *'Kommen Sie heraus, you bastards'* at the same time throwing bombs down as fast as they can, one feels that this study of language was a waste of time.[17]

There were inevitable casualties, often to young officers leading these raids. After one of them, the 2/20th Londons received a concerned message from Bulfin: 'Hope all have returned, and wounded sent back.'[18] However, he was pleased with the outcome of these forays across no-man's-land:

> I have no hesitation in saying that we always knew the German units in front of us, and if any unit was withdrawn to be sent down to the Somme we knew of it fairly soon, and communicated the move to Corps Head-quarters. Some of this information was highly valuable, and the Division received many complimentary messages.[19]

The division was building a solid reputation in the Arras sector, and the corps commander, General Sir Charles Fergusson, evidently thought highly of it. Bulfin had every reason to feel positive about his new division and, indeed, the recovery of his own reputation. But a surprise awaited him and his men.

'Under orders for the Balkan Front'

In late October tension mounted as orders arrived for the division to hand over to the 3rd Canadian Division. It was warned to go into the GHQ reserve area to the south-west, anticipating a move to the Somme, where Haig's offensive was grinding on; the Territorials were keen to live up to the deeds of their sister battalions there. But rumours abounded that this was not to be, and that another theatre of war awaited them. Having moved to the rear area east of Abbeville by the end of the month, Bulfin was visited by Haig on 1 November with this news:

> That the 60th as being one of the strongest Divisions on the Western Front had been selected to proceed to Salonika … Very sorry that he was compelled to part with the Division, particularly as it had been so highly reported on by the Army Commander under whom it had served.[20]

The year before, on 6 October 1915, the Austro-German armies had attacked across the Danube, meeting resistance from the hardy Serb army. Five days later, the Bulgarians had launched into eastern Serbia, driving a wedge between the Serbs and the French and British reinforcements newly arrived at Salonika (now Thessaloniki), the port of Macedonia. The doughty Serbs, driven west through the Albanian mountains, were evacuated to the island of Corfu, later to be re-equipped and join their Allies at Salonika in the spring of 1916. The failure to come to the timely aid of Serbia – the 'forgotten ally' – remains 'one of the remarkable blind spots in the strategy of the Allies'.[21]

The Allies, alerted too late to the danger facing Serbia, had hurriedly gathered together French and British divisions and dispatched them to Salonika under the command of the politically scheming French General Maurice Sarrail. He had recently been sacked by Joffre from the Western Front, to the embarrassment of the French government. Amongst the British troops was Bulfin's old 28th Division, rushed from the killing fields of Loos. Advancing up the Vardar River, the leading elements of the expeditionary force clashed with the Bulgarians and were forced back on Salonika. The British General Staff called for an evacuation, aware that the Gallipoli failure had already drained any vestige of Allied prestige from the

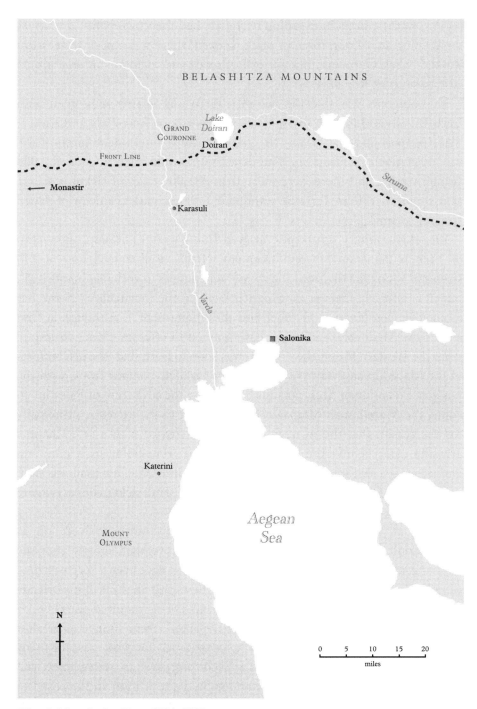

Map 8. Macedonian Front 1916–1917.

region. But the French, urged on by Joffre, had their own political motives for keeping a coalition force in place. Indeed, there was a need to reassure Russia, check German influence over Greece and maintain an operational base to support Romania.

The outcome was that the Salonika force was further reinforced with fresh British and French divisions as well as troops from Italy and Russia. The German jibe that 'it was the greatest Allied internment camp of the war' had much justification. The expedition would suck in over 400,000 British troops, and there were more than 481,000 cases of sickness at one time or another. John Terraine commented, 'This marked a nadir of Allied strategic planning'.[22]

Into this 'military sump-pit'[23] arrived Bulfin's 60th Division, the victim of French demands for reinforcement, 'fresh, well-trained and at full strength'.[24] For the division, the move had come as 'a veritable bombshell', but in a soldierly manner it 'resigned itself to the inevitable'.[25] Some felt a 'peculiar combination of relief and disappointment'.[26] Although at first glance the Mediterranean might have seemed to offer an attractive respite from the Western Front, the division was soon to learn that 'the discomforts of the Macedonian theatre of war were unparalleled on any front, with the possible exception of Mesopotamia'.[27] Lacking the adventure of Palestine to come, the Macedonian campaign tested morale to the extreme, principally for the reason that the men, unlike those in France with a safe Channel crossing close behind the front, were cut off from home by a long and dangerous sea journey. Not only was there no home leave, but mail was slow, creature comforts lacking, the climate extreme and sickness everywhere; getting home required a serious wound or illness.

Bulfin at least had the companionship of his newly arrived son as ADC. Eddie reported to Divisional HQ on 4 November, shortly after the announcement of the new posting, and this would have been a very welcome tonic for his father, especially following the news that all three of his brigade commanders were to be replaced, 'their services being required elsewhere'.[28]

The divisional history described its departure from France as a 'slow and protracted affair', a restrained choice of words for what was, for many units, a miserable experience. Trains arrived from seven to twelve hours late, whilst men and horses waited at stations 'in a sea of mud and exposed to very inclement weather'.[29] After eleven days' entraining, all was complete on 25 November, and the division headed south to Marseilles and sunnier climes. The first brigade to set sail was 179 Brigade, escorted by destroyers for protection from the active submarine threat in the Mediterranean.

Divisional headquarters landed at Salonika on 8 December. As they sailed in, an officer recorded:

We came up through the various minefields protecting Salonika, taking a zigzag course. On either side of us were several biggish steamships, which had been run ashore after being torpedoed by German U boats. Salonika looked most attractive from the sea, with its various minarets and villas scattered among the trees; but, on closer inspection, after landing, we found it anything but attractive, with its filthy lanes, abominable roads, and squalid buildings.[30]

A soldier of the Civil Service Rifles added: 'The quayside swarmed with cut-throats of all Balkan races and the thought struck me, for one, that if I saw Piccadilly again I should be lucky.'[31]

The arrival of the 60th Division, to join the 'Allied Army of the Orient' as the French exotically termed it, brought the British force up to six infantry divisions, all under the command of Lieutenant General Sir George Milne, later to be CIGS in 1926. Milne had been the senior staff officer (MGGS) at Second Army when 28th Division had its disastrous initiation to the Ypres Salient in early 1915, so he knew Bulfin. The British force was split into two corps, the 60th to be under Lieutenant General Sir Henry Wilson (not the future field marshal) in XII Corps. Bulfin's old 28th Division was quartered in the other corps, XVI, alongside its sister formation from Ypres, the 27th. Cyril Falls' assessment of Bulfin's division on arrival, in the official history of the campaign, was measured:

The 60th … was not yet at its best, but containing excellent material, as it was later to prove in Palestine. It had been for six months in France, but had not been on the Somme front, and so had not been engaged in any action bigger than a trench raid.[32]

The 'military sump-pit' of Salonika

The Allied front was some miles inland from Salonika, extending from the Struma River in the east to Monastir and the Albanian mountains in the west. The British held the right of the line, from the mouth of the Struma and then westwards to Doiran and the Vardar river. The strongly entrenched Bulgarian army dominated XII Corps from the Belashitza mountains. At one point, known as the Grand Couronne, above the Doiran lake the land rose to some 2,000ft.

At the time Bulfin's men were sailing from France the Salonika front was in deadlock, the last offensive action having been the taking of Monastir the previous November. Constant rain and snow storms now made operations well-nigh impossible. But General Sarrail had plans to use the newly arrived 60th Division. He was concerned that a hostile force of German-leaning Greek Royalists was threatening his rear from Thessaly and ordered General Milne to mount an expedition to repulse them. Milne, although unconvinced of the threat, directed Brigadier General Edwards and his 179 Brigade, with some engineers and artillery, to head for Katerini in the shadow of Mt Olympus, south-west of Salonika, to defend the Allied rear.

As storms and floods had broken the railway, the brigade, less the transport which went by road, set sail down the coast on the night of 10 December, three weeks after arriving in Salonika. It was ill-starred journey. On arrival at the local port, they found a storm had destroyed the jetty, leaving the troops to wade ashore:

> I had wild visions of a second Gallipoli landing, but the whole thing was a most appalling anti-climax. We arrived on a deserted beach sopping wet, with no sign of human life for miles around.[33]

After dark, the two battalions of the Londons set off for Katerini. Back at their landing place, another gale had hit the shore, requiring the lighters to be towed back to Salonika, but not before the remaining baggage had been swept off the decks into the sea. By the 12th the whole brigade had occupied Katerini, whilst the local Greeks, although sullen at first, 'showed themselves friendly';[34] the supposed Greek Royalist opposition made no attempt to confront the British.

On 13 December Bulfin arrived to inspect the position and recorded a local delegation making an unusual request to him:

> The most popular regiment in the Brigade was, undoubtedly, the London Scottish. While I was criticising the tactical arrangements with Brigadier-General Edwards at his Head-quarters, I found a deputation had come, headed by the Mayor and Elders of the town, while a crowd of two to three hundred men had formed up in the streets outside. The Mayor made an address expressing the feelings of the inhabitants as being full of pride in having so many British Regiments quartered on them. Their conduct … was exemplary; they were immensely popular … but, he went on, the real reason of his coming to see me was, that some two hundred men … had come to ask if they might join the London Scottish.

Bulfin diplomatically turned down the request but suggested they form a town guard. Although they were disappointed, ' I understood later, that they learnt English words of command, and were drilling in accordance with English ideas.'[35]

Military duty on this outpost line through the winter weather was harsh, but once spring arrived with no sign of war, 'this Katerini venture proved to be a lucky break in our active service … We can look back on our three months as a pleasant interlude.'[36] Although the officers 'enjoyed woodcock shooting such as Ireland at its best cannot match',[37] the men found it less enjoyable, being 'volunteered' as the brigadier's beaters and peppered by pellets.[38]

Meanwhile, the rest of the division had deployed north of Salonika to the area of Lake Doiran, as General Sarrail planned an Allied-wide spring offensive against the Bulgarians. Bulfin was put in command of this 10-mile section of the front. An early tactical lapse, when a large patrol from 180 Brigade was ambushed in daylight by the enemy, was an unhappy reminder for Bulfin of 28th Division's shaky start in the Ypres Salient. But a successful retaliatory raid quickly restored 60th Division's honour. The ground and weather were often atrocious, with violent storms sweeping away the bivouacs in the rocky hills, but the men were not to know it would prove an excellent training ground for the Judean Hills, where the division was to fight its way to Jerusalem at the end of that year. One regimental history gave this gloomy description of Macedonia:

> That depressing land of barren scrub and rocky hills, of quagmire-tracks in winter and dusty, parching plains in summer, a land of lizards and of tortoises, a land which seemed as bare and rough and inhospitable as any land could be.[39]

But as spring arrived it was soon very evident to the division that the war here was in complete contrast to their time opposite Vimy Ridge. The enemy was generally entrenched some 3 to 4 miles distant; no-man's-land, even at its narrowest point, was never less than a mile deep. With the apricot orchards and mulberry groves bursting into blossom, and fields carpeted in wild thyme and flowers, some took a more positive view: 'Macedonia in spring [was] a very lush, rich country with plenty of wildlife … it was the quietest war we ever had.'[40]

179 Brigade had their own adventure when ordered to march up the Vardar valley from Katerini and join their comrades near Karasuli. It became a piece of folk history for those who marched the 100 miles in seven consecutive days, laden down with full kit, across rough ground and raging rivers, facing all the vicissitudes of the Balkan weather. It was known variously as the 'Katerini' or 'Karasuli Trek', and 'no man who did that march will ever forget it'.[41] One soldier of the London Scottish died of exposure before medical help could reach him, and another succumbed in hospital.

The spring offensive that April gave the division the opportunity, for the first time, to go on to the attack, albeit in a supporting role to the main assault by the two other divisions of XII Corps. 60th Division was initially tasked with making a diversionary night raid against a strongly fortified position called the Nose, a task delegated to 180 Brigade, in the event led by a force from the 2/20th Londons. Although not on the scale of the Western Front, or what was to follow in Palestine, nevertheless it was a bloody fight. Initially, they penetrated the enemy's first line with a Bangalore torpedo;[42] they then came under heavy fire from Bulgarian trench mortars and were forced to retire, with the loss of twenty killed and seventy wounded. Their divisional commander kept a close eye on events from a nearby hill, as enemy searchlights swept the slopes.

Further operations were launched in May, with 60th Division ordered to support 26th Division, again in the vicinity of Lake Doiran. 179 Brigade was given the lead, mounting a silent night attack with the bayonet. Little serious resistance was met, and when counter-attacks occurred, although supported by heavy artillery, they were well beaten off. By the end of the month the advance had petered out in the foothills, with little headway achieved against the Bulgarians still entrenched in their lofty mountain positions. This was mirrored across the whole Allied front, and on 24 May General Sarrail issued orders for offensive operations to cease. Although the 60th Division had played a subsidiary role in the Battle of Doiran, it had cost the British some 5,000 casualties, a quarter of the losses in the entire Salonika campaign.

In late May calls were being made for men and animals for Egypt. On 1 June General Bulfin received orders that the division was to embark for the Middle East without delay. Bulfin himself sailed into Alexandria in the colourfully named *Minnetonka* on 19 June, a month later being mentioned in General Milne's dispatches for his services in Salonika. Earlier in the spring, the King of Italy had made him a Commander of the Military Order of Savoy for his part in the campaign.

There were few regrets at leaving Macedonia. Charles Jones of the Civil Service Rifles summed it up bluntly:

There was an unsatisfactory feeling about the Salonika front. There was apparently no hope of any successful advance, and one stood an excellent chance of getting killed quite uselessly, on some futile errand without hope of result … In general there was air of futility and neglect about the front, a feeling of being cut off from home in more ways than one.[43]

An encounter between the Bulgars and Bulfin's men on the Doiran front in many ways summed up the Macedonian campaign. Bulfin always maintained a picquet in the Vardar valley, to prevent the enemy penetrating between his lines and the French to his west. One day, three Bulgarian soldiers, sick of war, decided to surrender. Wading down the river they came upon the 60th picquet, all of whom were fishing. After the Bulgars were shouted at to go away as they were disturbing the fish, the disconsolate enemy moved on and finally surrendered to an Army Service Corps unit 6 miles behind the front line. Life would be very different in their next theatre of war.

As far as Bulfin was concerned, the decision to move the 60th Division to Egypt would have profound consequences for his career. He now had the opportunity to serve once again under his old master, Sir Edmund Allenby, in markedly more promising circumstances than in 1915.

Chapter 10

1917
Palestine – 'Jerusalem by Christmas'

Allenby takes command and Bulfin gets his corps

Unlike Bulfin's old 28th Division, left to fester in Macedonia until the end of the war, the 60th had the good fortune to be the beneficiary of a Cabinet decision to reinforce the Middle East. Whether it was selected because of its growing reputation under Bulfin's command, or simply because it remained at near full strength after the spring offensive, is unclear.

Since becoming Prime Minster at the end of 1916, David Lloyd George, disenchanted with the Westerners' attritional strategy on the Western Front, was casting his eyes eastwards to the Holy Land. His motive was not just to deprive the CIGS (Field Marshal Sir William Robertson) and Sir Douglas Haig of the divisions then being released from the 'unprofitable Salonika adventure'. His siding with the Easterners had as much to do with his longer-term aim for Britain, a full role in the Middle East once the war was won. In the immediate term, with Britain's morale low after almost three years of war, he needed a victory – 'Jerusalem by Christmas'. There was also military sense in advancing towards the Holy City, so as to threaten the Turks' plans to mount their counter-offensive (called '*Yildirim*' or 'Lightning') to recapture British-held Baghdad.

The Egyptian Expeditionary Force, under General Sir Archibald Murray, had during 1916 driven the Turks from the Sinai desert, thus strengthening the security of the strategically vital Suez Canal. Murray was a talented administrator, understood the critical importance of logistics and had succeeded in traversing the 120 miles of the Sinai with a railway, wire-netting road and water pipeline. This considerable achievement paved the way for an offensive into Ottoman-held Palestine. However, he was not an inspiring or effective commander in battle. After two attempts at breaching the Turkish defences at Gaza were repulsed in the spring of 1917, the first only just failing, London felt there was a need for a new leader and more troops to reinvigorate the campaign. Lloyd George accepted the CIGS's recommendation of General Sir Edmund Allenby.

Robertson was aware that relations between Haig and Allenby in France were strained. Allenby, an imposing figure with a reputation for fierce temper and blunt speaking, had been in command of the Third Army at Arras, where his 1917 spring offensive had started well but soon became bogged down with high casualties. On hearing the news that he was being recalled to London, he was initially dismayed at being moved to Egypt. Only after seeing the PM did he appreciate the possibilities that lay before him.

When Allenby set out for Cairo, the 60th Division was waiting to embark at Salonika. At the Gaza front was a young Captain John Harding, then serving in 54th Division; he had fought at Gallipoli, been wounded at First Gaza and later became a field-marshal and CIGS. Not normally used to seeing any officer more senior than his divisional commander, he clearly recalled Allenby's arrival in the desert as having an impact similar to General Bernard Montgomery's taking over of the Eighth Army a quarter of a century later.[1] Allenby galvanized his new command, seasoned and high quality troops but 'cynical and discouraged … Like the Israelites of old, weary of the hardships of the desert'.[2] Turfing his headquarters staff out of the comforts of Cairo, he moved them close to the front, with the words 'Staff officers are like partridges: they are better for being shot over.'[3] Going round his units, he made it clear to all, even the hard-bitten Australians, that he meant victory. 'My word, he is a different man to Murray … Allenby breathes success and the greatest pessimist cannot fail to have confidence in him', recorded Meinertzhagen.[4] Such was his impact that a signal was devised to warn units of his impending approach – 'BBL' for 'Bloody Bull's Loose', from his longstanding nickname.

Nevertheless, Allenby was fortunate in inheriting not only a well established logistic system but also hardened troops and an operational plan which contained all the guile and daring so often lacking – and seldom possible – on the Western Front. The commander of the Eastern Force on the Gaza front was Lieutenant General Sir Philip Chetwode, a fellow cavalryman well known to Allenby from before the war, with 'one of the keenest and quickest brains in the Army and a remarkable eye for ground';[5] a dapper, energetic man with a nasal drawl, his baronetcy gave him the inevitable nickname of 'the Bart'. He was supported by a talented staff officer, in the shape of

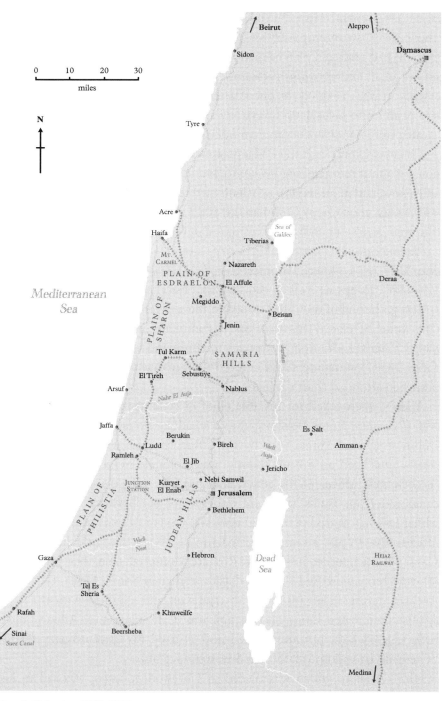

Map 9. Palestine 1917–1918.

Brigadier General Guy Dawnay, although some less gifted thought him 'theoretical', a contemporary swipe at those cosseted on the staff. The two of them had crafted a plan of manoeuvre to overcome the Turkish defences, set out in an appreciation[6] presented to Allenby shortly after his arrival. In essence, it was to exploit the open flank to the east of Gaza, cut off the enemy and push on to Jerusalem. Chetwode also wanted to prove that his beloved cavalry were not obsolete on the modern battlefield.

The new Chief, with the PM's promise of the reinforcements he needed, now set about reorganizing his command into two corps, largely of infantry, and a powerful mounted force. Allenby wrote to the CIGS on 19 July: 'Bulfin will make a good Corps Commander, and I shall be glad to have him. I know him well, as a staunch fighter.'[7] Bulfin's star had risen at last.

Placing Bulfin in charge of XXI Corps, he gave Chetwode the other infantry one, XX Corps. Desert Mounted Corps (DMC), consisting of ANZAC and Yeomanry troops as well as the Imperial Service Camel Brigade, was the largest gathering of mounted troops in the war. To the considerable envy of Chetwode, he placed this force under command of Lieutenant General Sir Harry Chauvel, the first Australian to command a corps (interestingly, all three corps commanders had entered their armies through the militia and none had attended Staff College).

Allenby then called for his able chief of staff from France, the cheerful Major General Louis Bols, noted as a steadfast brigade commander under Bulfin at Second Ypres. Sent by the CIGS to liaise with Allenby and his staff – and keep an eye on them – was Colonel Archie Wavell, probably the brightest officer of his generation and later a field marshal.[8] He soon came under the 'Bull's' spell and would serve as Chetwode's chief of staff, whilst Dawnay moved to be Bols' assistant. One of Allenby's key intelligence officers, due to play an important part in deceiving the Turks before Third Gaza, was the unorthodox Colonel Richard Meinertzhagen, that troublesome officer who had crossed Bulfin a decade earlier in South Africa. Out in the Arabian desert, inspiring the Arabs to revolt and combine with the Allies against their hated Ottoman masters, was T. E. Lawrence. Allenby never fully trusted him, but appreciated and utilized his extraordinary talents. 'The Bull' had an unusually gifted team under him.

60th Division, which was placed in Chetwode's corps, was sad to lose their GOC. One of Bulfin's brigade commanders, Brigadier General Freddie Carleton, had a premonition about his move:

I like more and more my Divisional General as one day succeeds another but alas I fear we are going to lose him as I am pretty certain he is going to get a corps. He ought to have had one long ago and would have if he had not been [indecipherable] outspoken in his views which I have always found sound. He has a nice boy about him as ADC.[9]

The adjutant of the 2/20th Londons wrote in their regimental history after the war:

Universal regret felt throughout the Division at the departure of Gen. Bulfin was tempered by the knowledge that he was receiving promotion long deserved. During the eighteen months of his command Gen. Bulfin had frequently had to make calls on the men which had taxed the capacities of physique and morale to the utmost. Those calls had invariably been answered with loyalty and enthusiasm. No Divisional Commander had earned the confidence and respect of his officers and men in a larger degree, as the writer had peculiar opportunities of observing. Probably no Division had a greater measure of divisional *esprit de corps* than the 60th. Certainly none was more infused through and through with the spirit of mutual help between units. How far this feeling was due to Gen. Bulfin's personality and leadership only those who actually served under him in the Division will ever realize.[10]

Adjutants, near the seat of power, often see their masters in a closer and thus clearer light than others, hence possibly his knowing comment about 'peculiar opportunities of observing'.

W. T. Massey, by today's standards the over-embedded war correspondent accompanying Allenby's troops, reflected the welcome given to 60th Division:

The 60th Division came from Salonika and we were delighted to have them, for they not only gave us General Bulfin as the XXIst Corps Commander, but set an example of efficiency and a combination of dash and doggedness which earned for them a record worthy of the best in the history of the great war.[11]

Allenby had brought with him a spare major general, Sir John Shea, who now took over the division, leading it with great success through the

Palestine campaign. Wavell considered him Allenby's best infantry divisional commander.[12]

Bulfin, promoted temporary lieutenant general, assumed command of his new corps on 2 August 1917. He took under his wing two experienced and proud territorial divisions which had fought through the earlier Gaza battles: 52nd (Lowland) Division led by Major General John Hill and 54th (East Anglian) Division commanded by Major General Sir Steuart Hare. The third was 75th Division, led by Major General Philip Palin, manned by West Country and Gurkha battalions recently gathered together in-theatre, the last division to be formed in the war. Predominantly a corps of infantry brigades, there was also a company of tanks from the newly formed Tank Corps. Allenby was confident about this new corps, writing to the CIGS in October, 'Bulfin has three good Divisional Generals.'[13] Two weeks later, Bulfin's divisions took over the Gaza front. The very next day, Allenby made his first visit.

Preparations for the Third Battle of Gaza

The crumbling Ottoman Empire in Palestine and beyond, in which Bulfin was about to make his mark, had for some time attracted the colonial ambitions of the British and French. By May 1916 the Sykes-Picot Agreement had been finalized, a secret Anglo-French arrangement whereby the region was split into post-war spheres of influence, with little sensitivity to local political, tribal and religious loyalties. Sir Mark Sykes, a Yorkshire landowner and MP for Hull, was a Green Howard Territorial who had served in South Africa and knew Bulfin. His nickname in the House of Commons was the 'Mad Mullah'. Sykes was commanding the 5th Battalion when war broke out, but because of his knowledge of the Middle East he was selected by the Foreign Secretary, Sir Edward Grey, to lead the negotiations with the Frenchman, François Georges-Picot. A year later, in November 1917, the Balfour Declaration was made public: it was to become one of the most controversial documents of the twentieth century. In a single sentence of sixty-seven words it boldly stated that the British Government viewed 'with favour the establishment in Palestine of a National Home for the Jewish people'. It was signed two days before Gaza fell to Allenby's forces, at which point Britain was in a position to make this pledge a reality.

In March and April 1917 Murray's two attempts at defeating the Turkish key defensive positions at Gaza had mainly failed due to reliance on a frontal assault, compounded by a confused command structure and insufficient artillery. The soldiers had fought resolutely but were let down by the generals and their staffs, a familiar echo from the Western Front. Chetwode's offering to Allenby, for the next attempt, was a more imaginative and bold approach.

The plan, as all sound plans should be, was simple. The Turks expected the main British effort to come, once again, against the strong defences of Gaza. Therefore every effort was made to convince the enemy that this was what would happen, with Bulfin's XXI Corps keeping their attention fixed on Gaza. This included the 'haversack ruse', successfully carried out by Meinertzhagen: he induced a Turkish patrol to chase him, pretending to be wounded and dropping a blood-stained haversack containing documents giving the impression that the main attack was aimed at Gaza. Meanwhile, the masterstroke would take the form of XX Corps appearing out of the desert and assaulting the Turkish left flank at Beersheba. At the same time, Desert Mounted Corps would carry out an audacious 30-mile sweep to Beersheba's east and round to its north. The 15-mile gap in the centre between Gaza and Beersheba would be held by the remaining yeomanry mounted division. The finale would be XX Corps striking north-west from Beersheba at the Turkish logistics hub of Tel es Sheria and, with DMC, rolling up the enemy line towards the Mediterranean. At the right moment, Bulfin's XXI Corps would then breach the weakened Gaza defences and pursue northwards. Success in cutting off the Turkish forces from the rear depended on three requirements: secrecy, water and animal transport. Key to this was the capture of the wells, intact, at Beersheba – in Arabic, *Bir es Sabe*, the Five Wells. In fact, the Third Battle of Gaza was a misnomer – it covered a much wider canvas.

Never before had Bulfin had such a force under command, nor had he had the chance to prepare so professionally for a major offensive. It was all very different to Loos, two years earlier. Forming a corps headquarters from scratch was one of his first challenges, even with two experienced divisions under him. He therefore brought with him his trusted chief staff officer (BGGS) from 60th Division, Brigadier General E. T. Humphreys, as well as his senior Gunner, Brigadier General Hugh Simpson-Baikie. His able senior logistics officer (AA&QMG), a Royal Marine Light Infantryman called Brigadier General St George Armstrong, commented after the war: '[Considering] Corps HQ had only been about 2 months in existence I feel quite certain that we could not have made the Administrative plans without the war experience in this area of commanders and staffs.'[14]

Bulfin was coming up for fifty-five and was, as a general, in his prime, but establishing a sound working relationship with one of his divisional commanders proved less than easy. Steuart Hare, who had led a brigade at Cape Helles in the fateful Gallipoli landings and had been in command of 54th Division through the first two Gaza battles, did not take kindly to the 'new boy' breathing down his neck: 'Corps Commander arrived 5.45 and stayed hovering for a good hour. Only got rid of him … by arranging for a failure of the electric light.'[15] Relations with Hare were to become more fraught in the approaching battle.

All through the desert heat of September and October, Bulfin had been training and preparing his troops. Although he was stripped of most of his transport to improve the mobility of XX Corps, he had been allocated the bulk of the EEF's artillery. In addition to moving his guns into position, he needed huge supplies of ammunition, water and stores. Despite having a more static role than Chetwode, his need for water was still a high priority. Royal Engineer parties were kept busy building light railways through the soft sand to the front line, to bring forward this and other critical items. Armstrong ensured, 'by the forethought of General Bulfin', that supply dumps were located close behind the front line trenches and well camouflaged.[16] In 54th Division alone some 100,000 man hours were expended digging telephone cable deep into the sand.[17] Strengthening the fortified strongholds along the Gaza front meant backbreaking and thirsty work for the infantry. Each attacking battalion carried out briefings, then rehearsals, on carefully prepared full-scale models of their objectives. All this time, secrecy was vital, so work was done mostly at night.

Breaking the Gaza – Beersheba line

Allenby issued his orders on 22 October, and over the next week the divisions moved into their concentration areas. On the night of 30/31 October Chetwode's infantry tramped by full moon across the open desert towards Beersheba. The night march went without a hitch.

Allenby would have preferred an earlier start in September to avoid battling through the Judean Hills to Jerusalem in the rainy season, but he needed time to get his formidable force prepared and trained. This now numbered some 80,000 troops against the 46,000 of the Turkish Eighth Army led by the German Kress von Kressenstein.

Four days beforehand, on 27 October, to distract the Turks from the move on Beersheba, Bulfin launched a furious diversionary bombardment on Gaza. For once, there was no shortage of artillery; he had at his disposal sixty-eight medium guns, two six-inch guns and 150 others; each battery fired 1,000 rounds per day. The heavier calibre guns concentrated on counter-battery work, destroying the Turkish artillery, and on the 29th British and French naval gunfire joined in from a powerful flotilla offshore. Seven of the heavy batteries had never been in action before and had only reached their gun positions five weeks before battle, but as Bulfin reported to Allenby, 'The artillery barrage worked like clockwork.'[18] It was the heaviest barrage carried out up to then during the war outside Europe. The Gunners were to be the unsung heroes of the Palestine campaign.

The assault on Beersheba opened at dawn on 31 October, and by midday XX Corps' infantry had captured the main defences in front of the town, thus fixing the Turkish garrison. Taking a leading part, and earning its spurs, was Bulfin's old division. Following its progress closely throughout the campaign, he found time to send a telegram to Shea on 1 November: 'Heartiest congratulations to 60th Division and its gallant Commander.'[19]

Meanwhile, on an even wider flank march, the Desert Mounted Corps swept round to the east of the town to capture it and the wells. On the success of this hung Allenby's plan – without water his advance would fail. It was an anxious time for the Chief, and by 3.00 pm, with the wells still in enemy hands and Chauvel's men held up by fierce Turkish resistance, he ordered him to seize Beersheba by dark. The 4th Australian Light Horse Brigade came to the rescue. In one of those dashing mounted charges made famous in the Palestine campaign, the light horsemen launched a direct attack on the town, forcing the enemy to withdraw. The wells were captured intact, and the EEF had successfully exposed the Turks' left flank.

Now the opportunity presented itself for XX Corps to storm the Turkish centre at Tel es Sheria, whilst DMC passed round the flank and intercepted the retreating Turkish army. Whilst XX Corps and DMC re-orientated themselves for this phase, it was Bulfin's turn to increase pressure on the Turks.

In order to distract the enemy into thinking that there would be an amphibious landing north of Gaza, companies of the Egyptian Labour Corps were marched down to the shore during the afternoon of 1 November, within sight of the enemy, loaded on to boats and sent out to sea. During the hours of darkness they came back again, but shipping lights remained on as a pretence of activity. Meanwhile, just before midnight, the first phase of the infantry assault began. The task was given to Hare's 54th Division, reinforced by Scotsmen of 156 Brigade from 52nd Division. Across a frontage of 5,000yds the men had to cross heavy sand, climbing dunes rising in places as high as 150ft, and take two objectives.

The first one, Umbrella Hill to the east of Gaza, was captured and held against heavy Turkish machine gun and artillery fire by the 7th Scottish Rifles, whilst to the east 75th Division was making diversionary attacks. The other objective, the small village of Sheikh Hasan overlooking Gaza's harbour, was identified as the key. It guarded the route along the coast and hence the enemy rear. In front of the village was a series of linked redoubts connected to a further redoubt and trenches behind; this was given to two brigades of Hare's division. To lull the Turks into thinking the attack on Umbrella Hill was just another raid, the brigades waited till 3.00 am before crossing the soft sand of the 1,000yd-wide no-man's-land. These attacks were supported by six tanks of the Palestine Tank Detachment, with two in reserve, but most broke down in the sand – Bulfin thought they 'were of little use to us'.[20] Navigation was made difficult for the infantry by cloud covering the moon and dust thrown up by the bombardment, and a number of units became disorientated and delayed. Command and control became fragmented in the hard fighting that followed, but by dawn on 2 November Sheikh Hasan was in British hands. Over the next two days the Turks responded by bringing up a reserve division – just what Allenby intended – and bravely counter-attacking the trenches held by Hare's increasingly exhausted infantry.

During this intense period of fighting, Bulfin was becoming frustrated with the hold-ups to progress, and the tension between him and GOC 54th Division came to a head. On 3 November General Hare let off steam in his diary:

4/Essex attacked Balak at 4.30 am & held it for 65 minutes and were driven out with 200 casualties. I then made up my mind that we must be content to hold what we have got. The Corps commander came in a.m. & talked rot for an hour. He is most captious & evidently thinks me and the Brigadiers to blame for not carrying out the whole programme. I wrote him a snorter in the afternoon & told him what I thought. I don't care a damn if I get the bowler hat. I won't hear men like Mudge & Ward [his brigade commanders] run down by that drivelling old dotard.[21]

Hare was, in fact, just five years younger than his senior officer. Nothing obvious seems to have come of this contretemps, but it was an indication of the pressure Bulfin and his generals were operating under during this Third Battle of Gaza.

By nightfall on 4 November both Bulfin's men and the Turks were running out of steam. British casualties were high, with 360 men killed, 400 missing and nearly 2,000 wounded. Wavell recorded of the action:

It reached practically all its objectives and fulfilled its mission of attracting enemy reserves to Gaza. But the losses of Twenty-first Corps were just double those that the Twentieth Corps and Desert Mounted Corps had suffered in the capture of Beersheba and showed how slow and expensive an attempt to break through on the coast would have been.[22]

To the east, Allenby's plans for the exploitation phase, to take Tel es Sheria and envelop the enemy rear, were encountering delays. The mounted troops were scattered, both men and horses tired out, and – critically – there was less water than expected. Similarly, Chetwode's infantry needed both replenishment and rest. The situation was complicated by the German commander von Falkenhayn's faltering counterstroke against Khuweilfe, 10 miles north of Beersheba, but this failed to divert Allenby's attention. By 6 November XX Corps was ready to overcome the Tel es Sheria defences, whilst Chauvel was given very clear orders to press through the narrow gap round Khuweilfe, attack the enemy 'with utmost vigour' and join up with Bulfin.

Now was the moment for Allenby to deliver his left hook. On 6 November Bulfin ordered 54th Division into Gaza the following morning. They discovered a town ruined and abandoned; to the great relief of the attacking troops, they had pushed an open door – 'Not a shot was fired at us and we advanced, unopposed, finding a vast quantity of ammunition and bombs left in the trenches.'[23] Allenby wrote to his wife: 'Gaza was taken by Bulfin, quite easily. The attack … went in with such a rush that Gaza became untenable. Everyone has marched and fought splendidly.'[24]

The official historian, Cyril Falls, summed up the Gaza battle:

> The British attack had achieved all that could have been hoped for; it had inflicted very heavy loss on the enemy, drawn in his reserves north of Gaza, as intended. But it had accomplished far more than this. It had, in conjunction with the operations of the XX Corps, brought about the evacuation of a very strong fortress, and opened a gateway for the swift advance which was to prevent the enemy from consolidating himself in his second line of defence.[25]

The next day, 75th Division, on the corps' right flank, after clearing the trench systems to the east of Gaza, linked up with 10th Division, thus closing the gap with XX Corps. But it was too late to trap most of the Turks now streaming north along the coastal plain.

The pursuit north across the Philistia Plain

The corps cavalry, followed by Hill's 52nd Division, were ordered to press on up the coast and further into Ottoman Palestine. But the Turks, to cover their retreating troops, had established themselves in strength on a formidable feature on the north bank of Wadi Hesi, a few miles north of Gaza; the British called it Sausage Ridge. Major General John Hill gave Brigadier General Pollock-M'Call's 155 Brigade the task of taking it from the left, with the Highlanders of Hamilton Moore's 157 Brigade in reserve. On examining the position, Pollock-M'Call considered it an unfeasible task, but Bulfin, who had ridden up to Hill's headquarters, 'decided the attack must be carried out as ordered'.[26] Both brigades, which had crossed the *wadi* at night, launched themselves at the ridge, closely supported by the divisional artillery, and after ferocious fighting and resisting a counter-attack, took their objective. 157 Brigade losses amounted to over 400, with only six out of eighteen officers of 5th Highland Light Infantry unwounded. In opening the route up the coast, Dawnay considered this 'mighty effort … hugely important'.

Allenby, realizing that the best opportunity to pursue the enemy now rested with XXI Corps and DMC rather than XX Corps, ordered all the latter's transport to be quickly switched to Bulfin's front, a 'really wonderful achievement' by the EEF logistics staff.[27] From the mouth of Wadi Hesi the navy was also able to help supply the troops pushing up the coast.

Bulfin was in his element, described by Wavell as having 'the drive and energy above the ordinary, and could be trusted to second the resolution of Allenby, who himself was constantly forward, watching events and ready to give a decision'.[28]

The Chief ordered Bulfin to push his other division, 75th Division, forward about 20 miles north-east of Gaza to support Chauvel's ANZAC Mounted Division (54th Division was left immobilized in Gaza). With Allenby's main effort now on the coast and the Philistia Plain, it was difficult to maintain the momentum of the cavalry pursuit, with re-supply stretched and horses short of water.

Although von Falkenhayn's Seventh Army threatened Allenby's right flank from the Judean Hills, the Chief was determined not to be distracted and kept to his plan to split the Turkish forces in two. Keeping the enemy's Seventh Army in the Judean Hills away from the coast, Allenby concentrated on defeating its Eighth Army, on its right flank. Pushing the cavalry up the coast towards Jaffa (now Tel Aviv) and Ramleh, he gave Bulfin the task of taking Junction Station. This was an important logistics and communications hub, run by the Germans, where the railway from Beersheba met the line linking Jerusalem and Gaza to the north. Its capture would split the two enemy armies, as well as providing vital facilities, especially abundant water.

With 52nd Division on the left and 75th Division on the right, Bulfin's troops pressed north-east towards Junction Station. Bulfin's orders set a start time, but the rest had the flexibility to adapt to the fluid situation. The Turks, although in dire straits and being pushed back at every turn, were not succumbing to a rout. Progress was slow, as the advancing troops continually encountered determined rearguard actions. On 10 November the infantry marched 13 miles against a scorching *khamsin* wind blowing in their faces, with eighty-two men falling out from one battalion. The next day, Dawnay wrote to his wife:

> Hill (52 Division) told me this was the third time in five nights that they had got in a night bayonet attack. They have been (52/75 Divisions) [advancing] with the greatest dash and determination.[29]

Two days later, Bulfin's two divisions closed up some 8 miles short of Junction Station. To the east, 'the Judean hills with their steep defiles, rocky spurs and deep re-entrants stood out in all the grandeur of dancing sunlight and deepest shade', as Captain E. R. Boyd eloquently wrote.[30] The key obstacle to taking the junction was the strongly held el Mughar Ridge to the west, in the path of the Yeomanry and 52nd Divisions. The mounted troops were called for, and in one of the finest examples of infantry, cavalry and artillery cooperation of the campaign, the Dorset and Buckinghamshire Yeomanry, supported by the Berkshire Yeomanry, fought alongside Brigadier General Pollock M'Call's Lowlanders of 155 Brigade and succeeded in capturing the ridge. Over 1,000 prisoners were rounded up and many enemy were killed, breaking the morale of the Turks.

Whilst this gallant action was going on, 75th Division's Gurkhas had cleared Mesmiyeh, on the railway line south of the junction, with their *kukris*. With the Turks retreating, Bulfin ordered 75th Division to capture Junction Station on the morning of 14 November. Brigadier General F. J. Anley, given the task with his 234 Brigade, lacked urgency in tackling this and was relieved of command the next morning. A golden opportunity was lost, as Kress von Kressenstein escaped on the last train. Alney's brigade-major, in a confidential note after the war to the official historian, was blunt:

> From the opening of the 3rd Battle of Gaza, General Anley was in a highly nervous condition, and by the night of the advance on Junction Station, he was in a state bordering upon breakdown.[31]

Dawnay wrote that day: 'After a fortnight's fighting and a fifty mile advance, I think the pursuit has about reached the limit of what is possible.'[32] Despite avoiding being encircled, as Allenby had originally planned, the Turks had nevertheless lost southern Palestine, and their two armies were split. In particular, the Seventh Army in the Judean hills was badly isolated, with its nearest rail access 40 miles away from Jerusalem at Nablus.

Through the Judean Hills to the Holy City of Jerusalem

Allenby now had to decide whether to stick to his original plan, to draw breath and allow his logistic chain to catch up, or make an immediate move on the Holy City. After three weeks' hard campaigning, his men and horses were tired and ragged, and his units urgently needed reinforcements. In 75th Division's case, it had marched over 70 miles in ten days since Gaza and had fought in nine actions.

But he was faced with a number of imperative reasons for a swift advance on Jerusalem: the approach of winter rains, an awareness that a substantial element of his force was likely to be withdrawn to the Western Front in early 1918 and, above all, the strategic gains to be had from not giving the harried Turkish Seventh Army a chance to regroup in the Judean hills. In keeping with his forceful nature, Allenby decided to move on Jerusalem – with a single day's break in offensive operations. At midday on 18 November he held a conference with his corps commanders at Bulfin's headquarters and issued orders for the next phase.

Keenly aware of the need to avoid any damage to the Holy City (a 6-mile clearance zone was ordered), his plan was for an indirect approach to encircle the city from the north-west, in many ways a more difficult and riskier operation than a direct assault. Keeping the Anzac and 54th Divisions, the latter fresh from marching up from Gaza, holding a defensive line on the Nahr el Auja River, north-east of Jaffa, he gave Bulfin the task of leading the advance eastwards into the Judean Hills. Palin's 75th Division would head up the only metalled road from Jaffa to Jerusalem with Hill's 52nd Division to the left (north). Barrow's Yeomanry Mounted Division would operate on its left flank, hoping to make a rapid strike through the hills and cut off the Turks retreating north. 'Allenby knew he could trust these divisions to force the passes and win Jerusalem, if skill and courage could do it. Nor would leadership be found wanting. Bulfin needed no urging to get the utmost out of his infantry.'[33]

XXI Corps' aim, once near Jerusalem, was to swing north-east, block the Nablus–Jerusalem road and force the Turks to give up the city without a fight. On 19 November, after crossing their start lines from Latron (75th) and Ludd (52nd), Bulfin's men entered the Judean hills. The country ahead was daunting, with rugged rocky hills of 1,500–2,000ft dominating deep valleys. On many of the precipitous ridges were perched small villages, often fortified by the Turks. Except for the main road, tracks were scarce and mostly impassable to vehicles and guns. Although the terrain was familiar to many who had served in India and fought on the North-West Frontier, it did not make for easy progress, fighting or re-supply. Bulfin's headquarters had its work cut out supporting the troops; simply getting winter clothing and rations forward to men still clad for the heat of the plains was a major challenge. This was not helped by heavy winter rain falling on the very first day. Many in XXI Corps remembered those early days in the hills – wet, cold, in ragged tropical clothing and half starved, to say nothing of the hard fighting – as the toughest of the whole war.

Nevertheless, good progress was achieved at first, with 52nd Division's leading troops reaching Beit Likia up a rock-strewn goat track by the first evening. 75th Division, on the main road, succeeded in dislodging the enemy from the village of Saris and, by the evening of 20 November, had claimed Kuryet el Enab, a larger settlement 2 miles further east. Helped by heavy rain and mist obscuring their approach, Brigadier General Huddleston's Gurkhas, strengthened by two British battalions from the neighbouring brigade, attacked the ridge covering the village. As the official history recorded:

> To General Bulfin, standing on the road near Saris, the first news of the success came when, above the rattle of musketry and the boom of the Turkish artillery, there were heard the shrill cheers of the Gurkhas and the deep-throated roar of the British troops, followed by regimental bugle-calls.[34]

This fighting was very much a brigade and battalion affair, the more senior headquarters being cut off by the difficult hill country from their forward troops.

Whilst 52nd Division made further progress, the Yeomanry were blocked at the well defended Zeitun ridge, west of Bireh and the Nablus road. On 21

November 75th Division continued its advance, now turning off the main road north-east towards Bireh, but was forced to abandon its artillery. They were now only a few miles from Jerusalem and were running into the main enemy defensive line. Near Biddu they were confronted with the dominating conical feature of Nebi Samwil, crowned by a distinctive mosque sitting on the remains of a crusader castle. It was here that the Prophet Samuel was reputed to be buried and where Richard Coeur de Lion turned back from the Holy City in 1192 during the Third Crusade. For centuries this site, holy to three faiths, had held the key to Jerusalem.

As the Holy City came into view, some officers and men of a religious persuasion felt a Crusader urge. Others were excited and fascinated by place names familiar from their Sunday school teaching. However, most were too exhausted to be spiritually uplifted. Captain Harry Milsom, a company commander in what was left of 5th Somerset Light Infantry, wrote:

> I regret to say few of us felt very reverent … in fact, the general thought seemed rather to be 'so that is the — place is it?' The truth is we were all dead tired, footsore and very 'fed-up-and-far-from-home-sort-of-feeling'.[35]

He was soon to be shot in the ankle and taken back on a camel.

In the fading light, two battalions of 233 Brigade (3/3rd Gurkhas and 2/4th Hampshires) supported by two battalions of 234 Brigade (123rd Outram's Rifles and 1/4th Duke of Cornwall's Light Infantry), all under-strength, rapidly assaulted this formidable objective. In fierce hand-to-hand fighting in the dark, the summit of Nebi Samwil fell to 75th Division, but the Turks still held the eastern slope and counter-attacked, with heavy artillery support, all the following day. 3/3rd Gurkhas' CO, Lieutenant Colonel G. K. Channer, in closing the courtyard gate to the mosque amid a cascade of bombs, bayoneted the German officer leading the attack. His men were forced to resort to rolling boulders down the hillside to disrupt the enemy. By the end of the battle they were down to one officer and sixteen men fit for action. Other battalions suffered similarly. After two further days' intense fighting, not only on this ridge but for 52nd Division at nearby El Jib, XXI Corps had shot its bolt.

On the evening of 24 November, with a heavy heart, Bulfin telegraphed Allenby, who had visited the front earlier, to say that he could not advance further without reinforcements and rest. Allenby realized that the Turks here were of a different calibre, and that a deliberate attack with new divisions was required. He signalled Bulfin to consolidate and hold his line, with this accolade: 'The Chief congratulates you and all under your command on the unflinching determination which has led to great successes under the most adverse circumstances.'[36] The fighting for Nebi Samwil and El Jib was XXI Corps' high water mark in its push for Jerusalem and was deemed some of the most savage of the entire campaign. 75th Division took, as its divisional badge, a heraldic key, to reflect the 'key' to Jerusalem.

In the next few days, whilst von Falkenhayn attempted and failed to disrupt the EEF's progress by a concerted counter-attack, Chetwode's XX Corps assumed the lead to take Jerusalem. The Lowland Scots of 52nd Division, delayed in the front line to cover this handover, were none too pleased. An angry Jock of the Royal Scots Fusiliers was heard to shout, as he threw bomb after bomb at the fleeing Turks:

> They mairched us a hunner miles! (Tak' that, ya — !) an' we've been in five fechts! (Anither yin, ya — !) and they said we wur relieved! (Tak' that, ya — !) and we're oot oor beds anither nicht! (Swalla that, ya — !)'.[37]

In his update to the CIGS, Allenby wrote: 'Thanks to the celerity with which Bulfin gained and held the hills, Chetwode has now got his divisions into position for further attack.'[38] Confronting equally testing conditions and fighting, 60th and 75th Divisions, now well supported by artillery, succeeded in pushing forward on a different flank. By dawn on 9 December it was evident the Turks had abandoned the city, and 60th Division had the honour of receiving the keys to Jerusalem. It would have been a small consolation to Bulfin that it was his old command who were first into the city.

The 'Gaza School'

Bulfin's part in the breaking of the Gaza line and then the pursuit to Jerusalem was crucial to Allenby's successes in 1917. Nevertheless, the Chief's acceptance of Chetwode's plan, and the difficulties XX Corps and

DMC encountered in turning the Turks' flank at Beersheba, generated some difference of views at the time and after the war. Championed by the 'Gaza School', the opposing view was that Allenby could have achieved a complete destruction of the Turkish Army in 1917 had he broken through with a much larger force at Gaza and then pushed through his mounted forces there rather than at Beersheba, thus enveloping the Turks. In essence, this would have predated Megiddo, a year later.

Lieutenant Colonel Clive Garsia, the GSO1 in Steuart Hare's 54th Division, was the leading advocate of the 'Gaza School', but his views seem not to have impressed GHQ prior to the battle. In 1920 he met von Kressenstein, the German commander at Gaza, in a Berlin hotel. The German, dressed in a blue Prussian frock coat adorned with the '*Pour le Mérite*', 'was surprised by our attack at Beersheba as he expected our main effort to be made along the coast', and although 'he thought we would have found Gaza a hard nut to crack', Garsia believed 'we would have walked straight through his Gaza front'.[39] Garsia wrote to the official historian, determined that this option should at least be recognized, which Falls duly did.[40]

It was logical that Allenby and Chetwode should have wanted to make full use of the EEF's mounted force and thus benefit from the freedom of manoeuvre the desert offered. Wavell, who wrote a well studied history, *The Palestine Campaigns*,[41] had his own agenda of demonstrating the benefits of cavalry mobility, as a precursor to mechanization, a post-war reform in which he would play a leading role. But the general repugnance at the idea of another frontal assault, after two repulses, unsurprisingly held sway. There was no stomach to copy the Western Front, especially when an open flank offered itself, whatever the attendant risks.

Bulfin did not formally record his own views on this argument. It would not have been in his character to openly criticize his Chief, and there was no mention of any difference of opinion in his correspondence with Falls after the war. However, Garsia, despite being an admirer of Allenby as the 'ablest general the British Empire threw up in the Great War', in his book on the Gaza battles, *A Key to Victory* , wrote:

At the time, the soundness of this plan [Allenby's Third Gaza] was questioned by a number of senior officers who had taken part in the

previous two actions [First and Second Gaza]. It was also criticised by
Lt. Gen. Bulfin, who had recently arrived with the 60th Division.

Garsia, later in the book, mentioned the 'advocacy of XXI Corps
Commander' and argued that Allenby 'must perforce have lent his ear to the
proposals which General Bulfin had hitherto urged in vain'.[42]

Whatever the case, in June 1918 Bulfin made a revealing remark to Dom
Bede Camm, a Downside monk serving as a chaplain in the campaign, when
they met for tea in Egypt. He confided that, in taking Gaza, 'he had done
it on his own and had not followed Allenby's pet plan which would have
been a failure. He struck at the right psychological moment.'[43] Assuming
Bulfin's private comments – made on the eve of his sailing home on leave and
evidently while unwinding – were correctly recorded, they certainly indicate
he lacked confidence in Allenby's plan and therefore was a supporter of the
'Gaza School'. Notwithstanding the immodesty and an unexpected degree
of disloyalty to his Chief, he felt that his success at Gaza had rescued Allenby.

The year 1918 would be a momentous one in both Europe and the Middle
East. For Allenby it offered further opportunities for his force to exploit the
advantages of mobility and surprise. His commanders would certainly rise
to the challenge, and Bulfin would be central to this. The successes his XXI
Corps had achieved, through its commander's 'fiery determination',[44] had
been a crucial element in giving Allenby the strong position he now held.
It is indeed possible, as some critics have argued, that Allenby could have
destroyed the Turkish armies in 1917 by attacking Gaza in greater strength.
However, generals in the field are denied the wisdom of hindsight, but not
the hard condemnation if a third frontal assault had failed.

Chapter 11

1917–1918
The Final Crusade – Jaffa to Beirut

The forcing of the River Auja

When on 11 December Allenby passed through the Jaffa Gate on foot, he led the first Christian force to enter Jerusalem in 700 years.[1] The Allied capitals around the world sang his praises, whilst the press extracted maximum propaganda value at a time when bad news was flooding in from elsewhere: the Western Front after Passchendaele and Cambrai, the Italian setback at Caporetto and, importantly, the collapse of Russia.

Bulfin was not part of the small military procession that, with suitable humility, entered the Holy City. He was on the coastal plain redeploying his corps, most of whom had enjoyed little time to recover from their exertions in the Judean Hills. The front of XXI corps extended just north of Jaffa, with 75th Division on the right to the east of the coastal railway, 54th Division in the centre astride it and 52nd Division on the coast; it was well supported by heavy artillery for counter-battery work. The next few days were spent overseeing some sharp actions as his divisions pushed forward, consolidating the western half of the EEF's line.

Bulfin's attention was focused on the last task ahead of him for 1917 – and a difficult one at that: the crossing of the Nahr el Auja (the Crooked River), flowing into the sea 4 miles north of Jaffa. The official history described the Auja as 'a formidable obstacle, forty to fifty feet in width and ten feet deep … The northern bank commanded the lower and much flatter ground to the south.'[2] Here the Turks had entrenched themselves, with good artillery support, in a dominating position with a view all the way to Jaffa. But unless the river was forced, enemy artillery would remain in range of the port, which was growing more vital by the day for Allenby's re-supply. Equally, getting north of this river was essential to provide a secure platform to launch any advance up the coast in 1918.

Major General John Hill's 52nd (Lowland) Division was given the challenge of forcing the river. Bulfin's natural instinct was to make best use of the additional heavy artillery he had been allocated and to overwhelm the Turkish defences. But Hill, concerned at how exposed his infantry would be whilst crossing the river, persuaded Bulfin that a surprise night attack, without the planned heavy bombardment, would give him the best chance of success.

Except for the bar at its mouth which was fordable, the river could only be crossed by military bridges or rafting. Lieutenant Colonel Lionel Fortescue Wells, the division's resourceful Royal Engineer commander, was soon put to task to devise a river-crossing plan. He set to, instructing a number of coracles to be made, initially as rafts but afterwards to be linked up and covered with decking as bridges for the infantry and pack mules to cross. Likewise two other infantry bridges were designed, using local wine casks lashed together to form a barrel bridge. Army carpenters and joiners formed a workforce, and amongst many other materials they used wooden orange boxes from the local groves.

The night of 20 December was chosen for the operation. Bulfin's original artillery plan was made available in the event surprise was lost and the crossing became 'noisy'. The only artillery fire would be a slow bombardment of the enemy positions, with bursts of machine gun fire, to disrupt any Turkish patrolling. During the run-up, a nightly programme of artillery bombardment and machine gun fire took place, similar to that on the night of the actual assault, so that the enemy would be lulled into thinking nothing unusual was happening on the 20th.

Detailed reconnaissance was also carried out. On the night of the 14th the commanding officer of 6th Highland Light Infantry, Lieutenant Colonel James Anderson, accompanied by a loyal subaltern, swam out to sea around the mouth of the river and landed behind enemy lines; in doing so, they were able to confirm the depth of the bar to be about 3ft and fordable, before they swam back.[3]

On the 19th and 20th cold squalls of rain blew in from the sea, not helpful for bridging but ideal for screening a night attack. With water levels rising, the Turks, already less than alert, did not expect the British to venture across the river. As night fell, with 'zero' hour set for 8.00 pm, the first of three columns of Scottish infantry crossed the river. By midnight, the first of the rafted footbridges had been completed and the entire 156 Brigade was across and attacking the Turks at the point of the bayonet.

At the mouth of the river matters were less straightforward. The Sappers had prepared a guide-rope and stakes, but when they attempted to find the markings for where to enter the river, the water level had risen with the rain. So Lieutenant Colonel Anderson, tasked to be first to cross the river with his battalion, stripped off again and found the crossing point, now 4ft under water. Not waiting for the guide-rope, he ordered his men to link arms and wade across. Turkish artillery had woken up by now, and his battalion took thirty casualties in reaching the enemy bank. The rest of 157 Brigade followed without trouble and rushed the trenches with the bayonet, finding a number of officers in their night clothes, then took their final objectives 4,000yds north by 3.30 am.

155 Brigade, crossing at the bend of the river, was delayed by the weight of the rain and mud slowing down their rafts, but the men were towed across, rather than wait for the bridges to be completed. The only serious enemy resistance was some sharp hand-to-hand fighting for 5th King's Own Scottish Borderers. Along the Auja, a firm bridgehead had been established by dawn and bridges were then used for the artillery to follow quickly.

The official history summed up XXI Corps' operation:

> The passage of the Auja has always been regarded as one of the most remarkable feats of the Palestine campaign. A great achievement it was, but its chief merits were its boldness – justifiable against troops known to be sluggish and slack in outpost work and already shaken by defeat – its planning, the skill of the engineers, the promptitude with which unexpected difficulties in the bridging of the river were met; finally the combined discipline and dash of the infantry which carried out the operation without a shot being fired before daylight and won the works on the right bank with the bayonet.[4]

Allenby was also impressed with this 'really well executed' operation.[5] 52nd Division's casualties amounted to 102, relatively light after the dour fighting in the Judean hills.

Bulfin did not allow his men to rest on their laurels but made them push on and take Arsuf, 8 miles north of Jaffa on the coast. With 54th Division on its right, and the Royal Navy supporting them from the sea, the advance continued, overcoming Turkish positions on the way. 54th Division had had its own fighting whilst the Auja was being forced. 11th Londons had to repel a determined Turkish counter-attack, during which Lance Corporal J. A. Christie won a Victoria Cross for single-handedly bombing the enemy, 50yds out in front of the British line.

On the afternoon of 22 December Bulfin rode up to 157 Brigade headquarters, inland from the coast at Jlil, and urged its commander, Brigadier General Hamilton Moore, to press on to Arsuf, over 2 miles to the north, and hold the high ground there. This achieved, the Jaffa flank was secured for Allenby. Bulfin must have been very satisfied with his corps' effort, in particular that of his intrepid Lowland Scots.

A prominent hill south of the river, which Bulfin had used to observe the battle, was soon named after him; he would base his headquarters, for Allenby's major offensive the following September, close by Bulfin Hill (Point 255).

Little respite

XXI Corps now had its first opportunity to draw breath after two non-stop months of hard marching and fighting. The war reporter Massey wrote:

> The troops received their winter clothing; bivouac shelters and tents were beginning to arrive. Baths and laundries were in operation , and the rigours of the campaign began to be eased … The men were in good health, despite the hardships in the hills and rapid change from summer to winter, and their spirit could not be surpassed.[6]

Even taking into account his propagandist style of writing, there was no doubt that *esprit de corps* was high. Nonetheless, Bulfin's men were exhausted and, with the worst winter rains in living memory, there was little respite for them.

In the midst of this military offensive, Anglo–French rivalry raised its head on Christmas Eve, as amusingly recounted by Sir Ronald Storrs, the recently appointed Governor of Jerusalem. Picot had decided to attend Mass, in some state and guarded by twenty *spahis* (North African cavalrymen of the French Army), at the Church of the Nativity in Bethlehem. Allenby, concerned to 'keep our end up', sent Bulfin and his staff to attend as well.

> Mass then began with two of the Franciscan friars emerging and ceremonially censing Picot, who bowed gravely in return: not a whiff for Bulfin … at about 1.30 a.m. an immense candle, 2 inches thick, was lit and presented to Picot: a 1-inch to Bulfin, and a small rook–rifle bore to the rest of us.[7]

For Chetwode's XX Corps north of Jerusalem there was still work to be done. The city needed to be made secure from Turkish artillery. A corps advance had been planned when a decoded enemy signal indicated that the Turks were about to mount a major counter-attack. During the night of 26 December they made a determined assault, focused against 60th Division's positions east of the Nablus road, but were beaten back with heavy casualties. The next day, Chetwode's divisions advanced, driving back the Turks, and succeeded in finishing off their last effort to retake Jerusalem. By the end of the year a 12-mile front had been established and the city was secure.

Allenby's 'butcher's bill' for 1917 had amounted to 18,000 casualties, light by Western Front standards, especially when viewed against what he had achieved. But over half of these casualties were in Bulfin's corps. The Turks had suffered far more, and crucially their morale had been badly shaken. General Erich von Falkenhayn, the former Chief of the German General Staff, had replaced von Kressenstein and succeeded in establishing some stability to their defence, at least north of Jerusalem. The antagonists' lines stretched from the Mediterranean to the Jordan valley.

The New Year brought satisfying news for Lieutenant General Bulfin, when his contribution to the successes of 1917 was recognized by a knighthood. He was dubbed Knight Commander of the Bath by HRH Prince Arthur Duke of Connaught at an investiture in Jerusalem on 19 March,[8] the day Allenby's generals had gathered on the Mount of Olives (see plate section, page 12). The previous time Bulfin had met the King's brother was during the royal visit to South Africa in 1910.

Allenby was keen to restart his offensive north along the coast in April but knew he required time to consolidate. Before any such operation could be mounted, his overstretched logistic tail needed to catch up. Roads had to be built, the standard-gauge railway extended, communications improved and supplies brought up – a huge task, not made any easier by the adverse weather. Also pressing was the need to secure his right flank across the River Jordan and, with it, make contact with Lawrence and Feisal's Arab army. Since his audacious taking of Aqaba in July 1917, Lawrence had led Arab tribesmen in guerrilla raids on the Hejaz railway, disrupting Turkish movement and tying down their troops. The hope now was to spread the Arab Revolt northwards to Damascus.

In London, the Prime Minister, buoyed up with Allenby's success, had written to the CIGS, Field Marshal Robertson, the day the liberator walked through the Jaffa Gate, seeking to exploit the opportunity to press north. After the failure of Third Ypres (Passchendaele) the previous November, Lloyd George had become set on giving priority to the Middle East. He wanted Aleppo captured and the Middle East campaign won or, even better, Turkey knocked out of the war. As a minimum, he wanted Palestine cleared of the Ottoman armies and their German leaders. Allenby was asked what force levels he needed for each option. His response was a request for sixteen infantry divisions and extra mounted troops. This was unrealistic, given what was happening in Europe. With the collapse of Russia on the Eastern Front, the Germans were free to transfer huge numbers of troops to the West. Intelligence clearly indicated that they intended to mount a major offensive in March, in the window before the Americans were ready to fight.

On the PM's direction, the South African General Jan Smuts was sent out to consult with Allenby and report back. Smuts' response, submitted on 1 March, was that the British forces in Mesopotamia, being the greater distance from Aleppo, should go on the defensive, whilst the priority for reinforcement should go to Allenby's EEF. Largely based on plans Allenby's staff had already worked up, he recommended that, once the EEF's right flank had been protected by the occupation of the Jordan valley, the main thrust should continue to be along the coast, clearing the Plain of Esdraelon and reaching Beirut as a final objective. The reinforcements, grudgingly agreed to by Robertson, were largely untested Indian troops. Bulfin's corps would, once again, be central to the success of these plans but would, as events turned out, have a strikingly different composition.

In February 1918 at Versailles Lloyd George had persuaded the Supreme War Council to agree the Allied strategy for the first months of 1918. Much against the CIGS's advice, which was to lead to Robertson's replacement shortly afterwards, the plan was to renew the offensive in the Middle East whilst the Allies remained on the defensive on the Western Front.

Amidst these arguments about strategy and force levels, Allenby decided that an early step should be made to take Jericho, to Jerusalem's east on the escarpment overlooking the Jordan valley, as well as the Wadi Auja to the north. This would allow him more room for manoeuvre, in preparation for any strike across the Jordan. 60th Division was tasked to take the lead into this desolate region, and after some sharp fighting by the Londoners and Anzacs, Jericho was seized on 21 February.

Allenby also wanted to drive the Turks finally out of the Judean hills and give himself more breathing space around Jerusalem, with an eye on the Samarian hills further north as a better base from which to mount future operations.

Whilst XX Corps advanced on both sides of the Nablus road, Bulfin's corps was tasked with moving its right flank forward to an old Crusader castle at Ras el Ain and bringing it in line, if not in contact, with XX Corps. The four-day advance of the two corps commenced in the first week of March, on an overall front of 26 miles to a depth of 5 to 7 miles. The Turkish Seventh Army responded with reinforcements, in places putting up a staunch resistance, but all objectives were won. It is easy to forget that the frontages and depths of even this relatively small operation would have been beyond the expectations – if not the dreams – of most Western Front commanders until later in 1918.

XXI Corps had an easier time than XX Corps, helped by being in less hilly country but especially because they enjoyed heavier artillery support. After the crossing of the Auja, Bulfin's front ran east and then south-east, now allowing his heavy artillery to enfilade the Turkish positions. In addition, infantry/artillery cooperation had become increasingly sophisticated, with field batteries leap-frogging, by sections, close behind the advancing infantry. XXI Corps' operation, as the official historian recorded, was:

> An interesting example of an attack by infantry in small numbers – only three brigades on a front of about seven miles – but strongly supported by artillery with good observation from the ground and from the air, against a position held mainly by machine guns … as it was, the casualties of the two divisions were only 104.[9]

This front, from Arsuf on the coast to the Shephaleh hills in the south-east, ended very much as the line maintained by Bulfin's men throughout the coming summer.

In March and May two large raids were launched across the Jordan, aimed at taking Amman, but they hit stiff opposition and were repulsed. It was Allenby's first significant setback. Nevertheless, with a third of the Turkish army based east of the Jordan, it did fulfil Allenby's intention of increasing the enemy's feeling of insecurity there, allowing him to concentrate on pushing north along the coast.

The first raid, led by Shea's 60th Division, had set off on 21 March, the day Ludendorff's *Kaiserschlacht* (Imperial Battle) fell on the Somme and came very close to breaking through the Allied line. It was the most critical time for the British Army in the whole war since First Ypres.

A summer of reorganization and training

The EEF was not immune to the crisis on the Western Front. In the scramble to restore manpower levels in Europe, two days later Allenby was ordered to send the majority of his battle-hardened infantry battalions and yeomanry regiments, plus supporting artillery and machine gun units, to the BEF, exempting the Australian and New Zealand contingents. In all, Allenby would send 60,000 British troops to the Western Front. In the case of Bulfin's corps, he would lose 52nd Division in its entirety, plus most of the British battalions from his 75th Division. In their place he received two Indian infantry divisions, 3rd (Lahore) Division and 7th (Meerut) Division, as well as Indian infantry battalions to replace those posted from 75th Division. The two divisions came from Mesopotamia, whilst the replacement battalions mostly came from India. By 1 April 52nd Division had handed over to 7th Division, sailing from Egypt on the 11th. The rest of the reorganization took place over the summer months, the last battalions arriving in early August.[10]

In line with the Indian Army system, each brigade had one British and three Indian battalions; Palin's 75th Division was reorganized on the same basis. The only division to be left untouched in the EEF was Hare's 54th (East Anglian) Division, although it would be joined by the *Détachement Français de Palestine et Syrie*. Bulfin now commanded a larger corps, of four infantry divisions, even if it had lost a good deal of its cohesion and hard-won battle experience. XXI Corps was now very much a multinational and multicultural Imperial force, with more Indian than British battalions (twenty-seven to twenty-one); about thirty per cent of the Indians were Sunni Muslims, their spiritual leader being the Ottoman Sultan in Istanbul. In many ways, it had become a new command. In Bulfin's view, of the Indian units joining in 1918, 'a few were certainly not as bad as others, but very few were approaching "good"'.[11]

With the exception of 54th Division and the old hands of 75th Division, the Corps was in varying states of inexperience, and much training was needed. Many freshly arrived units also required reorganizing to ensure, where possible, there were enough commanders at each level with some knowledge of battle. Half had seen service in India and Mesopotamia, but many were raw troops; one third had never fired a rifle, and many battalions lacked signallers, machine-gunners or drivers. A training school was established in Egypt at Zeitoun, grandly titled the Imperial School of Instruction, with new units rotating through; one of the staff was Captain Hugh Cumberbatch, Bulfin's ADC two years earlier.[12] It received much criticism for its poor standard of instruction and lack of equipment. Better training would be carried out within the Corps area, where battalions and brigades were welded together, then introduced gradually – not in all cases, as events turned out – to the front line. There they were initiated into patrolling and raiding to gain combat experience. It was a major task and achievement to bring the Corps to a state in which it was capable of operating as an effective fighting formation. Bulfin's experience of raising 60th Division, as well as his less happy early months with 28th Division, stood him in good stead. But for some of Bulfin's Indian troops, before any concerted training could commence, Allenby had other plans.

The Chief had decided to turn a blind eye to the War Office's ban on offensive operations and to mount a small number of limited pre-planned operations to further improve the British line. In XXI Corps' case, it was given the task of biting off a Turkish Eighth Army salient on the coastal plain, the objective being Berukin, which had at its back a sweep of marshes. The Australian Mounted Division would be attached to exploit any breakthrough achieved by the infantry. It was thought the marshes would be a considerable obstacle to any EEF cavalry advance once the rains arrived, but they turned out to be almost dry come September. If the Turkish forces could be trapped around Berukin and the large number of guns there captured, a significant prize would be won. In some ways it would be a small rehearsal for Allenby's masterstroke in the autumn. It was the first taste of action for the Indian troops of 7th Division, who were to be in support of the leading division, the 75th – and also the last Middle East action for many British infantry battalions. Bulfin had just recovered from a week off duty with bronchitis.[13]

Although Berukin was captured by the end of the opening day, 9 April, 75th Division met strong resistance, even counter-attacks by German *Asien Korps* battalions, and were not helped by the enemy holding captured orders and marked maps. Such was the intense fighting that nineteen-year-old Rifleman Karanbahadur Rana, of the 2/3rd Gurkhas, won a Victoria Cross for covering the withdrawal of his battalion with his Lewis gun as the enemy closed in on him. The advance was continued with difficulty the following day, but by the 11th it was evident that it was hard holding on to what had been gained. The heavy rate of casualties was becoming counter-productive. Bulfin, after visiting General Palin and carrying out a personal reconnaissance of the front, consulted Allenby, who eventually decided to cancel the operation. 75th Division had lost 1,500 men, twice the casualties of the enemy. It had been an ambitious yet costly exercise, and Bulfin's first setback since his Corps had exhausted itself in the Judean hills the previous autumn.

Whilst the Desert Mounted Corps, as well as the 60th Division, suffered a miserable summer maintaining a presence in the intense heat and humidity of the Jordan valley, XXI Corps was left to hold its current line by the coast and to get on with training and recuperation. Although home leave was denied to most of the EEF, Bulfin was given permission to take a month off, visiting the Vatican en route through Italy. Bulfin had asked, whilst passing through Cairo, for an audience with Pope Benedict XV, but it is not known whether this was achieved.[14] Accompanied by Eddie, he sailed out of Alexandria on the Japanese destroyer *Yanagi* on 18 June; it was his first time home to see Fanny and Eileen for over two years. When the two men returned, Eddie escaped Corps headquarters to earn his spurs on a six-month attachment to 2nd Leicesters in 7th (Meerut) Division, taking part in the battle ahead and winning the Military Cross.

Allenby's plan for Megiddo

By July 1918 it was apparent that the German offensive on the Western Front had failed, with both sides reverting to the static warfare of the past four years. Despite the government becoming resigned to the European war dragging on well into 1919, Lloyd George was keen to resume the offensive in Palestine.

In the Middle East the Turks' attention had turned to the Caucasus, wanting to take advantage of Russia's collapse. In Palestine their force levels on the coast had been reduced, fearing an offensive to the east of the Jordan. Morale was low, desertions high, and tensions continued between the German and Turkish command chains. Liman von Sanders nevertheless took the opportunity to restructure his command in Palestine, placing his headquarters in Nazareth, with Seventh and Eighth Armies west of the Jordan and Fourth Army to the east. On the coastal plain Bulfin's adversary was Eighth Army commanded by Djevad Pasha, based at Tul Karm.

Although Allenby had been ordered to maintain a stance of 'active defence' in 1918, a plan had been germinating in his active mind since the beginning of the year. The outcome of this venture would, in future years, be lauded as one of the finest masterstrokes in British military history. It would also establish Allenby as arguably one of the few great captains of the First World War. Unlike Third Gaza where, on arrival, Allenby had adopted a largely pre-prepared appreciation, the September offensive was of his own devising. He never divulged whether any lessons from Third Gaza influenced his thinking. True to his cavalry instincts, he was keen to maximize the shock effect of his formidable Desert Mounted Corps, the largest cavalry force ever gathered in the war, and he focused on launching a lightning advance, after the summer heat but before the winter rains, once his infantry had breached the Turkish defence line. Conscious that the Turkish army was in a vulnerable state after its string of defeats and relying heavily on its rail network, he concentrated his mind on the need to sever these lines at certain strategic points and paralyse his enemy. A key part of the plan would involve linking up with Feisal's advancing Arab army east of the Jordan, with the early capture of the rail junction at Deraa. On 1 August he issued secret orders to his corps commanders.

It was the opposite of Third Gaza, where his main effort had been against the Turkish left flank, deceiving the enemy into thinking he would attack at

Gaza. This time he intended, with a massive local predominance in infantry and artillery, to break through on the coast, whilst making the enemy believe he would strike east of the Jordan. Close behind the infantry, Allenby planned to release his cavalry divisions on the coast, to pour through the breach (the 'G' in 'Gap' yearned for all the war by cavalrymen) and get in behind the Turkish lines to encircle them.

But over the next three weeks Allenby grew more ambitious as he realized the weakness of his enemy and the possibilities open to him. After a morning ride, the Chief strode into his HQ and presented his plan to the staff. On 22 August he startled his corps commanders with new orders. Wavell described it thus:

> It was a daring plan ... There is no parallel in military history to so deep an adventure by such a mass of cavalry against a yet unbroken enemy. But Allenby had not made up his mind lightly, and there was no shaking it by the suggestion of difficulties. He left it to his staff and to his Corps commanders to work out the details of the design.[15]

The DMC was now given a far more distant objective: El Affule, a key railway junction deep in the heart of enemy territory, just south of Liman von Sanders' headquarters in Nazareth. El Affule lay on the Plain of Esdraelon or Megiddo (the biblical site of Armageddon), and reaching it would involve a continuous ride, crossing the hills of Samaria, of some 50 to 60 miles. From there, 5th Cavalry Division would press on up the coast to Haifa, and 4th Division, east to Beisan. Meanwhile, the infantry divisions of XXI Corps, like a large gate with its hinges in the foothills, would take over the role previously allocated to the cavalry. After making the breach, they would have hard marching ahead of them to sweep north to Tul Karm and then east, rolling up the enemy line of defence as far as Nablus and Sebustiye. To the east, Chetwode, frustrated at his XX Corps being stripped to two divisions, would attack north astride the Nablus road, aiming to tie down the Turkish Seventh Army and stop it from reinforcing the coast. Across the Jordan, the Anzac Mounted Division and Lawrence's Arabs would threaten the Fourth Army. All this time, the British and Australian air squadrons, which enjoyed air superiority, would play havoc with enemy headquarters and communication centres, then harass the retreating enemy.

An enemy intelligence map, captured later at Nazareth, showed no sign of any concentration by Allenby on the coast. Liman von Sanders had been totally deceived, and the Turks were about to be crushed.

XXI Corps breaches the line on the Plain of Sharon

The opening act was given to Bulfin's XXI Corps. Allenby knew his man and was confident he would provide the 'battering ram' to breach the Turkish defences on the coastal plain – 'It was here, by the Mediterranean shore, that the success or failure of the whole adventure would be determined.'[16]

Besides his four divisions, Bulfin was given Shea's 60th Division and the 5th Australian Light Horse Brigade, as well as French and Italian units. Importantly, the Force's heavy and medium artillery was concentrated on his front. It was the most powerful force he had ever commanded, with a greater striking power than Sir John French's BEF in 1914. It presented Bulfin with the greatest challenge and opportunity of his career.

One of his first tasks was to ensure secrecy in the preparations, and to this he gave his full attention. 60th Division, as well as the cavalry divisions, all moving by night from the Jordan valley, had to be hidden in the orange and olive groves north of Jaffa, with no visible increase in the number of tents; provision had been made for the new arrivals to share the tents of those already there. Daylight activity in the camps was banned and the watering of the horses strictly timed. Rehearsals over similar ground were carried out by each attacking battalion. Crucially, the RAF's superiority succeeded in denying any prying eyes from enemy aircraft.

Another important job, which brought Bulfin into some tense discussions with the cavalry generals of General Sir Harry Chauvel's Desert Mounted Corps, was to coordinate the positioning of the mounted divisions and, critically, the moment when they would be released, immediately after the infantry had cleared the way and the guns had moved forward. All this had to be tied up with a complicated artillery fire plan. Bulfin's experience of the *arme blanche*, since his days as a cavalry brigade-major in the Boer War, was evident when agreeing the timing with Major General Sir George Barrow, the commander of the 4th Cavalry Division – a general of huge experience who was considered to be one of the finest cavalry leaders of the war; he had also led an infantry division in France. Barrow, conscious of how fleeting the opportunity for effective pursuit could be, was keen 'there should be no repetition of the distressing delays which marred the Battle of Cambrai'.[17] Barrow reported Bulfin's reaction :

I know you damned cavalry fellows: you'll go getting in the way of my people, obstructing their movements, masking their fire, delaying them – in short, making a damned nuisance of yourselves if I let you go before we are all clear.[18]

It would have been a meeting to behold. But Allenby had been insistent that:

General Chauvel was held responsible that his movements in no way hindered the attack of the XXI Corps by interfering with its supporting troops or masking the fire of its guns … General Bulfin was responsible for opening the doorway, and on the success of his initial attack the whole operation depended.[19]

Allenby left Chauvel and Bulfin to sort out the detail.

A solution was reached whereby the cavalry divisional commanders were able to place themselves, or a staff officer, at the two infantry divisional headquarters concerned, ensuring not a second was wasted in pushing on. Fortuitously, the four generals concerned had served together in the Indian cavalry. In addition, Chauvel's headquarters was sensibly sited within a mile of XXI Corps HQ under Bulfin Hill. In the event, the breach was made so swiftly that the mounted troops swept through earlier than scheduled.

'On the eve of the assault he [Bulfin] circulated the message: "Time is our enemy, not the Turks", as the watchword he demanded every man, including the Indians, should learn.'[20] XXI Corps' well crafted operation order, issued two days before battle, made clear the need to 'crack on':

If the total destruction of the enemy's forces in front of us can be achieved by 48 hours' concentrated exertion, the results will more than repay any hardships endured …The Corps Commander therefore expects commanders to take risks and act with the utmost boldness with their leading troops.[21]

Brigadier General Salt, Bulfin's new BGGS, and the corps staff had planned the operation with considerable skill. The date of 'zero hour' was a closely guarded secret and only released to brigade commanders and below two days beforehand. Ronald Savage, on Allenby's staff, recorded the moment:

> At 4.30 on the morning of September 19th we gathered, a group of twelve officers, outside the door of the Chief's house … as we watched and waited. Suddenly Allenby's voice boomed out 'Zero!' and looking up towards the front, we were treated to a remarkable sight. Along the whole front, as far as the eye could see, some fifteen miles from Rafat to the sea, there leapt up a sheet of flame, interspersed with a myriad of red and green Verey lights, followed a few seconds later by the thunderous roar of the artillery.[22]

A few miles north from Allenby's HQ at Bir Salem, the Gunner staff of XXI Corps were masterminding a fire plan of concentrated intensity. With no preparatory bombardment, the guns had opened with a seventeen-minute barrage, 300 guns together, the heavy guns and howitzers aiming for the enemy batteries and the field guns targeting the Turkish trenches and wire. It equated to one gun every 50 metres.

On an absolutely still night, during the short period of darkness between the almost full moon setting and first light, the battalions had silently left their 'start lines', carefully marked with white tape, and crept across the 1,000yds of no-man's-land towards the enemy wire. As the barrage descended, Bulfin set his infantry loose. Timings had been so well coordinated that within minutes, before the Turks could recover, the assaulting troops were through the wire and in amongst the first line of enemy trenches with rifle, bomb and bayonet, well supported by a creeping artillery barrage, machine guns and naval artillery. Although there were varying degrees of resistance along the front, the shock effect of this early example of *blitzkrieg* was overwhelming.

Assaulting on a five-division frontage, the decisive point was concentrated into a 10-mile area. On the coast Bulfin had placed his trusty 60th Division with the Australian Light Horse on the shore, given a key task of opening a breach for the cavalry to disgorge on to the Plain of Sharon. Having lost nine London battalions to France, this was the division's first chance to see how the Indian replacements would fare in serious battle. There was little need for concern as many were Punjabis, men with a long martial tradition, and they rose to the challenge. Through the gap poured the 5th Cavalry Division, streaming north along the coast.

The centre of gravity lay in the middle on a front of only 3 miles where – from west to east – the 7th (Meerut), 75th and 3rd (Lahore) Divisions aimed for the main Turkish defences around Tabsor and El Tireh further north. After subduing these, they swept east. To the 7th's left, Barrow's 4th Cavalry Division cantered through. Evidence was widespread that the enemy's will to fight was rapidly collapsing. The 7th was commanded by Major General Sir Victor Fane, an Indian Army officer of great experience, but who Bulfin thought was 'inclined to be pigheaded',[23] maybe just the character to overcome the Turkish defences. In his division, one wounded *naik* (lance-corporal) of 92nd Punjabis with four wounded comrades took the surrender of an entire 150mm howitzer battery. In 125th Napier's Rifles, another Indian unit of the brigade, Captain T. W. Rees with six men captured another battery, whilst in the same battalion forty riflemen took two hundred prisoners and six machine guns.

On the right, in the foothills, was 54th Division, supported by the French, acting as the important pivot on which the rest of the corps would wheel right. Here the strongest resistance was met but was soon overcome.

The enemy commanders' ability to respond to this onslaught had already been severely damaged. During the night a single Handley Page bomber had attacked their central telegraph and telephone exchange at El Affule, whilst a few hours later other aircraft had targeted the headquarters of Seventh Army at Nablus and Bulfin's adversaries, Eighth Army, at Tul Karm. Allenby had been quick to appreciate the potential of airpower. T. E. Lawrence was not alone in recognizing that the British and Australian air squadrons played an 'indispensable part in Allenby's scheme'.[24]

Shea's 60th Division, on the coast, had the furthest to march, their target the HQ of the Turkish Eighth Army at Tul Karm, but Shea could be relied on to push his men onwards. By 5.00 pm they had captured the town, hurriedly vacated by Djevad Pasha, while the Australian Light Horsemen pursued those escaping along the road to Nablus, many of whom were cut down from the air. It had taken 60th Division just over twelve hours to fight their way across 16 miles. Private E. C. Powell, accompanying Shea's troops, vividly described the ordeal:

We marched all day, on and on, scorched by the sun, parched with thirst, nearly dead with fatigue and want of sleep, struggling painfully through heavy sand...night came and still we were marching … I thought to myself, 'If we who are advancing feel like this, my God, what must the Turks feel who are retreating?' [To his flank he noted the encouraging sight of] long columns of cavalry passing us at the canter.[25]

On a similar September day in 1191, Richard the Lionheart had defeated Saladin's army along this very coastal stretch.

Surprise complete, Bulfin's men, at a stroke, had destroyed the Turkish XXII Corps in front of them. Refet Bey, its commander, became a fugitive behind British lines for a week until he slipped through to Tyre. XXI Corps had successfully completed all the objectives set by Allenby for the opening phase of his lightning campaign. The opened gate now provided a secure shoulder for the DMC to speed north.

The cavalry charge north

An aircraft flying over the Plain of Sharon that morning would have witnessed an unforgettable and historic sight: in a broad and deep swathe, ninety-four mounted squadrons – some in slouch hats, others in helmets and many in turbans – raised dust clouds as they rode relentlessly north across the desert sands.

Major General MacAndrew's 5th Cavalry Division had been set loose through 60th Division's gap at 7.00 am and by noon they had covered 25 miles up the coast. During the night the leading elements had crossed the western pass of the Samarian hills and disgorged on to the Plain of Esdraelon, cutting the railway line to Haifa. A detachment was rushed 10 miles north to Nazareth, but due to a language misunderstanding just missed Liman von Sanders, who managed to escape the town in his pyjamas.

The 4th Division made similar progress, reaching the Musmus Pass, the eastern way through the hills, as darkness fell. After a delay caused by one of his brigade failing to locate the obscure entrance to the pass, the Lancers eventually found their way through, and as dawn lit up the houses of El Affule before them, they bumped into a Turkish regiment ordered to block them. Two squadrons of 2nd Lancers, under the command of a thirty-year-old captain, charged them with levelled lances and, in a shock action worthy of their arm, rode down forty-six Turks and took into custody the remaining 470, losing one Lancer and twelve horses for their efforts. By 8.00 am they had ridden into El Affule, closely followed by the Australian Mounted Division.

By nightfall that day, thirty-six hours after making the 'G in Gap', the DMC had blocked the escape routes of the Turkish Seventh and Eighth Armies. Already Eighth Army was close to being destroyed as a fighting formation.

XXI Corps' pursuit

Throughout 19 September Allenby had placed himself at Bulfin's HQ. Content with XXI Corps' progress, he moved on to see Chetwode and then travelled to Chauvel's HQ at Megiddo on the 21st. He was quickly coming to appreciate he could embolden his plan even further.

By the evening of the 19th, with the second phase of reaching Nablus and Sebustiye in their sights, Bulfin had ordered his reserve brigades and battalions to take over the lead. Given little time to rest, they marched on at dawn the next day, from the Plain of Sharon into the foothills to the east.

For the enterprising Irishmen of 1st Connaught Rangers, in Major General A. R. Hoskins' 3rd Division, their most welcome booty that night came in the capture of a number of German field kitchens (*Goulasch Kanonen*) filled with nourishment; in regimental folklore it became known as 'The Night of the Soup'.[26]

The next day, the Corps pushed on along the rough tracks of the Carmel hills, overcoming the Turkish rearguards despite meeting stubborn resistance in places. The 3rd Division encountered the German reserves under Colonel von Oppen but by a skilful interception succeeded in capturing over 400 of them.

By the afternoon of the 21st, the 5th Australian Light Horse, with a detachment of armoured cars, had entered Nablus. That same day, Sebustiye's garrison surrendered en masse to 60th Division. For XXI Corps, the battle was won. Casualties amounted to 3,378 in total, of which 446 were killed or died of wounds. They had taken over 10,000 prisoners and almost 150 guns, with huge amounts of small arms and ammunition. Bulfin's infantrymen, tired but in high spirits, had the satisfaction of having turned the key and opened the door to Allenby's success. The official history's assessment was that 'The XXI Corps had thus completed one of the most overwhelmingly successful operations of the war.'[27] In his report Bulfin paid warm tribute to his staff, in particular Brigadier Generals Salt and Armstrong, and to the endurance of his troops, especially the astonishing marching power of his Indian infantry.

The Chief had been keeping his cards close to his chest, whilst his corps commanders were focusing on the task in hand, but on 26 September he called them together at Jenin and revealed the next objectives of his campaign – Damascus and Beirut. Turning to his chief logistics officer, he asked, 'And what of the supply situation?'

The reply was, 'Extremely rocky, sir.'

'Well', Allenby responded, 'you must do your best.'[28]

All of Palestine had fallen in a week, with 50,000 prisoners taken. But 40,000 Turks were thought still to be between the EEF and Damascus. Allenby wanted the job finished, and on into Syria he headed.

By this time Bulfin had established himself at Haifa. One of his many visitors was Sir Ronald Storrs, who came to stay at the monastery on the top of Mount Carmel that Bulfin had occupied for his quarters, with its superb view over the Bay of Acre. Storrs recorded: 'He was obliging enough to have the private chapel … converted into my bedroom, a goodish concession for a fervent R.C.'.[29]

On to Beirut

Whilst Allenby ordered the Desert Mounted Corps to push on to Damascus, a ride of 100 and 140 miles for Barrow's 4th Cavalry and Hodgson's Australian Mounted Division respectively, east of the Jordan Lawrence and the Arab Army rode north to join them. At Deraa Barrow's troopers witnessed the horrific excesses of the Arab irregular soldiers' revenge on the Turks. Harassing the miserable remnants of the Turkish Fourth Army streaming north, the first regular unit entered the oldest inhabited city in the world on 1 October.

The chaotic aftermath in Damascus – and the treachery of Anglo-French imperial ambitions for Feisal's Arabs, with its immense implications for the Middle East today – are beyond the scope of this book. But soon Bulfin would be caught up, albeit at a less complicated level, in the political fall-out of military victory as he headed up the Mediterranean coast.

Bulfin's corps was widely scattered, mostly marshalling hordes of prisoners back to the rear areas, when Allenby issued orders for one of his divisions to make for Beirut. 7th Division was best placed, as a battalion had reached Haifa, already captured by 5th Cavalry Division, in motor lorries the day before. Further advance up the coast was made difficult by the lack of a coastal road; there was only a 6ft wide track. A major obstruction was the 'Ladder of Tyre', a 1-mile section of giant steps hewn out of the rock on a promontory. When the Corps Commander drove up to assess the obstacle, he was advised by the division's senior Sapper, Lieutenant Colonel E. F. J. Hill, that the demolition he planned might take the entire cliff into the sea.

> General Bulfin demanded 'time for a couple of cigarettes' in which to consider the problem; then ordered the attempt to be made. It was completely successful. The whole length of the cliff road was made practicable for wheeled transport in the course of three days.[30]

The completion of the road was largely due to the hard graft of Indian pioneers. Bulfin's car was the first to use it, assisted by much pushing. Meanwhile, the Glasgow Yeomanry, the corps cavalry regiment, was told to push on to Tyre, once the famous Phoenician capital but now an insignificant port. They reached it on 4 October.

On the same day that Allenby was resolving how Damascus should be governed, news reached him of a coup in Beirut, the second city of Syria, by pro-Feisal Arab nationalists keen to stake a claim for the Lebanon. Concerned about a clash between them and French troops, a Royal Navy motor yacht was sent to establish the facts. At dawn on 6 October it found the French destroyer *Arbalète* in the harbour and French transports unloading stores, whilst Sherifian irregulars roamed the city.

Allenby was keen that Bulfin get there promptly. On the evening of 8 October the leading elements of 7th Division entered Beirut after heading up the excellent coastal road at speed, accompanied by their corps commander. Bulfin and his troops were welcomed enthusiastically by the city's inhabitants, many of them highly educated Christians benefiting from the American university. The Germans had left the city a week before, and about 600 Turks were handed over as prizes. No delay was had in establishing firm governorship, and Bulfin moved his headquarters into the Deutscherhof, the main hotel, that day. In accordance with the Sykes-Picot Agreement, Colonel de Piépape, the commander of Bulfin's French detachment, was installed as military governor of Beirut, and other French officers were appointed to Tyre and Sidon. French troops were brought in by ship from Haifa and took over the policing of the three places, putting down any unrest from Sherifian fighters.

On 15 October Allenby visited Beirut, where Bulfin's headquarters had moved to 'a palace belonging to a wealthy Syrian';[31] they both had to make it clear to Picot and de Piépape respectively that the Lebanon was not a French colony and that they remained under the Chief's orders. The French were to become more of a headache than the Arabs to these British generals turned imperial administrators.

Allenby, partly urged on by London, decided to press on north to Aleppo and Tripoli. The former was taken by MacAndrew's tireless 5th Cavalry Division, the latter by XXI Corps on 13 October. A final cavalry charge by the Mysore and Jodhpur Lancers 5 miles north of Aleppo on 26 October was followed by news of the Turkish Armistice five days later.

Bulfin was eventually to meet Feisal in late November, shortly after the Great War ended. The Emir had arrived suddenly with his delegation in Beirut, en route by British warship to Marseilles, where he was met by Lawrence, then to England. Picot was away in Cairo at the time, and Bulfin took the opportunity to entertain Feisal to a formal dinner, where he was introduced publicly as 'His Royal Highness, the Emir Feisal, Commander-in-Chief of the Arab Forces'.[32]

A few days later, Sir Mark Sykes, on a three-month Foreign Office mission to assess progress in the region, visited Beirut and stayed with Bulfin, 'an old brother officer of the Green Howards'.[33] Sykes, weakened by an exhausting tour, died of Spanish influenza three months later whilst attending the Paris Peace conference, a month short of his fortieth birthday.

Allenby's victory was remarkable. In five weeks his army had advanced 350 miles, capturing 75,000 Turkish and German prisoners and 360 guns, whilst suffering 6,000 battle casualties (853 dead); the number of enemy dead is unknown. Three Turkish armies had been destroyed and Palestine, Syria and Lebanon freed from Ottoman rule.

Reflections

The Palestine campaign has frequently been portrayed by historians through the prism of Allenby's dominating personality, the romantic appeal of Lawrence of Arabia and the Arab Revolt, and the heroic charges of the cavalry and yeomanry. However fascinating these aspects may be, they have led to one significant observation on the nature of command being obscured.

There is no doubt that Allenby, on taking over the EEF in the summer of 1917, invigorated a demoralized force. But what made his achievements so impressive in the context of the First World War was above all his organizational ability: welding together such an exotic medley of an army into a modern fighting machine, integrating air and naval power to boot, as well as benefiting from the many new developments in training and technology from the Western Front. T. E. Lawrence, not a natural admirer of the military class, recognized 'the perfection of this man who could use infantry and cavalry, artillery and Air Force, Navy and armoured cars, deceptions and irregulars, each in its best fashion!'[34] Part of that ability was Allenby's success in moulding a command and staff structure that had the capacity and skill to fight and win a large-scale campaign.

As such, Allenby understood the operational level of command and exercised it superbly, a rare talent in the First World War. Admittedly he was facing an inferior foe when compared to the German army on the Western Front. The legacy of Megiddo and the subsequent deep thrusts into enemy territory can be found in the German *blitzkrieg* of 1940, Wavell's Operation Compass in North Africa two years later, and even Operation Desert Storm in Iraq in 1990. Allenby understood that deception, overwhelming power at selected points and deep penetration, allied with speed and dexterity, led to the enemy suffering strategic paralysis and being overwhelmed. It was, at least for the attackers, much less costly in human lives – one of the reasons why more EEF veterans survived the Great War than those who had served in France and Flanders. Indeed, Wavell regarded Allenby as 'the best British general of the Great War'.[35] To succeed thus, he was fortunate to have been served by an unusually able team of field commanders and staff officers.

A perhaps more mundane reminder came from Falls:

The old truth … that the cavalry virtually always has to seize the opportunities made for it by the infantry and artillery. Lieutenant

General Bulfin's infantry smashed the opposition so thoroughly, opened so wide a breach, and swept so clean that the three Cavalry divisions … met practically no opposition until they got behind the Turks.[36]

Nevertheless, Bulfin did not hold back in commenting on Falls' draft chapter when the latter was writing the official history:

Generally I notice the Mounted Troops 'get all the fat' … but if the poor old infantry had not cleared the ground and so make it possible to start in safety, they never could have brought off their splendid effort. Had the XXIst Corps muddled their job – well, Amen!!![37]

Bulfin evidently enjoyed serving under Allenby, a commander who trusted him and allowed him to flourish. This is confirmed in his letter to Edmonds after the war about the 'nightmare' of Loos and serving under Hubert Gough.[38] The only matter which seemed to irk him, as Falls recorded Bulfin remarking, was 'Allenby's obvious preference for Chetwode, a more outstanding character. "Ah, it was always Philup this an' Philup that, and Philup th' other".' But it was Bulfin who was given the key role at Megiddo, whilst 'Chetwode was left to demonstrate with two divisions in the Judean hills'.[39]

The Battle of Megiddo, or more precisely the battle of Sharon, was undoubtedly the apogee of Bulfin's career. He had been able to bring together all his strengths: detailed preparation, administrative care, steadfastness and tenacious fighting spirit. The hard-won lessons of his previous battles had honed him into a thoroughly effective infantry corps commander, skilled in the employment of artillery and the other arms. Allenby described him, in his Dispatch, as showing 'great ability as an organizer and leader in high command'.[40] Bulfin – and the British Army– had come a very long way since the low point of 1915.

After their heady successes in Palestine and beyond, Allenby and Bulfin's fortunes would continue to be tied together in the Middle East well into the post-war period – but much less to a soldier's taste.

Chapter 12

1919–1939
The Shadows Lengthen

'I haven't the foggiest idea what is going to be the future in the Near East'

It would be easy to assume that the Armistice heralded an easier life for a soldier. For Edward Bulfin, however, unlike the citizen soldiers under his command waiting anxiously for demobilization, the heavy weight of responsibility would show no signs of lightening.

Allied victory over the Ottoman Empire, bringing in a long period of acute and complex instability throughout the region, only added to the burden of Allenby and his generals. They were responsible for 'the maintenance of order and the establishment of an impartial, non-political administration' over some million Palestinians, Syrians, Lebanese and Armenians, to say nothing of the huge Egyptian population soon to add to their worries. As Allenby confessed in March 1919, even after the Paris Peace talks had started at the beginning of the year, 'I haven't the foggiest idea what is going to be the future in the Near East.'[1] It would be some time before the fog cleared. In the meantime, the victor of Megiddo and his corps commanders, the latter allocated regions of responsibility, could only turn to their hard-won experience, applying the tenets of 'imperial policing', and to a deep well of common sense.

Their task was not made any easier by the Allied declaration, the previous November, of a seemingly open-handed promise to set up 'national governments and administration that shall derive their authority from the free exercise of the initiative and choice of the indigenous population';[2] this was influenced by Woodrow Wilson's principles of popular self-determination. Bulfin, as a regional commander, had to deal not only with raised political expectations, set against a backdrop of Turkish refusal to disband their forces in accordance with the Armistice, but also with banditry in the remote area of Cilicia, the desecration of Christian churches, lawlessness and intercommunal fighting. It came to a head at the end of February when Muslims in Aleppo attacked an orphanage, murdering a hundred Armenians. On top of this, Bulfin and the other generals had to deal with French officialdom, which was increasingly high-handed and prone to intrigue. A crisis point was reached when the lack of conciliation shown by the French to the Arab peoples of Syria caused Sir Mark Sykes to conclude with Allenby that 'any attempt to foist a French administration on Syria would be violently opposed by the majority of Muslims and Orthodox Christians'.[3] By his military victories, Allenby had made Britain the paramount power in the region and Lord Curzon, the Foreign Secretary, did not intend to waste this position: 'I would sooner come to a satisfactory agreement with the Arabs than I would the French.'[4] However, Lloyd George, with an eye on Britain's wider post-war priorities, required the support of Clemenceau at the Paris Peace Conference. He had come to a private deal with his French counterpart in London the previous December. Britain would keep Palestine, thus securing the vital Suez Canal, as well as the rich oil deposits around Mosul in what became northern Iraq, whilst France would take Lebanon and Syria, the latter under direct rule, not jointly with the Arabs.

Bulfin remained in command of his XXI Corps, with its headquarters still in Beirut, although many of his battalions were about to be sent back to Europe as part of the Army of Occupation or to be demobilized. During a short respite, he had his portrait painted there before Christmas by the war artist James McBey. He looked very much the resolute, albeit tired, victor (see plate section). But given the poisoned chalice of this turbulent region covering Lebanon, Syria and Cilicia, once Allenby had made his official entry into Beirut on 13 January, Bulfin hastened north to tour his 'patch'. From Cilicia he reported that the locals were a 'hardy race of hillmen who are very independent', the Turks in the past having been unable 'to enforce their laws throughout this region'.[5] In early February, a 'brawl' in Alexandretta involving Armenian soldiers, recruited by Picot, caused Bulfin to report that they were 'utterly useless as soldiers and are a standing menace to their officers'.[6] War's end is always less than tidy, as modern day politicians and generals keep having to relearn.

Another great problem now started to impinge on commanders and staff. In a largely citizen army soldiers expected demobilization to start soon after the Armistice. But the demand for manpower to meet the post-war policing of the region, as well as delays due to the Army's flat-footed bureaucracy, inevitably caused unrest. This soon began to manifest itself amongst both Anzac and British troops, many of whom had been serving in the Middle East since 1915, with home leave a rarity. Fears about being at the rear of the queue for jobs back home only added to their unhappiness. The first indications were post-celebratory riots in the base camps in Egypt immediately after 11 November, soon spreading to the smashing up of Egyptian shops. The worst incident was in December, when Anzac soldiers, angered by the murder of one of their comrades by a Bedouin, sought revenge by destroying the local village of Surafend close to GHQ, killing and wounding thirty people and incurring the wrath of Allenby. Trouble continued into 1919, with dependable units such as the Gloucestershire Hussars in Aleppo and the Middlesex Yeomanry in Damascus demonstrating against these delays; unrest even spread to Bulfin's old division, the 60th, burning down a cinema at its base camp. In many ways the greatest concern when it came to keeping the Army's wheels in motion was a strike in the Ordnance workshops at Qantara and Haifa in February. Nevertheless, local commanders managed to handle these incidents with more success than in northern France and southern Britain, where major and widespread post-war mutinies were taking place in the Army.

On 12 March 1919 Allenby was summoned to Paris to give his views on the situation in Palestine, Syria and Lebanon. In his absence, Bulfin was placed in overall command of the EEF and was immediately faced with a further severe test of character.

Revolt in Egypt – 'The Egyptian Problem'

Up to the outbreak of the First World War, Egypt was still nominally a province of the Ottoman Empire. However, Britain, with a substantial garrison based there since 1882 to secure the Suez Canal, also provided civil servants to oversee the Egyptian government. Needing to protect the vitally important Suez Canal from any Ottoman threat, the British Government had declared the country a British Protectorate. The Egyptians were unwillingly drawn into the war against their Muslim brethren, providing the Egyptian Expeditionary Force with food and transport and, in a move which lost the support of the once loyal *fellaheen* (agricultural workers), 123,000

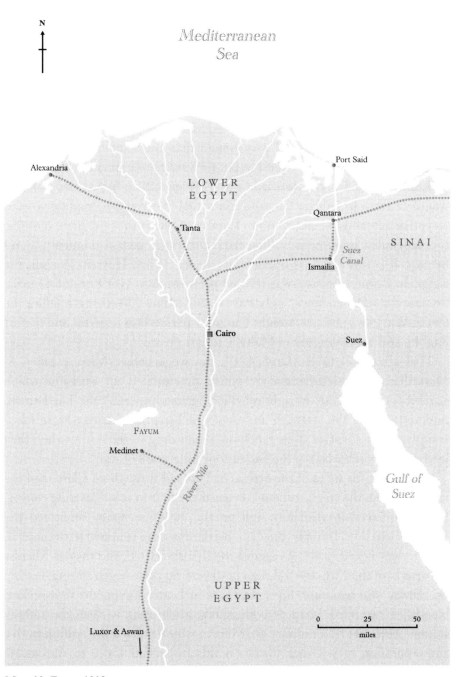

Map 10. Egypt 1919.

conscripted labourers. By the end of the war, the country was suffering from food shortages and inflation. Anti-British sentiment across all classes created a climate ripe for agitation.

Sir Reginald Wingate, Britain's long-standing High Commissioner in Cairo, received early warnings of an increasingly active independence movement in November 1918, when leading politicians, led by Said Zaghlul, demanded the same treatment as other Arabs when it came to self-determination; in fact, they argued that they were far more capable of conducting a well-ordered government than their northern neighbours. Wingate supported their request to put forward the Egyptian case in person in London, but Curzon refused. The Foreign Office hoped the problem would go away. In January Curzon, concerned that Wingate might give in to Egyptian demands, recalled him to London. During the next three months, the nationalist movement, calling itself the *Wafd*, gained momentum and by March it was given its opportunity to act. When Hussein Rushdi, the Egyptian Prime Minister, was refused permission to visit London to make his case for independence, riots started. Sir Milne Cheetham, holding the fort in Wingate's absence, sought Curzon's permission to arrest and deport Zaghlul and his colleagues to Malta. Curzon agreed.

That afternoon of 8 March 1919, the week before Allenby sailed to Marseilles, this high-handed response precipitated an uprising which quickly turned into an outright rebellion against imperial rule. The British, underestimating the strength and depth of Egyptian feelings, were taken completely by surprise. This rebellion would drag in the Army, when they least needed such a task at the end of four long years of war.

By evening the news of the arrests had spread throughout Cairo, and the next morning, the city's students, as usual the first to react, starting rioting. Strikes followed immediately, and on the 10th the police requested the Army's assistance. Initially, the demonstrations were confined to the capital, but the very next day, attacks against the British started, and the day Allenby departed, on the 12th, the *fellaheen* in the countryside began rioting, tearing up railway and telegraph lines. At Tanta in Lower Egypt, the first serious bloodshed occurred when demonstrators, attempting to rush the railway station, were met by a military guard force which opened fire, killing twelve and wounding fifty. Other towns on this important Cairo to Alexandria railway line experienced similar outbreaks of violence over the next few days. On 17 March disorder in the Fayum, a vast and rich agricultural oasis south-west of Cairo, became violent, when a 4,000-strong mob attacked the railway station in Medinet, as well as some houses where 2,000 Europeans had gathered for protection. They were driven off by 150 men of the 46th Punjabis, suffering heavy casualties. The next day, eight unarmed British and Australian servicemen were murdered whilst travelling by train north from Luxor in Upper Egypt, and their bodies brutally desecrated. Lurid reports claimed that the assailants drank the blood of one of them, whilst women ululated in delight.[7] With the country increasingly out of control, the sizeable European community throughout Egypt was reminded of the horrors of the Indian Mutiny some sixty years earlier, as well as the more recent Boxer Rebellion of 1899–1901.

Bulfin first heard news on the 14th whilst at GHQ at Ramleh in Palestine, where he had moved on Allenby's departure. He recorded:

> The reports from Egypt indicated coming danger: a spirit of lawlessness and destruction appeared to be growing and I decided to proceed at once to Cairo in order to deal with the trouble on the spot.[8]

He had his first experience of the scale of the violence when his train was stopped outside Minat al Qamh, between the Suez Canal and Cairo, where two hours before 3,000 rioters had tried to rush the station. They were beaten off by fifty Australian dismounted cavalrymen after a minute's rapid fire – at least the same number of rioters lay dead and injured. Although a hardened campaigner, Bulfin must have been unsettled by the level of violence. Further on, the railway and telegraph lines had been cut, so he completed his journey by motor with an armoured escort, reaching Cairo on the evening of the 17th.

Bulfin 'will stand no nonsense'

Faced with the prospect of an ungovernable country, its capital cut off from the provinces except by air, he immediately appreciated the need for firm and rapid action. In concert with Sir Milne Cheetham, the first step was to issue an appeal to local politicians and leaders. Bulfin called together the Committee of the Party of Independence as well as a gathering of local notables and told them:

> So far only defensive measures had been taken, but that it seemed necessary now to begin taking offensive measures which might entail considerable loss of life. It was the duty, therefore, of every Egyptian to assist the authorities and to act in such a way as to avoid the bloodshed and suffering which would result from such measures. He concluded by solemnly declaring that he intended to do his duty and expected them to do theirs.[9]

Calling also on the Egyptian Sultan, Fu'ad, Bulfin explained that 'he had the necessary forces to repress agitation, and intended to do so, but that from what he saw of tenacity and extension of outbreak, no repression could be effective which was not of the severest.'[10] The Egyptians, not surprisingly, were taken aback by his 'severe attitude',[11] but Bulfin was not a man to mince his words.

The corridors of power in London were anxious. As the Foreign Office memo of the day to Curzon summarized it, 'Position still ['very' struck out in Curzon's blue crayon] serious. Genl Bulfin has arrived.'[12] The memo further noted that the CIGS and Director of Military Operations had been consulted, insisting that 'there are ample troops' and that 'Gen. Bulfin is a good reliable officer who will stand no nonsense.'[13]

Bulfin, after conferring with General Watson commanding the troops in Egypt, was already setting to work – 'I drew up a simple plan to be followed.'[14] The plan consisted of a clear four-phase operation, and to assist him he had the good fortune of having as chief of staff the young Brigadier General Archie Wavell, who had taken over the post from Louis Bols on the latter's departure with Allenby to Paris. Wavell thought Bulfin 'an exceptionally stout-hearted, level-headed soldier, the right man for the job.'[15]

Cheetham, accepting that 'possible measures should eventually succeed … but only at the expense of considerable bloodshed and the creation of great bitterness', had little option but to support Bulfin's plan. As he said, 'Drastic military action is now justified and unavoidable.'[16] Given the lack of an effective response from the local politicians – 'I completely failed to induce them to take any part', Bulfin admitted[17] – he kept his word. Martial law, imposed on the 11th, was carried through with grim determination.

Two threats faced Bulfin. First was the isolation of Cairo, cut off from rail and telegraph links, especially to the ports of Alexandria and Port Said, with the consequent danger of a critical shortage of food and oil. The second was the vulnerability of outlying towns in Upper Egypt, poorly protected by weak or non-existent garrisons.

The initial part of the four phase response was to restore communications immediately between Cairo and Alexandria. At the same time Bulfin sent a column up the Nile by river-boat to Aswan to evacuate European families and bring them safely to Cairo; this latter task he gave to the trusted Brigadier General Huddleston. The second phase was re-opening the railway to Port Said and third, that to the south. Finally, once rail links were restored, he moved out eighteen flying columns, supported by a hundred aircraft, to clear the country close to the railways, restoring order and re-establishing civil government. Superimposed on this were early steps to secure control over the vital Fayum region. Bulfin was also concerned at the danger of a fanatical outbreak by the desert Bedouin, so he placed bombing squadrons of the Royal Air Force on stand-by at strategic airfields.

All this required a considerable force. The numbers were there in Egypt, but many were scattered in demobilization centres and had handed in their weapons and equipment. In particular, mounted troops were needed, but in many cases the men were in one camp and the horses in another. At a time when most soldiers were eagerly waiting demobilization, it was a significant administrative and management challenge to respond to the situation effectively.

The final task, of re-establishing civil government throughout the country, was met by sub-dividing it into seven areas and allocating a general to each one, with sufficient troops for the task. Bulfin was fortunate in having such experienced divisional commanders as Shea, Palin and Fane, the first being sent south with a strong mobile column to restore control of Upper Egypt.

Less than a week after Bulfin's arrival in Cairo, Cheetham was wiring London that the 'vigorous language and action of C-in-C has had a sobering and reassuring effect'.[18] As Lawrence James wrote in his biography of Allenby, 'No time was wasted in executing Bulfin's orders. Although nowadays forgotten, the four-week suppression of the Egyptian uprising matched in ferocity the campaigns of the Indian Mutiny.'[19] In the first six days of the revolt, over 1,000 died, including 75 British, Anzac and Indian soldiers.[20]

It was in many ways providential, at least for the British, that the *Wafd* had not waited a few weeks to initiate the uprising. If they had done so, the ongoing demobilization would have left Bulfin with too few troops to cope. Critically, the RAF would not have had the planes, or the flying boats of 64th (Naval) Wing operating up the Nile, both of which played such a crucial part. Not only were aircraft vital in maintaining contact with Upper Egypt, but they were effective in bombing and machine-gunning crowds attacking unguarded railway lines and stations.[21] It was the first time aircraft had been widely used in such an aggressive role.

For some soldiers, angered by the murder of their unarmed comrades and their 'demob' being further delayed, it was an opportunity to seek revenge on a country where they had felt 'ripped off' by tradesmen they deemed dishonest and a people they generally despised. This was not just a European racist view: a secret telegram to London reported that Indian troop morale was 'all sound, and contempt for Egyptians to be general'.[22] Nevertheless, operational reports at the time reflected many cases of courage and restraint shown by isolated troops threatened by overwhelming numbers.[23] Although the Army claimed that 'vindictive repressive measures were rigorously avoided',[24] doubtless over-harsh treatment was handed out at times, especially during village searches. By the standards of the time, which would be deemed unacceptable today, the British viewed it as a firm and measured response to what was seen as a rebellion. *The Times*, in a leading article on 2 April 1919 reflecting much establishment opinion, found Bulfin's robust stance 'reassuring'. General Gwynn, in his military textbook *Imperial Policing* wrote:

> With the exception of those cases in which a definite attack which had to be repelled was made, there was little loss of life. No steps in the nature of vindictive or oppressive punitive measures were taken, and the troops showed admirable restraint.[25]

But the fact that every eleventh round was removed from machine gun belts, to prevent prolonged firing against rioting mobs, indicated that restraint needed to be enforced.

The Egyptians, understandably, had a very different perspective. The *Wafd* circulated a charge-list during the Paris Peace Conference of alleged atrocities, including murder, rape and robbery. How much was propaganda is difficult to prove, but the Milner Mission later that year did admit to one officer having shot five suspects without a court martial, and flogging being used to extract information.[26]

A popular song, sung throughout Egypt at the time, demonstrated how difficult it would be for the British to put the genie of independence back in the bottle:

Pardon, Ya Wingate!
You've taken our corn.
You've taken our maize.
You've taken our camels.
You've taken our cattle.
You've taken our money.
You've taken our young men.
For God's sake leave us our lives![27]

Allenby, after only two days in Paris, was called upon once again to come to his nation's aid. The seriousness of the 'Egyptian Problem', with Britain shaken by the murders on the train, led to Lloyd George urgently seeking the King's approval to Allenby being appointed immediately as Special High Commissioner to Egypt, with pro-consular powers. He left Paris on 22 March and set sail from Marseilles on the suitably named destroyer HMS *Steadfast*, arriving in Cairo on the 25th. He certainly seemed content with the way Bulfin was handling the crisis, writing a covering note to Bulfin's report submitted to the War Office: 'The operations were carried out by General Bulfin to my entire satisfaction.'[28]

'On his [Allenby's] arrival in the country, the situation was, for the most part, calm on the surface owing to the military measures which had been taken.'[29] Allenby, in writing to Chetwode, found 'things better that they seemed and I think they are calming down'.[30] But trouble continued well into late May, with civil strikes threatening any return to normality. The burden of responsibility was at least lightened for Bulfin by having Allenby close at hand.[31]

One of Bulfin's most taxing tasks was how to handle those elements of the EEF who were thoroughly disgruntled at being held back from going home.

The situation became so serious that strikes and mutinies had spread from the base at Qantara to Ramleh and Haifa. Allenby warned London of the danger and, under pressure, it was agreed to speed up the demobilization process. During June, some 26,000 troops received their long-awaited discharge.

During this time, the Special High Commissioner's attention was very much concentrated on finding a peaceful political solution to Egypt's future. To London's consternation and to many of his soldiers' anger, the 'Bull' felt that a conciliatory note was the only way forward, a view also supported by Bulfin. By the time the latter was able to sail home on 7 November on H.T. *Caledonia*, Allenby, with two and a half years still to serve in Cairo, was left grappling not only with the 'Egyptian Problem', but also with the greatest of the post-war Middle East power struggles, that of the future of Syria. For Lieutenant General Sir Edward Bulfin it would not be his last experience of the region, but it would be his final operational command. It was one in which he had displayed his usual sense of duty and moral courage, to a level of robustness difficult to envisage and, many may argue, to defend today.

Ireland – 'The Frocks are frightened'

The Bulfins had taken a house in Kensington and there they savoured his first Christmas at home since 1913.[32] The tired general had little time to recuperate before his wealth of experience was being called upon again, this time in his country of birth, Ireland.

The immediate post-war years presented the government with, in Keith Jeffery's words, a 'crisis of Empire'.[33] Although the continued occupation of Mesopotamia, Palestine and Egypt placed an unwelcome burden on Army manpower, what troubled the government most was the re-eruption of unrest in India and Ireland, traditionally the focuses of the Army's attention.

When the Home Rule Bill of 1914, put on hold until the end of the war, was finally enacted, the exclusion of the six counties of Ulster served to unite the Nationalist and Catholic population in opposition. Throughout 1919, the Irish nationalist guerrilla campaign, known as the War of Independence, intensified, with attacks first against the RIC and then the army. By the new year of 1920 internment without trial was imposed and the south-west counties of Cork, Tipperary, Kerry and Limerick were placed under martial law; others followed later. The month Bulfin returned home, the Army had over 30,000 troops in Ireland (thirty-four infantry battalions, amongst them 2nd Green Howards sent to Tipperary).

On 11 May 1920 the Cabinet met to discuss the precarious state of security there. Sir Henry Wilson, the CIGS, wrote in his diary:

The Frocks are frightened … As usual I found the Cabinet hopeless. They are terrified about Ireland and, having lost all sense of proportion, thought only of that danger, and completely forgot England, Egypt, India, etc., in all of which we are going to have trouble – and serious trouble.[34]

It was at this meeting, chaired by Bonar Law (in place of the Prime Minister David Lloyd George, sick at the time), that Bulfin's name came to their attention.

General Sir Nevil Macready and an irritable CIGS were in attendance. Macready had recently been appointed C-in-C in Ireland[35] and he came to London with a long shopping list of additional military and police resources he needed, amongst them extra infantry battalions and mechanical transport to improve troop mobility. Although the Cabinet agreed 'the present situation is so serious' that 'all requirements … should be promptly met',[36] in the event it was decided Macready would delay as long as possible in calling for the eight battalions earmarked.

Macready was also seeking a senior officer to oversee the police forces in Ireland.

My own idea was that this official should if possible be an Irishman, and a Roman Catholic, but without any leanings towards any political party, possessing at the same time powers of organization and experience in handling men, especially his own countrymen. It may be thought that such a combination could hardly be found in one man. As a matter of fact I had in my mind's eye the one individual who combined the essentials for this post, and who after a distinguished career during the war was at the moment unemployed, Lieutenant-General Sir E. Bulfin … the one and only man I could personally recommend as fitted in every way for this post.[37]

Winston Churchill, present as Secretary of State for War and Air, suggested a scheme for raising a special force of 8,000 former soldiers to reinforce the Royal Irish Constabulary. Macready had briefed the Cabinet that 'the whole RIC might collapse at any minute & the Dublin Metropolitan Police were absolutely useless'.[38] As Churchill wrote to the King's Private Secretary:

> [Macready] wished to take General Bulfin as Head of the Police to reorganize both the RIC and the Dublin Metropolitan Police and to build up a composite Secret Service from the four separate and uncoordinated departmental branches which are at present dealing with Irish matters. This is an appointment of great importance.[39]

The Cabinet agreed that Bulfin was the man needed. Wilson sent for him later that day, but 'he flatly refused to take on the job'.[40] Churchill was similarly rebuffed:

> I thereupon sent for General Bulfin, who flatly refused on the grounds that as a Catholic and an Irishman it would be distasteful to him to do any work of this kind which was not of a purely military character.[41]

With his customary stubbornness and moral courage, Bulfin had made it clear that he was not prepared to order policemen to fire on his own countrymen. He was still very much an Irishman at heart. For Macready 'it was a misfortune I never ceased to regret'.[42] The poisoned chalice was passed to Major General Hugh Tudor, an ambitious Gunner acquaintance of Churchill, with no experience of 'policing', who failed to heal the damaging rift between the police and the Army.[43] That 'special force' would evolve into the infamous and hated 'Black and Tans' and the Auxiliaries.[44]

Bulfin's employment since returning from Egypt had not been particularly high-profile. In April he had been temporarily appointed, along with Lieutenant General Sir Walter Braithwaite, to, as reported Churchill to the House of Commons on 4 May, 'tour the country and put the case for the Territorial Army before meetings of employers … and it is hoped that during the next six months every employer in the country will have been approached, either individually or through the medium of the central or local employer associations'.[45] His refusal to take on the post in Ireland meant that, in a shrinking army with too many generals to employ, he had killed any chance of ever being selected for further advancement.

It would be fascinating to discover how much Bulfin knew of the depth of involvement of his relations, Eamon and Catalina ('Kid') Bulfin, in Ireland's independence struggle at this time. Interestingly, there was no mention at the time, in the London or Dublin press, of this family link.

After Eamon's deportation to Argentina he had been busy as de Valera's representative there, drumming up support and raising funds for the War of Independence. His sister 'Kid' was living more dangerously, carrying messages and hiding caches of weapons and ammo for the IRA volunteers in Dublin. Some descendants today believe Edward Bulfin had long before cut his ties to the republican side of the family, indeed to Ireland herself.[46] The former might have been the case, but not the latter.

Regimental loyalties

Bulfin now turned his attention and energies to his regiment. Since assuming the appointment of Colonel of the Green Howards at the height of the First Battle of Ypres, he had taken every opportunity to stay in touch with battalions at the front. A fortnight after the Cabinet meeting, he was able to gather his brother officers together for the first post-war regimental dinner in London. It was a sadly depleted gathering (see plate section).

Bulfin continued to hold his old 60th Division in great affection and also attended its annual dinner in London a month later. A telegram was dispatched that evening to Sir John Shea, still in Palestine: 'We drink the health of the gallant General who commanded the Sixtieth Div: at its zenith. We miss you tonight. General Bulfin.'[47]

The regimental matter which most concentrated Bulfin's mind on his return to England was his desire to formalize its treasured and distinctive nickname of 176 years. After the Great War, when war correspondents had frequently confused the names of the seven regiments with 'Yorkshire' in their titles, Bulfin was clear it was time to make the 'Green Howards' its official designation. In time-honoured fashion when it came to such contentious matters, the War Office appointed a committee to resolve this and other regimental submissions for name changes. Bulfin devoted himself to championing the Green Howards' claim and, in Army Order

509 of 1920, success was achieved. On New Year's Day 1921, 'Alexandra, Princess of Wales's Own Yorkshire Regiment' became 'The Green Howards (Alexandra, Princess of Wales's Own Yorkshire Regiment)', shortened to 'The Green Howards', as its previous title had been abbreviated to 'The Yorkshire Regiment'.[48]

Bulfin confided to a close friend, soon afterwards, that the name change had not found favour in one important quarter, namely with his sovereign. King George V had called for Bulfin to tell him 'in very plain terms that the Regiment had insulted his mother', the Dowager Queen Alexandra, by in effect demoting her to brackets, adding inaccurately that 'you are the only regiment in the Army who are called after a commoner'; he seems to have forgotten the Duke of Wellington's Regiment.[49] Queen Alexandra, as the regiment's Colonel-in-Chief, had received Bulfin at Marlborough House on 1 December, her seventy-sixth birthday, for a report on her regiment and been presented with a green and white bouquet and an inscribed 'Roll of Officers'. This gracious and much loved royal figurehead, now very deaf, would have been too discreet to divulge whether she indeed felt insulted. Bulfin called on her regularly until her death five years later.

Earlier that summer of 1920, Bulfin was awarded an honorary degree by his old university. On 30 June he collected his *honoris causa* from the Provost of Trinity College Dublin in a college theatre packed with staff and students, who heard an oration given in Latin:

> A remarkable soldier now stands before you who was once a student in our halls … To this illustrious son of our country and our college, who has deserved so well of the Empire and is now to receive our academic laurels, we assuredly owe all the applause that we can give.[50]

On coming forward, he was given a 'tremendous ovation by the students'.

Whilst in Dublin he called on the Commander-in-Chief, General Macready, before spending two days with the 2nd Battalion of his regiment in Tipperary. It was probably his first visit back since 1913, and offered the added bonus of seeing his son, then employed as the battalion's intelligence officer.

The battalion had been in Ireland since mid-1919, and it was a loathsome posting. Back in England, civil unrest and strikes meant that all leave and courses were cancelled. Poorly recruited, with veterans still war-weary and new recruits ill-nourished and poorly educated because of the war, the battalion's first job was guarding police stations. 'We hate our job here, but none of us would like to leave Ireland without first seeing an end to Sinn Fein and its despicable tale of murder, robbery, intimidation and anarchy', recorded a regimental officer at the time.[51]

The year 1921 was a quiet one for Bulfin, still a serving officer, but waiting to hear of any future employment. That summer, he attended the unveiling of the regiment's war memorial in Richmond, the ceremony carried out by Sir Hugh Bell, Gertrude Bell's father and a friend of Bulfin, in his capacity as Lord Lieutenant of the North Riding.

In October he returned to Ireland, to pay a second visit to the 2nd Battalion. By 1921, with increasing rebel violence, their work had become a good deal more serious. An emboldened IRA had begun operating flying columns, usually about twenty-five strong, and this required a commensurate response. Army patrols of up to three platoons, often composed of volunteers, moving on bicycles and wearing rubber-soled boots, sometimes in shorts, covered up to 25 miles a day. With the fine summer weather and a more active role, morale rose. In May at Lackelly a Green Howard patrol of ten men and three policemen, led by a subaltern, ran into an IRA ambush. In the exchange of fire at least five rebels were killed and a number wounded. Placing the dead on farm carts, the patrol continued on its way, only to be attacked in a five-hour running battle by 200 rebels. In all, ten rebels were killed and thirty-five wounded, the Green Howards losing one man seriously injured.[52] Despite the intensity of this counter-insurgency role and the inevitable distaste of the Irish for the Crown forces, aggravated by the atrocities of the 'Black and Tans' and the Auxiliaries, the regiment seemed to maintain remarkably cordial relations with the local people.[53]

By the time Bulfin arrived on Friday 7 October, the rebels were losing heart and the British government was under pressure to find a way to halt this unhappy conflict. In July a truce had come into effect, prior to the Anglo-Irish Treaty that December, by which the South gained dominion status as the Irish Free State.

Bulfin's visit took the traditional form of a welcoming dinner with the officers, followed by a tour the next day around the battalion area, including visiting the scene of the action at Lackelly. At a Church parade on Sunday he addressed the whole battalion, commending by name those soldiers who had performed so well, 'a matter of deep satisfaction to him as Colonel of the Regiment'.[54] He returned to London by mail train the next day. Such a visit, especially the chance to be with his soldiers again, would have given the ageing general, now rather in the wilderness, a great lift.

Final posting – India and Iraq

Shortly afterwards, Bulfin received welcome news of gainful employment, albeit not in a senior command. He was to carry out the distinctly unglamorous task of Commissioner for the Disposal of Surplus Stores in India and Iraq, stationed in Delhi. Sailing to Bombay in late December 1921, he was soon involved in helping to draw down a British and Indian Army increasingly under pressure to find cuts. It was his first voyage east of Suez since 1890. The Commander-in-Chief there was General Lord Rawlinson, the man who had gossiped about him and his division in 1915, but who proved to be a successful C-in-C at a turbulent time for India.

By 1919, the peoples of India – 'the jewel in the Crown' of Empire – had an air of expectancy. The collapse of Tsarist Russia, amongst other events, and the British public's admiration and gratitude for the part Indian troops had played throughout the widespread campaigns of that truly World War, had raised expectations. But the heavy-handed response to what were seen as subversive activities surrounding the campaign for Home Rule merely encouraged Gandhi's passive resistance movement. Demonstrations and strikes spread throughout India. With the Punjab in turmoil, on Sunday, 13 April 1919 Brigadier General Reginald Dyer responded to a public demonstration at the Jallianwala Bagh in Amritsar by ordering his soldiers to open fire. In ten minutes 1,650 rounds were fired, killing about 400 and wounding 1,500 trapped and unarmed civilians. 'The British Raj was never the same again', wrote V. Longer, an Indian historian of the Indian Army. 'The Indian attitude towards the British changed; resentment, anger and hatred grew. A point of no return had been reached.'[55]

At the same time, the army in India was having to cope with the Third Afghan War throughout the summer of 1919, as well as a perennially troublesome North-West frontier, sucking in troops and aircraft on punitive expeditions. On Lord Rawlinson's arrival as C-in-C in November 1920, later supported by Lieutenant General Sir John Shea as his CGS, he was confronted with the Esher Committee's recommendations to reorganize the Army. This evolved two years later, under the Inchcape Committee, into finding significant savings in expenditure and manpower. It was in this atmosphere of an 'Empire in crisis' that Bulfin arrived in India, tasked with overseeing a drawdown of stores and equipment from India as well as Iraq, the latter still administered for military purposes from Delhi.

The Iraqis, like the Indians, had yearnings for independence. But after the British victory over the Ottomans in Mesopotamia, the League of Nations, in 1920, declared the area a mandate under British administration. A four-month rebellion followed, referred to today as the Great Iraqi Revolution, which was only crushed by troops brought in from India. Realizing that the country needed to move to a degree of independence, but not wishing to give up influence in the region – or relinquish control of Iraq's rich oil potential – London appointed Sir Percy Cox as High Commissioner. His task was, in effect, to create an Arab state, complete with its own government and constitution. This was the opportunity to repay Hussein, the Sharif of Mecca, for his support during the Arab Revolt; and so, in August 1921, the British placed his son Feisal on the throne of this most ancient kingdom, now demarcated by arbitrarily drawn borders, although many were based upon the previous Ottoman administrative areas.

The new Colonial Secretary, Winston Churchill, with T. E. Lawrence and Gertrude Bell, had been busy at the Cairo conference that spring deciding the future of Iraq. Gertrude Bell, 'the Queen of the Desert' and the most influential woman of her time in imperial decision-making, appointed Oriental Secretary, declared, 'We have got our King crowned.' It would take until 1932 for the mandate to run its course and for Iraq to be admitted to the family of nations. Bulfin arrived at an unsettled time of British 'divide and rule'.

He spent the year and a half travelling his huge estate, a role which would have suited his administrative strengths, whilst enjoying the freedom to re-acquaint himself with those he had known during his earlier days in the Middle East.

In February 1922, soon after his arrival, he was in Baghdad joining a big Sunday lunch party hosted by the Naqib's eldest sons, with the new King, also Sir Percy Cox and his wife, Gertrude Bell, the Commander-in-Chief of

Iraq and others. Bulfin knew the Bell family well from Yorkshire. Gertrude wrote back to her father warmly about him: 'There was also General Bulfin, whom I rather love (he sends you many messages).' She painted an illuminating picture of the occasion:

> Lunch was a terrific function, about 15 courses. The effort to find a common denominator of language is unspeakably exhausting and I usually end by relapsing relentlessly into Arabic. The King and C-in-C talk what you might call the worst French in the world if you hadn't heard that of Lady Cox, while neither she nor the C-in-C have a word of Arabic which was the sole language of our hosts.[56]

A few days later she threw her own dinner party, inviting Bulfin as well as some prominent figures he had known in Syria: 'Sir Edward and Sasun Eff [minister of finance] got on splendidly and the General, who is very quick and clever in his appreciation of people, at once recognized Sasun's great qualities.' Later, she had lunch with Bulfin, seeking his views on how the country was 'finding its feet'.[57] He seemed to be doing a good deal more than merely disposing of surplus stores.[58]

Whilst in India, he was also able to visit the 1st Battalion of his regiment serving in Secunderabad. It had been languishing in India throughout the Great War, and it was the Third Afghan War, toiling in the defiles of the Khyber Pass, which rescued it from oblivion. The year before Bulfin's visit, it had the thankless task of tackling Jewish-Arab fighting in Palestine, as a result of the League of Nations' mandate there.

Retirement

By the end of April 1923, his task complete, Bulfin sailed back from Bombay to England. The Bulfins had taken a house in Walmer, one of the Cinque Port towns in Kent, most likely to be close to Fanny's brother at Ramsgate. A great regimental friend from Boer War days, James Fearon, lived nearby in the town. Adjacent to Walmer, at Deal, the government in 1925 had given the castle – 'this funny little Tudor fort' – to Allenby as a gift from a grateful nation. Although the Allenbys, a restless couple in retirement, spent little time there before moving to London, they would have kept in touch with the Bulfins as neighbours; the two generals regularly attended EEF dinners together. There Bulfin spent the next seven years of his life, finally retiring from the army on New Year's Day 1926, having been promoted full general the previous May.

It was a time when the Great War commanders were fighting 'the battle of the memoirs', whilst official and unit histories were also being written. James Edmonds and Cyril Falls sent him drafts of chapters they were preparing on the Western Front as well as the Palestine campaigns. He was asked to write forewords to various records of the war, and the one he helped with most was that of 60th London Division. Sadly, and understandably given its unhappy existence, a record of 28th Division was never produced.

One of the most controversial memoirs was that of General Sir Horace Smith-Dorrien, sacked by Sir John French in 1915. Bulfin, who had commanded 28th Division under him in Second Army, was included in the circulation of a draft of his manuscript for comment.[59]

In one foreword he wrote Bulfin made some revealing remarks which give an insight into why this private man did not write his own memoirs. The work in question was that of Captain Hyndson of the Loyal North Lancashires, whose men had fought so steadfastly in Bulfin's brigade in 1914. Bulfin opened the foreword thus:

> Since the Great War we have been inundated with a flood of literature dealing with the numerous impressions, experiences and mistakes of the Higher Command. These outpourings are inflicted on the long-suffering public by Generals, Staff Officers, Chaplains and Press Correspondents, but remarkably few from that splendid product of the British Army – the Regimental Officer. I suppose he instinctively abhors publicity; by training silent, he leaves it to others to do the talking. The books dealing with the late War are 'Thick as autumnal leaves that strew the brooks of Vallombrosa'.[60]

Bulfin identified strongly with the regimental officer, as he had always done throughout his career.

The New Year of 1927 was spent in Ireland. On return, he and Fanny paid their farewells to the 1st Battalion the Green Howards, as they sailed from Southampton for peace-keeping duties in Shanghai. His advice to his departing Yorkshiremen was typically soldier-like: 'You must not get rattled, but keep your rifle bolts well oiled.'[61]

In the spring he returned to France to unveil a memorial in Béthune before spending a few days in Ypres, where he had the opportunity to admire the newly built Menin Gate memorial (unveiled by Field Marshal Plumer on 24 July).

That summer, he travelled to Lancashire to inspect his old school's Officer Training Corps, as well as to Yorkshire to see territorial units of his regiment. Whilst there, he took the opportunity to visit Mount Grace Priory and offer his condolences to Lady Bell, whose stepdaughter Gertrude had died from an overdose of sleeping pills in Baghdad the previous July. He also lunched with his old ADC, Hugh Cumberbatch, and his wife.

A happy family occasion took place in September of that year when his daughter Eileen was married in London, to John Holmes of the King's Dragoon Guards. She produced his only grandchild, Peter, four years later. Sadly, they were divorced before Bulfin's death in 1939.

Two years later, tragedy struck the Bulfin family, with the news that Eddie had died in Palestine. The general had seen many of his contemporaries lose their sons in the war. Most prominently was Allenby, whose 'boy' Michael was killed on the Western Front in July 1917, shortly after Allenby arrived in the Middle East; he was an only child. Relieved that Eddie had survived the war, it must have been an especially hard blow for Bulfin and Fanny to lose him now.

Eddie was still serving with 2nd Green Howards when the battalion, en route to Shanghai in August 1929, was dispatched from Egypt to Haifa. The exhausted and overstretched local police had been unable to cope when serious rioting in Jerusalem spread further afield, with widespread massacres of Jews and attacks on their *kibbutzim*. For the next two days the thirty-year-old Bulfin and his company experienced the gamut of internal security duties: dispersing riots, protecting houses from looting and burning, chasing armed gangs and generally attempting to keep the peace between Jew and Arab.

Whilst leading a force sent to assist the police in Jenin in the Galilee district, Eddie became very sick, constantly retching as he discussed the situation with the police commander, John Faraday. Eventually persuaded to hand over to his sergeant, he was admitted to the Jewish hospital at Safed, where ptomaine poisoning was diagnosed. Twenty-four hours later, on 30 August, Faraday went to visit him, but the nurses held out no hope and, in the absence of a Catholic priest, a Greek Orthodox one was found to administer the last rites. Faraday set on record, in a letter to the author's father, what followed: 'A little while later, Eddie Bulfin died, with Faraday holding his hand. Just before he expired, from somewhere he conjured up the strength to shout aloud, twice "Up, the Green Howards".'[62] Some in the regiment thought he had been poisoned by coffee he had taken in an Arab café, but Faraday's view was that it could be traced to some bully beef sandwiches prepared by the mess in Egypt, which was the only food Bulfin had eaten. He was buried the following day on Mount Carmel, close to where his father had served a decade earlier. It was a month before he was due to start studying at the Staff College.

Among Eddie's effects returned to his grieving father was his watch, which the general then sent to Faraday, with a visiting card on which was written: 'From my dear boy for much kindness. To Captain J. A. M. Faraday, Palestine Police, Safed, Palestine'. Marked on the back of the stainless steel waterproof watch was 'Maj. Gen. E. S. Bulfin', suggesting it was first worn by the general in 1915 or 1916.[63]

The year before, Eddie had completed three years as adjutant. He was an immensely popular officer in the regiment, with an 'irrepressible sense of humour', and everyone had high hopes that he would go far in his profession. As with many men of his age who lose a son, especially an only one, it is unlikely his father ever fully recovered.

Bulfin, now sixty-six, responded by immersing himself in his beloved regiment, travelling frequently the long distance to Yorkshire for various events and reunions. In September 1931 he attended the annual reunion in Richmond, and in proposing the toast at dinner, he described the Green Howards as 'the best spirited regiment in the British Army'.

As old soldiers know, attending the funerals of one's comrades gathers pace with the years. For Bulfin this was no exception. In July 1932, aged seventy-six, Field Marshal Viscount Plumer, Bulfin's commander during Second Ypres, died. Buried in Westminster Abbey, 'Old Plum and Apple' was given the honour of being interred in the secluded Warrior's Chapel, a few yards from the tomb of the Unknown Warrior. Amongst the host of mourners on that humid summer day, watching the coffin pass by draped in the same faded Union flag used at Haig's funeral four years earlier, was Bulfin. In November he attended the funeral in Wiltshire of his old divisional commander from South African days, Lord Methuen,

On 20 September 1934 he took the salute on Alma Day, as the 1st Battalion marched past at Portland in Dorset, captured for posterity by Pathé News.[64] It marked the fiftieth anniversary of his commission in the regiment and, in recognition of this, he was presented with a set of four Irish silver candlesticks, made in Dublin in 1750. It would be the last appearance with his Yorkshire soldiers, as a 'long and distressing illness'[65] began to set in. His final evening with his officers was a regimental dinner in June the following year.

On 14 May 1936 Bulfin lost his old Chief. Allenby died suddenly, from a blood tumour on the brain, and his ashes were interred five days later beside the remains of Plumer. It is not recorded whether Bulfin, by now a sick man, was among the many senior military figures, led by Field Marshal Sir Philip Chetwode, paying their last respects at the funeral. It was a strange act of fate that placed Plumer and Allenby, two of the most widely respected and successful Great War military figures, next to each other in such an honoured resting place. Bulfin was fortunate to have served under both of them.

After Walmer and a number of years living in Brighton, by 1936 the Bulfins had moved to Boscombe, part of Bournemouth, a mile from his younger brother Ignatius.[66] It was the same seaside town that C. S. Forester's central character in *The General* retired to. Two years later, on 20 August 1939, General Sir Edward Bulfin died of heart failure; he was seventy-six. Within a fortnight of his death, the country he had fought so hard to defend was once again at war with Germany.

The funeral took place three days later with full military honours, preceded by a Requiem Mass. With due ceremony, of which he would have approved, the coffin, draped in a Union Jack, was borne to the grave by warrant officers and sergeants of his regiment, followed by a sergeant major carrying a cushion on which were the General's orders and decorations. A firing party fired three volleys over the grave and a bugler sounded the Last Post and Reveille.[67] Leading the many military mourners was the recently retired CIGS, Field Marshal Sir Cyril Deverell, Colonel of a fellow Yorkshire regiment (the West Yorkshires), who had served as a brigade-major under Bulfin at Second Ypres. Also present was Lieutenant Colonel Patrick Butler, another Stonyhurst old boy, who as a young captain had watched the wounded 'tower of strength' walk back to the dressing station in the Ypres salient a quarter of a century before.[68]

This servant of the Empire, a devout Catholic to the end, is buried in an easily missed corner of Wimbourne Road cemetery in Bournemouth, close to the graves of two of his sisters. On the unpretentious headstone, above his name and decorations, is inscribed 'Here sleepeth until the great reveille sounds'.[69]

Chapter 13

Epilogue

'That hideously unattractive group, the British Generals of the First
World War, whose diaries reveal hearts as flintlike as the texture of
their faces.'

The military historian John Keegan made this remark in his 1978 review of
John Terraine's *To Win a War*, the latter at the time often ploughing a lonely
furrow in defending Haig and his generals' reputations.[1] It reflected a long-
standing perception, which survives even today, that anyone who could send
so many men to their death must be callous or incompetent.

Forty years on, historians have added a great deal to the understanding
of generalship in that war and of those in positions of command, leading
to a more informed and balanced assessment. Whether they are seen as less
'hideously unattractive' by the general public is more difficult to judge.

However, a general's job is to win victories on the battlefield, not to be
attractive. As Montgomery's chief of intelligence commented after a later war,
'Nice men don't win wars.' What is more profitable for military historians is
to assess whether men such as Bulfin can be admired and respected in their
profession of arms, by scrutinizing the part they played. To reach any useful
conclusions it is essential to judge them by the standards of their day, not
the twenty-first century.

In recent years, driven partly by the centenary of the First World War,
there has been a plethora of books on the major battles as well as, at one
end of the spectrum, the first-hand experiences of the ordinary soldier
and, at the other, a fresh analysis of the high command. What has often
been missing in the past, but is now being better addressed, is the study of
junior and middle-ranking generals – those commanding brigades, divisions
and corps – whose part is of equal significance and interest. It is hoped the
present book will help to fill this gap in the historiography of that war.

The man

Unlike most Irish generals, Bulfin was not from the landed gentry. Nevertheless, he was brought up imbued with the values and ethos, reinforced by his time at Stonyhurst, of a typical late Victorian public schoolboy. Essentially, these reflected a muscular Christian faith and a belief in the Empire, grounded in a strong sense of duty: service above self. As Peter Parker put it, 'The schools and their ethos exacted a loyalty which seems to have been virtually unshakeable' throughout the Great War.[2]

Unfashionable in our more egalitarian and self-centred age, these values were extended to the ideal of the British officer of the late-nineteenth century, for whom a paternalistic responsibility to one's soldiers was central. Relations between officers and men were far from familiar, but they were founded on mutual respect and often a degree of affection; other ranks admired bravery in their officers but were suspicious of foolhardy glory-seeking, hoping their commanders knew their job and would take care of them. In an age of deference, soldiers expected their officers to be gentlemen and maintain a certain distance.

This basis of leadership, especially amongst platoon and company commanders, provided the backbone to a regimental system able to sustain morale and discipline through the long four years of world war – the British Army was the only one that did not break. Bulfin expected nothing less from his officers or himself.

In accepting the often high casualties incurred in the Great War, generals such as Bulfin were not so much callous as seeing it to be their duty not to let their personal feelings overcome their responsibilities to wage war – a mindset not confined to British generals. Nevertheless, such a stoic and unsqueamish view can be difficult for later generations to understand or accept.

For many British officers the regiment was – and still is – central to their loyalties, even after leaving the colours. For Bulfin this was no different. Indeed, he was Colonel of his Regiment for twenty-five years. From an early age he learnt to put his men first and, even as a senior officer, he always retained a strong empathy for the regimental officer and soldier. Bulfin's 1914 diary, and his letter to Edmonds about Second Ypres, demonstrate that he never lost this touch.

Losing his father at a young age, and then his elder brother Joseph and sisters, must have had an impact. Bulfin's steely will would have been partly forged by this. Nevertheless, despite photographs and portraits depicting him as long-faced and often gloomy, he had a lighter side. Good company, with a lively sense of humour, his appreciation of the importance of concert parties and regimental bands, to maintain his troops' morale, was evidence of this.

A further key influence was his Christian faith. He was a proud Catholic[3] and devout Jesuit, his ADC's diary carefully recording his weekly attendance at Mass, even at the height of Second Ypres and Loos. His preface to the Stonyhurst War Record (see Chapter 1) reflected his moral compass: 'Honour all men, love the brotherhood, fear God, honour the King.'

The fact that Bulfin was Irish as well as Catholic was not unusual in itself. Many such served in the Army in the war, but few reached senior rank and none climbed higher than Bulfin. In an age when suspicion of Catholics was still prevalent, and when Home Rule for Ireland had been a dominant political issue in the run-up to the Great War, this was exceptional. Although Bulfin left his country of birth at an early age, he returned a number of times, firstly to go up to Trinity before joining a local militia and, penultimately, to be given an honorary doctorate by his old university. He also married a fellow Irish Catholic. The time he spent serving under General Sir William Butler, another Irish Catholic, in Cape Town would have given him an even stronger sense of identity and loyalty to his mother country – and possibly also a wariness of politics. Added to this was the fact that many generations of the family canvassed and fought for nationalist and republican causes, both inside and outside Ireland. Bulfin never lost his Irishness.

An obvious question is this: why then was he trusted so much by the British establishment? It is inconceivable that the Army was unaware of his family connection to those involved in the Easter Rising and later War of Independence. Despite this, throughout his career he was seen as a loyal and patriotic soldier of the Empire. Today it may appear difficult to reconcile these seeming contradictions. One historian, well versed in the complexity of Irish loyalties, has commented:

There is a whole lost class, that of the 'Castle Catholic' military/ imperial class, who combined a belief in Empire with a desire for Irish self-determination and whose memory needs to be retrieved. Theirs is a strong and honourable tradition, now largely air-brushed from history.[4]

In the letters left by his cousin William there is no mention of Edward, and it is clear that the nationalist side of his family, not surprisingly, had largely cut ties with him during his adult life.[5] Nevertheless, the passage of time has led to a growing awareness of Edward Bulfin's achievements, and he deserves to be better known.

The general

Generals, on all the warring sides, are sometimes thought of as fully formed when the Great War started. It is easy to neglect the fact that, whilst the first war of the industrial age unfolded in all its technological complexity and ferocity, they were still learning and developing as commanders.

The small regular British Army, with its experience of the Boer War, had seen more recent fighting than the continental conscript armies of France and Germany. In the aftermath of South Africa it had digested many lessons in battlecraft and the development of initiative. This gave the British Expeditionary Force, for its size, a distinct tactical edge in 1914; but many of the lessons learnt in South Africa had little relevance for the sheer scale of what was to come. Indeed, the infantry's tendency, even as late as Second Ypres, to dig in on forward slopes to gain better fields of fire, as they had done on the veldt, incurred huge casualties from crushing German artillery.

As with most of his generation, Bulfin had earned his spurs during the Boer War, in his case as a brigade-major and then column commander. The hard marching and fighting under Methuen, in particular, had taught him much and given him a steely core and an adaptable mind. But the intervening years offered little hint of what was to happen to his career in 1913. Bulfin's appointment to command the Army's premier infantry brigade, despite his not having attended staff college or commanded a battalion, on the face of it seems difficult to explain. However, it can only be a clear sign that the Army recognized his considerable soldierly and leadership qualities. Patronage would doubtless have played a part: it was less important than a generation earlier, but not dead. It is not clear which of his previous superiors would have been key in championing him, but Sir Charles Douglas was his most likely patron. What this does demonstrate is that the pre-war Army was more meritocratic than it is often given credit for.

Bulfin was to prove the Army right. One of a small band of outstanding brigade commanders in 1914, he was admired throughout the BEF as a stout-hearted warrior. Haig's 'tower of strength' accolade, given to him during the fighting on the Chemin des Dames above the Aisne, was reinforced by Bulfin's stubborn resolve, initiative and fighting spirit in the desperate days at First Ypres. His powers of leadership and command were rewarded with promotion in the field to major general. He was even remembered in an Australian obituary as having 'Won Fame at Ypres'.[6]

Unquestionably, 1915 was a miserable year for him. Not fully recovered from his wounds, and given the impossible job of hastily marshalling together unprepared staff and units into a fighting formation – a 'rotten arrangement' – he and 28th Division were soon struggling in the Ypres Salient. Learning to shoulder the wider and more complex responsibilities of divisional command epitomized the sharp learning curve demanded of many generals, all at a time when the Army was undergoing the largest expansion in its long history. It comes as no surprise that he must have found this one of the most challenging times of his career.

Once Second Ypres started, he proved himself once again a doughty fighter, but his division paid a terrible price for holding this sacrosanct soil with such stoic courage. The lack of an effective artillery response, against German shelling often burying his soldiers alive, was such a handicap that it turned into a political scandal. Moreover, the Army's adherence to an offensive spirit, and its stubborn doctrine of retaking lost ground at all costs – despite its saving Ypres – exposed many weaknesses in the Army's approach to fighting on the Western Front. Second Ypres also served to highlight the frequent inability of senior commanders, without radio communication, to influence the battle once it was joined. Bulfin learnt some hard lessons during this bitter struggle. What he would not have known then was that serving under Allenby at this time would rescue his later career.

Loos was his nadir. His division, thrown late into battle by the high command and then handled recklessly by Gough, never recovered any coherence or striking power. Bulfin, still in poor health, was unable to influence effectively the close-quarter fighting around the Hohenzollern Redoubt, and exasperation overtook him by the time his third brigade was ordered to reinforce disaster. Although Bulfin had gained useful experience in divisional defence at Second Ypres, he made a poor job of trying to mount coordinated attacks in the chaotic and labyrinthine conditions of Loos. He knew he had not performed well at Loos and acknowledged that Edmonds had let him off lightly in the official history.

Doubtless worn out by a long year of fighting, by the end of 1915 Haig's description of him as his 'tower of strength' had a hollow ring to it. However, standing up to Hubert Gough and being sent home to rest was, perversely, a lucky break for Bulfin. He did not accompany his old division, outcast to Salonika, but was given the task of raising and training a territorial division. It seemed an unpromising appointment for someone who, under more propitious circumstances, could have expected a corps command by then. Nevertheless, it was a wise one, offering him breathing space to recover his strength and confidence. More importantly, commanding 60th London Division gave Bulfin the chance to exercise his exceptional powers as a trainer and organizer, something for which he had gained notice when preparing 2 Brigade for war in 1913/14. It also allowed him precious time to weld his Londoners into a fighting formation with a renowned identity and esprit de corps, an opportunity denied him with 28th Division. With his customary drive, he threw himself into the task.

An unnamed commanding officer ('T. B. L.'), during Bulfin's time commanding 60th Division, made some revealing remarks about him:

> As a man his greatness was due to the fact that he set his house of defence very high. He showed this by his devotion to duty and his care for the private soldier. Officers of the old Expeditionary Force had a sense of duty which came as a revelation to us civilian soldiers, and Bulfin showed it by his actions and his behaviour more than any other that I met. He inspired us by his mere presence, and his influence extended down through the lowest files of the non-commissioned officers to the men in the ranks … The situation was at times unpleasant, especially when he took you aside and spoke to you very quietly and low. At such time he fixed you with two steel-grey eyes, and the rays from these seemed to go like gimlets through your breast-bone and meet somewhere in your spinal marrow. But, if his criticism was severe, his praise, when it came, was generous and unstinted … this spirit of aiming at far more

than you ever thought possible he instilled into the furthest corners of every unit, great and small, and it was that, I believe, that made us so great a division.[7]

After 60th Division had started to gain a solid reputation under Vimy Ridge, the next posting to Salonika, rather than the expected Somme offensive, could have sunk him into oblivion. But the demand for reinforcements to the Egyptian Expeditionary Force, under Allenby's new command in 1917, gave Bulfin his greatest career opportunity since taking command of 2 Brigade in 1913. Allenby knew his man, and the recommendation for corps command was Bulfin's chance to exercise high command and reach the apogee of his career. Released from the static confines of the Western Front, Bulfin, like many generals – and none more so than Allenby – flourished in the more mobile and open environment of the Palestine campaign. General Shea was not alone in 'finding great happiness to fight there'.[8]

Not everyone enjoyed serving under the 'Bull', but Bulfin evidently did so; he was not a man to be pushed about. Without doubt, what allowed Bulfin to show his powers of leadership and organization to the full was that he knew he was trusted, a comfort he had not enjoyed under Gough at Loos. Allenby, in his own words, understood that 'when a man knows he is trusted, he can do things'.[9]

Bulfin, without the brilliance of Chetwode or the dash of 'Light Horse Harry' Chauvel, was seen, in contrast, by some as a 'battering ram' and a 'bludgeon',[10] descriptions he resented. However, the tasks given him in Palestine, particularly at Megiddo, required a degree of battering – to harness mass and overwhelming power at the decisive point, in order to penetrate the Ottoman defences.

Bulfin could not have been a better exemplar of why a hardened infantry general was needed in such times as the breakthrough at Third Gaza, the advance through the Judean hills to Jerusalem and the relentless pursuit at Megiddo the following year. That is why Allenby had chosen him as a corps commander, and without him Allenby would never have succeeded at Third Gaza and Megiddo. *The Times*, in its obituary of Bulfin, wrote that 'Perhaps no British General of his time understood so well the temper of British infantry and what could be expected of them'[11] – one might add, Indian troops as well.

But this 'battering ram' label does raise images of lack of imagination or care for casualties. Of course, to achieve such success, strength of purpose and a certain ruthlessness were vital. Nevertheless, such large-scale operations – he had five divisions and unprecedented artillery support under command at Megiddo – required a considerable degree of care and imagination in planning and preparation, as well as in execution. Indeed, Bulfin's tendency at times to micro-manage could irritate his subordinates. His care for his soldiers is well documented, but how imaginative he was is more difficult to evaluate. If obstinacy, as shown at Second Ypres and Loos – where he had little option but to comply with the overall plan of battle – equates to lack of imagination, he stands charged as such. But the nature of command in battle is more complex than that: the flip side of obstinacy or stubbornness is often steadfastness and resolve. The initiative he showed at Modder River and during the First Ypres counter-attacks certainly required imagination. Perhaps one gets closer to Bulfin's perspective on the subject by noting his somewhat ungrateful remark, in conversation with Dom Bede Camm in Cairo in 1918, that 'Haig has no more imagination than my boot.'[12] Gertrude Bell, not one to respect those of inferior intellect, sought Bulfin's counsel in Baghdad in 1922, and thought him 'very quick and clever in his appreciation of people'.[13] Bulfin was no dullard.

He was to show these same characteristics of firmness of purpose, dependability and some ruthlessness once again, in his decisive putting down of the Egyptian uprising in 1919. His refusal of the police role in Ireland the next year should not have surprised anyone who knew Bulfin. As *The Times* obituary wrote, 'He had moral as well as physical courage, and his readiness to speak his mind to superior authority did little to further his own interests.'[14]

In 1933 Allenby penned a tribute, inevitably fulsome, to 'his old and valued friend' for Bulfin's regiment. But his Chief ended with some telling words: 'There is no one I would rather have as a colleague in battle; no one I would less like to have as an opponent.'[15]

Bulfin was an admirable soldier, drawn from an adventurous Irish family steeped in its country's turbulent history. The story of his trials and triumphs of generalship, the considerable contribution he made to Allied victory in the First World War, and his place in the birth pangs of the modern Middle East deserve better recognition, not only in Britain but in Ireland too.

Appendix

The Career of General Sir Edward Bulfin KCB CVO

Date	Rank & Appointment	Place
6 November 1862	Born	Rathfarnham, Dublin
1873–1883	Education	Stonyhurst, Kensington, Trinity College Dublin
1884–1896	Lieutenant and Captain, 2nd Bn The Yorkshire Regt	Ireland, England, India and Burma (Kachin Hills)
1897–1898	Captain, Garrison Adjutant	Richmond and Dover
1898–1899	Captain, ADC & Assistant Military Secretary to C-in-C	Cape Town
1899–1902	Captain, Bde-Maj and then DAAG 9 Infantry Brigade, Bde-Maj 4 Cavalry Brigade, Major, Column commander	Boer War, South Africa
1902–1904	Brevet Lieutenant Colonel, DAAG 2nd Division	Aldershot
1904–1906	Lieutenant Colonel, Second in Command, 1st Bn Royal Welch Fusiliers	Aldershot
1906–1910	Colonel, AA&QMG, Cape of Good Hope District	Cape Town
1911–1913	Brigadier General, GOC Essex Infantry Brigade (TF)	Brentwood, Essex
June 1913–November1914	Brigadier General, GOC 2 Infantry Brigade. Promoted Major General 26 Oct 14, appointed Colonel of the Regiment, wounded 1 Nov 14	Aldershot, France and Belgium. BEF's Retreat from Mons, Marne, Aisne and First Ypres
December 1914–October 1915	Major General, GOC 28th Division	Winchester, Ypres Salient and Loos
December 1915–August 1917	Major General, GOC 60th (London) Division	Warminster, Arras, Salonika and Egypt

Date	Rank & Appointment	Place
August 1917–March 1919	Lieutenant General, GOC XXI Corps	Palestine, Lebanon and Syria
March–November 1919	Acting C-in-C EEF and GOC XX Corps	Egyptian Uprising
1920	Turned down Ireland post, TA role.	England
December 192–August 1923	Commissioner for the Disposal of Surplus Stores in India and Iraq	India and Iraq
May 1925	Promoted General	
January 1926	Retired	
20 August 1939	Died	Boscombe, Bournemouth

Notes

Introduction
1. Jones, Spencer (ed.), *Stemming the Tide: Officers and Leadership in the British Expeditionary Force 1914* (Helion, Solihull, 2013).
2. Haig diary: he refers to his 'tower of strength' twice, 20 September 1914 and 1 November 1914.
3. Robertson papers, Allenby's letter to CIGS, 19 July 1917.

Chapter 1: 1862–1898 Early Life (pp. 1–17)
1. *Times History of the War in South Africa 1899–1902* ed. by L. S. Amery (London 1902), Vol. II, 350.
2. Barnett, Corelli, *Britain and Her Army 1509–1970: A Military, Political and Social Survey* (Allen Lane The Penguin Press, London, 1970) 314–15. However, Ian Beckett, in his book *The Army and the Curragh Incident 1914* (Army Records Society, 1986), questions the conception that the Army's highest ranks were dominated by the 'Anglo-Irish', one study showing that of the 108 major generals on the active list in July 1914 only 12 of the 89 whose origins could be identified, were Irish – and two of these were Catholic (p. 3). Bulfin was a brigadier general at the time.
3. Summary of Conveyances held by Estate Solicitors for Woodtown Park, Rathfarnham.
4. The term 'Castle Catholic' was coined by Irish republicans to refer to those Catholics who identified themselves with the British establishment, centred on Dublin Castle. It applied particularly to those wealthy middle class Catholics who lived on the south side of Dublin City. Another label was 'West Briton', used by William Bulfin, Edward's first cousin.
5. *Freeman's Journal*, January 1871.
6. Stonyhurst College term reports 1873–6, Stonyhurst College Archives.
7. *Stonyhurst Magazine* No. 341, July 1940, 393–4.
8. O'Connor, Steven, *Irish Officers in the British Forces, 1922–45* (Palgrave Macmillan, London, 2014) 62–3. One who followed Bulfin to Stonyhurst was Paul Kenna, whose parents were from Co. Meath and who would win his Victoria Cross at Omdurman with the 21st Lancers. Mortally wounded in command of a yeomanry brigade during the calamitous Gallipoli campaign in August 1915, he is buried in a seldom visited graveyard on the lonely promontory of Lala Baba hill overlooking Suvla Bay. Coincidentally, he lies alongside many soldiers of Bulfin's own regiment, who had been the first to land and take that hill.

9. *Stonyhurst Magazine* No. 341, July 1940, 391.

10. Cardinal Manning Papers, Diocese of Westminster Archives Ma 2/7/10. Memorandum of Association, 24 February 1877.

11. Ibid. Letter from Monsignor Capel to Canon Gilbert, Maundy Thursday 1877.

12. Register of Enrolled Students, Trinity College Dublin Archives. Bulfin is listed as aged twenty-one.

13. Army List 1882.

14. Ibid. 1884.

15. In the 1740s regiments were named after their colonels. Serving in Flanders at the time were two regiments commanded by a Colonel Howard, one by Thomas Howard and the other by Charles Howard. A means of distinguishing between the two was vital. The answer was simple. The senior regiment, later the 3rd of Foot, wore facings of buff. That of Charles Howard wore green. So it was that these two regiments became 'The Buff Howards', shortened to 'The Buffs', and the other, 'The Green Howards'.

16. Jeffery, Keith, *Field Marshal Sir Henry Wilson: A Political Soldier* (Oxford University Press, 2006) 11.

17. Powell, Geoffrey and Powell, John, *The History of the Green Howards: Three Hundred Years of Service* (Pen & Sword, Barnsley, 2002), 105. Bulfin sailed from Portsmouth to Bombay in the troopship *Euphrates*.

18. *Stonyhurst Magazine* No. 341, July 1940, 391.

19. During the Crimean War, in September 1855, the Russians had built substantial defences around Sevastopol, one strongpoint being the Redan facing the British. The Green Howards, then the 19th Foot, formed part of the assault. Casualties were high, with most of the senior officers hit. A seventeen-year-old Lieutenant Dunham Massy, left commanding the Grenadier Company, was first into the Redan and, although badly wounded, stood on the wall to encourage his men forward. For the rest of his life he was known as 'Redan' Massy. He won immediate promotion to Captain, more rewarding in those days than receiving the newly minted Victoria Cross. This event would have been vivid to those serving some thirty-eight years later in Burma. See *The History of the Green Howards*, 93–4.

20. *Green Howards Gazette* Vol.1, 1893, 100.

21. Ibid. Vol. XLIII, No. 546, 1939, 113–14.

22. *Catholic Encyclopaedia* entry on General Sir William Butler.

23. Lady Wolseley to General Sir Garnet Wolseley, letter 25 December 1884, quoted in McCourt, Edward, *Remember Butler; The Story of Sir William Butler* (Routledge & Kegan Paul, London, 1967) 173.

24. Beckett, Ian, *Oxford Dictionary of National Biography* entry on General Sir William Butler, Vol. 9, 237–40.

25. McCourt, Edward, *Remember Butler; The Story of Sir William Butler* (Routledge and Kegan Paul, London 1967) 140.

26. Ibid. 141.

27. *GHG* Vol. V, No. 60, March 1898.
28. Butler, Sir William, *Sir William Butler: An Autobiography* (Constable, London, 1911) 387.
29. Ibid. 387–8.
30. Ibid. 400.
31. Letter from John Bulfin, Bulfin family papers.
32. Headlam, Cecil (ed.), *Milner Papers 1897–9* (Cassell, London, 1931) 402–3.
33. Butler, Elizabeth, *From Sketch-Book and Diary* (Adam & Charles Black, London, 1909) Part III 'The Cape', 91–123.
34. *The Sketch*, 16 December 1914, 11.
35. Butler, Elizabeth, op. cit. 91-123.
36. Ibid.
37. Butler, Sir William, op. cit. 449.
38. McCourt, op. cit. 227.
39. Ibid. 230.
40. Strachan, Hew, *The Politics of the British Army* (Oxford University Press, 1997) 102–3.
41. McCourt, op. cit. 230.
42. Butler, Elizabeth, op. cit. 91–123.
43. *The Times* obituary of General Sir Edward Bulfin, 22 August 1939.
44. Strachan, op. cit. 116–17.
45. Henry Wilson was very much the 'political general' of Bulfin's generation. There is an illuminating vignette from Bernard Fergusson, who was ADC to Wavell some years later: 'When I first went to serve with him [Wavell], I made some jejeune remark about Henry Wilson having been "a political general"; he took me up on this cliché, and listened to my flounderings as he made me define exactly what I meant. I don't think he held much of a brief for Henry Wilson, but he did at least impress on me that it was part of a soldier's training to understand the ways of politics without becoming involved in them.' Fergusson, Bernard, *Wavell: Portrait of a Soldier* (Collins, London, 1961) 95.

Chapter 2: 1899–1902 The Boer War – 'No end of a lesson' (pp. 18–44)
1. Pakenham, Thomas, *The Boer War* (Weidenfeld & Nicholson, London, 1979) 84.
2. *London Gazette*, 10 November 1899.
3. Dixon, Norman, *On the Psychology of Military Incompetence* (Jonathan Cape, London, 1976) 59.
4. Colvile, Maj. Gen. Sir Henry, *The Work of the 9th Division in South Africa 1900* (Edward Arnold, London, 1901) 23–4.
5. Extract from letter from Michael Bulfin to his brother William, 14 January 1900 (from Derrinlough), National Library of Ireland, MS 13811 (3).
6. Kinnear, Alfred, *To Modder River with Methuen* (J.W. Arrowsmith, Bristol, 1900) 67.

7. Methuen to his wife, 18–21 November 1899, quoted in Maj. Gen. Sir Frederick Maurice and staff, *History of the War in South Africa 1899–1902* (Hurst & Blackett, London, 1906) Vol. I, 214.

8. Belfield, Alfred, to his wife 20 May 1900 (146/118), Belfield Papers, 8111-29-1, National Army Museum, London.

9. P. S. Methuen to M. E. Methuen, 19 November 1899, Methuen Papers, Wiltshire and Swindon History Centre.

10. Methuen to Colonel Verner, quoted in Pakenham, op. cit. 189. Also *The Times History of the War in South Africa 1899–1902* ed. by L. S. Amery (London, 1902) Vol. II, 322.

11. Farwell, Byron, *The Great Boer War* (Allen Lane, London, 1976) 91.

12. Gurney, Russell, *History of the Northamptonshire Regiment 1742–1934* (Gale & Polden, Aldershot, 1935) 287.

13. Ibid. 288.

14. Conan Doyle, Sir Arthur, *The Great Boer War* (London, 1901) 133.

15. Kinnear, op. cit. 76.

16. For the British, the victory at Belmont was at a cost of 4 officers and 71 men killed, and 21 officers and 199 wounded, against some 100 Boer deaths; in 9 Brigade's case, the Northumberlands suffered the most heavily, with 12 killed and 40 wounded.

17. Pemberton, W. Baring, *Battles of the Boer War* (Pan Books, London, 1969) 51.

18. Pakenham, op. cit. 191.

19. Kruger, Rayne, *Good-bye Dolly Gray* (Cassell, London, 1959), 112. The officer in question was Major Plumbe of the Royal Marines, accompanied by his Jack Russell 'Dickie'.

20. Methuen's Dispatches dated 19 February 1900, TNA, WO 105/6.

21. Report on the Action at Enslin by Colonel Money CB Acting GOC 9th Brigade, 26 November 1899, TNA WO 32/7891.

22. Report on Enslin by Lord Methuen, 26 November 1899, TNA WO 32/7891.

23. Pakenham, op. cit. 192.

24. Kinnear, op. cit. 99,100.

25. Ibid, 103.

26. Menpes, Mortimer, *War Impressions Being a Record in Colour* (Adam & Charles Black, London, 1901) facing plate 42.

27. Methuen to Buller 2 December 1899, TNA WO 132/15.

28. *The Times History of the War in South Africa 1899-1902* ed. by L. S. Amery (London 1902) Vol. II, 350.

29. Maurice, op. cit. 253–4.

30. Major-General Pole-Carew's Report on the part taken by the IXth Brigade during the action at Modder River of 28 November 1899, dated 29 November 1899, TNA WO 132/15.

31. Wood, Walter, *The Northumberland Fusiliers* (Grant Richards, London, 1901) 170.

32. Pemberton, op. cit. 74.

33. *The Times History of the War in South Africa 1899–1902,* Vol. 2, 359.

34. Walker, H. M, *History of the Northumberland Fusiliers* (John Murray, London, 1919) 432.

35. Pole-Carew Dispatch 29 November 1899, TNA 132/15.

36. Methuen's Report on Modder River, TNA WO 132/15.

37. Methuen's order of the day after Modder River, 30 November 1899, TNA WO 132/15.

38. Pemberton, op. cit. 75.

39. Pole-Carew, a close member of the Roberts ring, was given to writing frequently to his old master, never wasting an opportunity to undermine Buller, as well as his own divisional commander. From the Modder River, he wrote on 21 December to the new Commander-in-Chief en route: 'Methuen did on the 11th at Magersfontein exactly what I think I told you ... I hoped he would not do. He rammed his stupid head against the strongest part of the Boer position, he could find – with the result heartrending – such a magnificent lot of men so mishandled! He has taken the stuffing out of the whole division – and now barring, perhaps, his personal staff – no man trusts him a yard.' Pole-Carew letter to Roberts, 21 December 1899, Earl Roberts Papers 7101-23-59, NAM, London.

40. Belfield, H. E., letter to his wife 19 February 1900 (146/48), 8111-29-1 NAM, London.

41. Jeffery, Keith, 'The Irish Soldier in the Boer War', chapter in *The Boer War: Direction, Experience and Image,* ed. by John Gooch (Frank Cass, London, 2000) 145–6.

42. Letter from Michael Bulfin to his brother William, 26 September 1900, National Library of Ireland, MS 13811 (3).

43. Pugin, the great Victorian designer and architect, famous for the interior of the Palace of Westminster, designed the Abbey in 1860; it was the first Benedictine monastery to be built in England since the Reformation.

44. Two years later, Roberts defended Methuen in the House of Lords: 'But I confess that when I made a careful survey of the Boer position I came to the conclusion that Lord Methuen had been given an almost impossible task. When I arrived at the Modder River... with a view of operating for the relief of Kimberley, I had at my disposal 45,000 men and 136 guns, of which 6,000 were mounted. This enabled me to make a wide turning movement, which with Methuen's smaller force was impossible ... I came to the conclusion that Lord Methuen could not be blamed for the failure to relieve Kimberley, and I decided, therefore, to keep him in his command.' Extract from Parliamentary Debates CIV, 10 March 1902. Part of lengthy supportive comments made by Lord Roberts in the House of Lords on the occasion of Lord Methuen's capture by the Boers at Tweebosch on 7 March 1902.

45. Historians customarily split the Boer War into three phases, the first being Buller's attempts to relieve the three besieged towns; the second, Roberts' arrival and driving the Boers from Bloemfontein and Pretoria, before his departure from South Africa

at the end of 1900; the third phase was Kitchener's guerrilla war of 1901–2 against the 'bitter-enders', with its blockhouses, concentration camps and mobile columns.

46. Belfield, H. E., letter to his wife 29 April 1900 (146/102), 8111-2901, NAM, London.

47. *ODNB* entry on Charles Douglas by Edward Spiers, Vol. 16, 636.

48. Robertson, William, *From Private to Field Marshal* (Constable, London, 1921) 195.

49. Miller, Stephen, *Lord Methuen and the British Army; Failure and Redemption in South Africa* (Frank Cass, London, 1999) 188.

50. Gurney, op. cit. 295.

51. Walker, op. cit. 444.

52. de Wet, Christiaan, *Three Years War* (Archibald Constable, London, 1902) chapter VII.

53. Pakenham, op. cit. 436.

54. Jeffery, op. cit. 147.

55. Belfield, H. E. letter to his wife 22 July 1900 (146/176), 8111-29-1, NAM, London.

56. Walker, op. cit. 446.

57. Gurney, op. cit. 298.

58. Belfield, H. E. letter to his wife 16 August 1900 (146/215), 8111-29-1, NAM, London.

59. Guest, Herbert, *With Lord Methuen and the 1st Division* (Klerksdorp, South Africa, 1902) 78.

60. Walker, op. cit. 447.

61. *The Times History of the War in South Africa 1899-1902* ed. by L. S. Amery (Sampson Low, Marston and Co., London, 1906), Vol. IV, 432. The Official History was similarly complimentary: 'Methuen took up the pursuit almost unaided … Methuen redeemed his earlier failures by his skill in this campaign.' Major General Sir Frederick Maurice and staff *History of the War in South Africa 1899-1902* (Hurst & Blackett, London, 1906) Vol. III, 450.

62. *GHG* Vol. VIII, No. 96, March 1901, 222.

63. Kitchener to Roberts, 24 November 1901, Earl Roberts papers, NAM, 7101/23.

64. *The Times History of the War in South Africa 1899–1902*, Vol. V, notes to 513–4.

65. Ibid., Vol. V, 514.

66. Ibid., Vol. V, 514.

67. Kruger, op. cit. 479.

68. *GHG* Vol. XI, No. 130, January 1904, 149.

69. Beckett, Ian, *The Victorians at War* (Hambledon Continuum, London, 2003) 241.

Chapter 3: 1902–1914 Inter-War Years (pp. 45–56)

1. Bulfin's War Office service records.

2. *Officers of the Royal Welch Fusiliers*, compiled by Major E. L. Kirby, 1997, 17.

3. The Green Howard COs in 1904 were as follows: 1st Battalion, based in Sheffield, commanded by Col Granville Egerton, formerly of the Seaforth Highlanders, born

in May 1859 and promoted Lt Col in May 1903. A veteran of Roberts' march to Kandahar, Tel-el-Kabir, Khartoum, and ended the First War commanding the 52nd Lowland Division in Gallipoli. 2nd Battalion, based in Cawnpore, India, commanded by Lt Col James Fearon, born in October 1856, promoted Lt Col in September 1902. A veteran of the Nile Expedition, the Tirah campaign and the Boer War, taking part in the battle of Paardeberg; a close friend and neighbour of Bulfin at Walmer, Kent, *Officers of the Green Howards 1688–1931* by Major M.L. Ferrar (Belfast, 1931) 281, 230.

4. *Officers of the Royal Welch Fusiliers* compiled by Major E. L. Kirby 1997, 9.

5. *Regimental Records of the Royal Welch Fusiliers* compiled by A. D. L. Cary and S. McCance, Vol. II 1816–1914, 304–7.

6. Death certificate, registered (after post-mortem) 7 July 1906.

7. Meinertzhagen, Richard, *Army Diary:1899–1926* (Oliver & Boyd, Edinburgh and London, 1960) 27–8.

8. *GHG*, 'Regimental Personalities' by General Sir Harold Franklyn, Vol. LXVI, No. 779, February 1959, 290–1.

9. Bulfin maintained his Green Howards connections whilst serving with the RWF. He attended the officers' annual dinner at the Ritz on 4 June 1908, whilst enjoying home leave from the South African winter.

10. A brave and devoted CO, Arthur Hadow was brought out of retirement in 1914 to raise the 10th Service battalion of his regiment, but was killed commanding them at Hill 70, during the battle of Loos, on 26 September 1915.

11. *The Times*, 8 November 1910.

12. Ibid., 1 August 1911.

13. *Report on Army Manoeuvres 1912*, TNA WO 279/47.

14. MacDiarmid, D. S., *The Life of Lt. Gen. Sir James Grierson* (Constable, London, 1923) 248.

15. Charteris, John, *Field-Marshal Earl Haig* (Cassell, London, 1929) 65–6.

16. Bulfin's War Office service records.

17. Charteris, John, *At G.H.Q.* (Cassell, London, 1931) 5.

18. Ryan Memoirs, quoted in Sheffield, Gary, *The Chief: Douglas Haig and the British Army* (Aurum Press, London, 2011) 61.

19. Sheffield, op. cit. 61.

20. Letter from Bulfin to Abbott of Downside concerning his son Eddie, 14 January 1913, from Woodtown Park, Rathfarnham, Co. Dublin. Downside Abbey Archives.

21. Aldershot Command: Comments on the Training Season 1913, TNA WO 279/53, 15, 16, 38.

22. Sutherland, John and Webb, Margaret, *All the Business f War: The British Army Exercises of 1913, the British Expeditionary Force and the Great War* (in association with the Towcester and District Local History Society, 2012) 24–33.

23. Ibid, 33.

24. Sheffield, op. cit. 62–3.

25. Beckett, Ian (ed.), *The Army and the Curragh Incident 1914* (Army Records Society, 1986). Telegram from H. P. Gough to J. E. Gough, Curragh, 20 March 1914, 197.

26. Ibid. Extract from Diary of Lt. Gen. Sir Douglas Haig 21 March 1914, 199.

27. Ibid. Haig diary 25 March 1914, 199.

28. Mallinson, Allan, *Too Important for the Generals: Losing and Winning the First World War* (Bantam Press, London, 2016) 326.

29. Gough, General Sir Hubert, *The Fifth Army* (Hodder & Stoughton, London, 1931) and *Soldiering On* (Arthur Baker, London, 1954).

30. Falls, Cyril, *Armageddon 1918* (Weidenfeld & Nicolson, London, 1964) 59.

Chapter 4: 1914 'A Tower of Strength' – The Retreat from Mons and the Battles of the Marne and Aisne (pp. 57–76)

1. Charteris, John, *At GHQ* (Cassell, London, 1931) 3.

2. *OH*, Vol. 1, Military Operations in France and Belgium August–October 1914, 10–11.

3. Mallinson, Allan, *Too Important for the Generals: Losing and Winning the First World War* (Bantam Press, London, 2016)

4. Haig, Douglas, *War Diaries and Letters 1914–1918*, ed. by Gary Sheffield and John Bourne (Weidenfeld & Nicolson, London, 2005). Haig started his diary on 29 July 1914, and included the events of 4 August, when the mobilization order was received at 5.30 pm.

5. Extracts from the diary of Lieutenant General Sir E. S Bulfin, KCB, CVO, who commanded the 2nd Brigade (1st Division) British Expeditionary Force 1914. 11 August, 1914 to 3 November, 1914. TNA CAB 45/140: Ypres: Authors A–L.

6. Gilbert, Adrian, *Challenge of Battle: The Real Story of the British Army in 1914* (Osprey, 2014) 134.

7. Smith-Dorrien diary 27 August 1914, TNA CAB 45/206.

8. Charteris, op. cit. 161.

9. Haig's I Corps Dispatches 24 September 1914, TNA WO 95/588. Maxse was removed from brigade command but recovered his career to command a corps by 1917. He emerged as a renowned trainer. Correlli Barnett considered him 'one of the ablest officers of his generation, a man of originality and drive, and a formidable personality'.

10. Needham., E. S., quoted in *The Great War – I Was There*, ed. by Sir John Hammerton (Amalgamated Press, London) Vol. 1, 117–18.

11. 2 Brigade War Diary, 28 August 1914, TNA WO 95/1267/1.

12. Needham, op. cit. 112.

13. *OH*, Vol. 1, Military Operations in France and Belgium August–October 1914, 242.

14. Mallinson, Allan, *1914: Fight the Good Fight* (Bantam Press, London, 2013) 407.

15. Spears, Louis, *Liaison 1914: A Narrative of the Great Retreat* (William Heinemann, London, 1930), 417.

16. Charteris, op. cit. 27.

17. *OH* Vol. 1, 269–70.
18. Hyndson, J. G. W., *From Mons to the First Battle of Ypres* (1935) 35.
19. Sheffield, Gary, *The Chief: Douglas Haig and the British Army* (Aurum Press, London, 2012) 82.
20. Harris, J. P., *Douglas Haig and the First World War* (Cambridge University Press, 2008) 83.
21. Ibid., 84.
22. Charteris, John, *Field-Marshal Earl Haig* (Cassell, London, 1929) 99.
23. Charteris, John, *At GHQ* (Cassell, London, 1931) 29.
24. Captain John Norwood was the first VC holder to be killed in the Great War.
25. Mallinson, op. cit. 416.
26. Spears, op. cit. 474.
27. Harris, op. cit. 89.
28. The patrol was led by Second Lieutenant Oswald Balfour, the nephew of Arthur Balfour, author of the Balfour Declaration.
29. Bolwell, F. A., *With a Reservist in France* (George Routledge & Sons, London, 1917) 48.
30. Extract from speech by General Sir James Willcocks DSO, Colonel of the Loyal North Lancashires, on the unveiling of the regiment's memorial near the Sugar Factory in 1923. Quoted in Kendall, Paul, *Aisne 1914: The Dawn of Trench Warfare* (The History Press, Stroud, 2012) 128, from *The Lancashire Lad*.
31. Sheffield, op. cit. 85.
32. Lomax covering letter to 2nd Brigade report, 2nd Brigade War Diary, TNA WO 95/1267.
33. Sir John French's order 16 September 1914, TNA WO 95/1235.
34. Charteris, John, *At GHQ* 39.
35. Haig Diary 20 September 1914.
36. *The Northamptonshire Regiment 1914–1918* (Gale & Polden), compiled under direction of the regimental history committee, 41.
37. 2 Brigade War Diary, 17 October 1914, TNA WO 95/1267.
38. Lieutenant General Sir William Franklyn was the father of Harold Franklyn, the subaltern who later wrote so bluntly on his CO in Cape Town in 1906.
39. Gardner, Nikolas, *Trial by Fire: Command and the British Expeditionary Force in 1914* (Contributions in Military Studies, No. 27, Praeger, Connnecticut, USA, 2003) 96.
40. Gilbert, Adrian, *Challenge of Battle: The Real Story of the British Army in 1914* (Osprey, 2014) 214.

Chapter 5: 1914 First Ypres – 'Clinging on by our eyelids' (pp. 77–94)

1. Beckett, Ian F. W., *Ypres: The First Battle 1914* (Pearson Education, Harlow, 2004) 80.
2. Charteris, John, *At GHQ* (Cassell & Co, London, 1931) 49.
3. Bulfin's diary 25.

4. LoCicero, Michael S., *'A Tower of Strength': Brigadier-General Edward Bulfin*, chapter on Brigade Command in *Stemming the Tide: Officers and Leadership in the British Expeditionary Force 1914* (Helion, Solihull, 2013) ed. Spencer Jones, 225.

5. Needham, E. S., quoted in *The Great War – I Was There* ed. Sir John Hammerton (Amalgamated Press, London) Vol. 1, 205.

6. Ibid., 205.

7. Hyndson, J. G. W. *From Mons to the First Battle of Ypres* (Wyman & Sons, London, 1932) 77. The foreword to the book is written by General Bulfin. Also see Chapter 13.

8. Bolwell, F. A., *With a Reservist in France* (Routledge, London, 1917) 75.

9. Hyndson, op. cit. 78–80.

10. Ibid. 80–1.

11. *OH Military Operations 1914*, Vol. II, 185–6.

12. Bulfin diary 26.

13. Ibid. 26–7.

14. Needham, op. cit. 205.

15. Bulfin diary 27.

16. The congratulations are recorded in field message and signal forms, contained in 2 Brigade's War Diary, TNA CAB 95/1267.

17. Coleman, Frederick, *From Mons to Ypres with French: A Personal Narrative* (Sampson, Low Marston & Co, London, 1916) 220.

18. Farrar-Hockley, Anthony, *Death of an Army* (Wordsworth Editions, Ware, 1998) 101–3.

19. Ibid. 104.

20. Quoted in *OH Military Operations 1914* Vol II, 191. From German official account by Otto Schwink, *Ypres 1914: An Official Account published by order of German General Staff* (Constable & Co, London, 1919).

21. Ibid., Vol II, 187.

22. Falls, Cyril, *The Life of a Regiment: The History of the Gordon Highlanders* Vol. IV 1914–1919 (University Press, Aberdeen, 1958) 26.

23. Bulfin diary 28.

24. Horne's letter to his wife, 27 October 1914, Horne Papers, Con Vol 1, IWM.

25. At the time of his death, Lieutenant General Sir William Franklyn was commanding the Third Army in England. He had been tasked with making a report for the Army Council on conditions in the BEF and had been travelling extensively in France. On returning to his headquarters at Luton Hoo, the home of Lady Wernher, he died suddenly and unexpectedly on the evening of 27 October 1914, aged fifty-eight. His son, Harold, was to follow his father as Colonel of the Green Howards on the death of General Bulfin in 1939 and rose to be a full general and Commander-in-Chief Home Forces in the Second World War.

26. *OH* Vol. II, 466. During First Ypres, 7th Division lost 372 officers and 9,493 other ranks.

27. The origin of the story is found in *The Immortal Salient*, a guidebook published after the war, compiled by Lt. Gen. Sir William Pulteney and Beatrix Brice, reviewed in *The Times* (Book of the Day), 3 February 1925. In the Green Howards Museum is a gavel presented by General Bulfin to the Officers Mess, made of wood from Sanctuary Wood, engraved 'In memory of Ypres October 1914'. The Wood had a special significance for him and his regiment. See the plate section.

28. Bulfin diary 29.

29. Ibid. 30.

30. *GHG* Vol. XXII, No. 261, December 1914, 142.

31. *OH*, Vol II, 304.

32. Quoted in Beckett, Ian F. W., *Johnnie Gough VC* (Tom Donovan, London, 1989) 193.

33. Carew, Tim, *The Vanished Army* (William Kimber, London, 1964) 217.

34. LoCicero, op. cit. 230.

35. Bulfin diary 30.

36. Butler, Patrick, *A Galloper at Ypres* (Fisher Unwin, London, 1920) 159–60. In the frontispiece there are charming watercolours by Lady Butler of her son's three chargers at Ypres. One, 'Brightness', has the caption in the artist's hand, 'Killed in Action'. A copy of the book is in the Prince Consort's Library, Aldershot. Patrick Butler, who rose to be a lieutenant colonel, attended Bulfin's funeral in Bournemouth in 1939 (*Green Howards Gazette*).

37. Bulfin diary 31.

38. Ibid. 31.

39. Bulfin's handwritten annotation to 'Information about the counter-attack of the 2nd Infantry Brigade, 1st Division, British Expeditionary Force, at First Battle of Ypres, in 31st October 1914, supplied by Lieut-General Sir E.S. Bulfin, K.C.B., C.V.O. – in 1914 Brigadier-General Commanding 2nd Infantry Brigade', 5. TNA CAB 45/140.

40. Ibid. 2. Bulfin's handwritten annotation to 'a hellish minute [rapid rifle fire]' notes 'Officers called it the "mad minute".'

41. Bulfin diary 32.

42. 'Information about the counter-attack etc', 3. TNA CAB 45/140.

43. *OH*, Vol. II, 337.

44. Bulfin diary 31–2.

45. Falls, Cyril, *The Life of A Regiment: The History of the Gordon Highlanders* Vol. IV 1914-1919 (University Press, Aberdeen, 1958) 20.

46. Harris, J. P., *Douglas Haig and the First World War* (Cambridge University Press, 2008) 104.

47. Beckett, op. cit.

48. Bulfin diary 32–3. Brigadier-General Edward Fanshawe came from a remarkable military family: three brothers, all of whom rose to command divisions or corps. Two would fight alongside Bulfin at First Ypres. Edward would replace the sacked

Hammersley in command of the 11 (Northern) Division after the debacle at Suvla Bay in Gallipoli in August 1915. His younger brother, Robert, was GSO1 in 1st Division until 20 September, when he took over from the sacked Davies of 6th Brigade (the latter had failed to come to Bulfin's assistance on 10 September during the battle of the Marne); Robert would command 6th Brigade throughout First Ypres.

49. Bulfin diary 33.
50. *OH*, Vol. II, 357.
51. Butler, op. cit. 171.
52. Haig diary 1 November 1914, TNA WO 256/1.
53. Bolwell, op. cit. 8.
54. Bulfin diary 34.
55. Robbins, Simon, *British Generalship on the Western Front 1914–1918: Defeat into Victory* (Frank Cass, London, 2005) 53.
56 Bourne, John, *ODNB* entry on General Sir Edward Bulfin, Vol 8, 571.

Chapter 6: 1915 Command of the 28th Division – 'A most rotten arrangement'
pp. 95–108)

1. Jones, Spencer (ed.), *Courage without Glory: The British Army on the Western Front 1915* (Helion & Co, Sollihull, 2015), xxiv.
2. Mrs Bulfin's letter to Father Ramsay at Downside School 10 November 1914, Downside Abbey Library. *The Sketch* of 16 December 1914, in its 'Small Talk' gossip page, wrote more lightly: 'General Bulfin, who had arrived home before the dispatch that made him famous, and had the pleasure of reading General French's praises while breakfasting in Sussex, is now making excellent progress. His own description of his injury (he wrote to a friend that his new great-coat had a hole in it and that a bit of wool had been blown from the back of his head) hardly did justice to the effectiveness of German shell-fire; but the coat is patched and the hurt is mended.'
3. Robbins, Simon, *British Generalship on the Western Front 1914–1918: Defeat into Victory* (Frank Cass, London, 2005) 85. Quote from Brigadier-General (then Major) Philip Howell: 'The fatal policy of trying to form new units (big units, like divisions) instead of drafting onto old ones resulted in a terribly big bill in the form of heavy casualties … even in formations like the 28th Division formed from "real good regular battalions".'
4. Of 28th Division's regular battalions, ten came from India and the remaining two from Egypt and Singapore.
5. Moody, R. S. H., *Historical Records of the Buffs (East Kent Regiment) 3rd Foot 1914–1919* (Medici Society, London, 1922) 27: 'The newly issued boots were not of proper quality: the heels came off and the nails went through. Later on, in France, the men experienced a good deal of unnecessary hardship on account of their boots, which to an infantry soldier are only of secondary importance to

his weapons.' Pearse, H. W., *History of the East Surrey Regiment* (Medici Society, London, 1923), Vol. 2, 88: 'The boots that had been issued at Winchester were by now found to be of very bad quality and gave much trouble.' The GSO1 Lord Loch's letters underlined the need for more 'gumboots' in the trenches.

6. TNA WO 107/19. Also quoted in Messenger, Charles, *Call to Arms: The British Army 1914–1918* (Weidenfeld & Nicolson, London, 2005) 65.

7. Snow, Thomas D'Oyly, 'Narrative of the 27th Division from the date of its formation to the end of its tour on the Western Front', TNA WO 95/2254, 1.

8. Ibid. 5.

9. Captain Hugh Carlton Cumberbatch's pocket diary of 1915 (unpublished and held privately by his family). This diary was traced in 2016 by the author and loaned to him by kind permission of Cumberbatch's granddaughter. A copy has now been lodged, with those of 1917 and 1918, in the IWM archives.

10. Moody, op. cit. 27.

11. Cumberbatch diary entry, 25 January 1915.

12. *OH Military Operations in France and Belgium Winter 1914–1915* Vol. III, 27.

13. Private papers of General Sir Horace Smith-Dorrien, diary entry, 8 February 1915, IWM 87/47/3.

14. By the time the three brigades had been exchanged, 28th Division had 'about 4,000 sick, 75% of whom were feet illnesses' (Loch's letter to his wife 13 February 1915, IWM box 71/12/1, file 1/2/2).

15. Smith-Dorrien diary, 17 February 1915, IWM 87/47/3.

16. Smith-Dorrien, letter to his wife, 18 February 1915, IWM 87/47/5.

17. Cumberbatch diary entry, 18 February 1915. 9 Brigade was from 3rd Division, whilst 13 and 15 (not 16, as Cumberbatch writes in error) were from 5th Division. 9 and 13 Brigades suffered similar difficulties and setbacks in holding the trenches they took over from 28th Division brigades.

18. Confidential correspondence between Sir John French and Sir Horace Smith-Dorrien concerning 27th Division's casualties in January 1915, due to frostbite and trench foot (afternote in Smith-Dorrien's own hand), Smith-Dorrien papers, IWM 87/47/7.

19. Messenger, Charles, *Call to Arms: The British Army 1914–1918* (Weidenfeld & Nicolson, London, 2005) 65.

20. Smith-Dorrien, letter to his wife, 21 January 1915, IWM 87/47/5.

21. Smith-Dorrien, letter to his wife, 6 February 1915. His efforts to return to England for some leave were being delayed: 'I am just off to see the 28th Divn … The incident which is keeping me is ridiculous … A certain Battln of new troops disgraced itself by leaving trenches & it is [*sic*] failed to re-occupy them – why I can't make out. Some-one is to blame & this is what I have to discuss. Forgive the disappointment.' (IWM 87/47/5).

22. Norman, T., *Armageddon Road: A VC's Diary 1914–1916* (Kimber, London, 1982) 102. Congreve's diary entry for 21 February 1915.

23. Loch, letter to his wife, 15 February 1915, IWM, box 71/12/1, file 1/2/2.
24. 28th Division War Diary. Memo to V Corps HQ dated 23 February 1915. TNA WO 95/2268.
25. Loch considered Wintour the best of the three brigade commanders. The Divisional War diary makes no mention of Wintour's departure, nor does the ADC's diary. He was posted to Plumer's staff at HQ Second Army as his senior administrative officer but was plagued by illness. Wintour's memoirs frustratingly finish in 1912, but he did leave a secret document recording his unhappiness at the conditions under which his brigade was operating in February 1915, with a note complaining that Bulfin never visited his troops (LHCMA, GB009 Wintour, File 3); the ADC's diary does record Bulfin visiting trenches and brigade HQs throughout this period, mentioning 85 Brigade on 13 February, but not stipulating 84 Brigade.
26. Lord Loch's letters to his wife are a fascinating treasure trove for any historian of the First World War, not only on the fighting in the Ypres Salient in 1915 but also on the culture of the Army at the time. Like most officers, he wrote to his wife on a daily basis, normally late at night before going to bed, even in the height of battle; letters often extended to four closely written pages. His wife Margaret, known as 'Mousie', on one occasion complained, 'Not necessary for you to write at such length each time – tiny line quite enough with a longer letter occasionally.' Her replies are full of promotion gossip and show a remarkable knowledge of the tactical situation on the Western Front. Loch, managing to circumvent the censor, even sent map references of trench fights to tie in with a copy of the same map she held at home. Another aspect which might surprise a modern reader was the efficient and fast postal service to and from the Salient. Loch, having chased his wife about whether she had succeeded in ordering some delicacies, had the generosity to share these amongst his brother officers: 'Loch produced asparagus and plovers' eggs for dinner' (Cumberbatch diary entry 6 April 1915).
27. Loch, letters to his wife, 20 and 21 January 1915, IWM box 71/2/1, file 1/2/1.
28. Loch, Report to HM The King, 19 April 1915, p. 6, IWM box 71/12/7, file 5/2/4.
29. Lord Loch papers. Private letter from Sir Clive Wigram, 23 April 1915, IWM box 71/12/7, file 5/2/4.
30. Cassar, George H., *Trial by Gas: the British Army at the Second Battle of Ypres* (Potomac Books, University of Nebraska Press, 2014) 23.
31. Oakey, Iris, 'Problems of Morale, Discipline and Leadership in the 28th Division January–October 1915' (MA Dissertation for University of Birmingham, Centre of First World War Studies, 2006).
32. Ibid., 39.
33. Discussion between the author and Iris Oakey, July 2016.
34. Loch, letter to his wife, 10 March 1915, IWM box 71/12/1, file 1/2/3.
35. Lady Loch, letter to her husband, 24 February 1915, Loch Papers IWM box 71/12/3, file 4/1/6.
36. Loch, letter to his wife, 18 February 1915, IWM box 71/12/1, file 1/2/2.

37. Ibid., 13 February 1915, IWM box 71/12/1, file 1/2/2.
38. Ibid., 23 February 1915, IWM box 71/12/1, file 1/2/2.
39. Cumberbatch diary, 26 February 1915.
40. Ibid., 27 February 1915.
41. Loch, letter to his wife, 25 January 1915, IWM box 71/2/, file 1/2/1.
42. Ibid., 13 February 1915, IWM box 71/2/1, file 1/2/1.
43. Home, Brig. Gen. Sir Archibald, *The Diary of a World War 1 Cavalry Officer*, ed. by Diana Briscoe (Costello, Tunbridge Wells, 1985) diary entry, 17 February 1915. Two days later, 'Sally' Home (GSO1 to 1st Cavalry Division) wrote: 'Hear 28th Div. are being relieved … This is the old story – new troops, new Officers, new everything and people expect it to work like a wound-up machine – the thing is absolutely impossible.'
44. Smith-Dorrien, letter to his wife, 27 February 1915, IWM 87/47/5.
45. Cumberbatch diary, 31 March 1915.
46. Norman, op. cit. 117. Congreve's diary entry for 23 March 1915. The brigade-major of 9 Brigade was Major Archie Wavell, later Field Marshal, who would serve again with Bulfin in Palestine and Egypt and observe him at close quarters.
47. Loch, letter to his wife, 11 April 1915, IWM box 71/12/1, file 1/2/4.
48. Cassar, op. cit. 28.
49. Smith-Dorrien papers, IWM 87/47/3 and 7.
50. Conan Doyle, Arthur, *The British Campaign in France and Flanders 1915* (Hodder & Stoughton, London, 1917) quoted on p. 42.

Chapter 7: 1915 Second Ypres – 'Desperate fighting in a desperate position' (pp. 109–123)
1. Cassar, George H., *Trial by Gas: The British Army at the Second Battle of Ypres* (Potomac Books, University of Nebraska Press, 2014) 34.
2. Bulfin, letter to Edmonds, 10 March 1925, TNA CAB 45/140.
3. Ibid.
4. 2nd Buff's War diary, TNA WO 95/2279. Also paraphrased in Moody, R. S. H., *Historical Records of the Buffs (East Kent Regiment) 3rd Foot 1914–1919* (Medici Society, London, 1922) 43.
5. Amongst the units of 50th Division was 4th Battalion the Yorkshire Regiment, commanded by a brother officer of Bulfin, Lieutenant Colonel Maurice Bell. This battalion would come under Bulfin's command for a period of the battle. The Bell family were well known ironmasters and colliery owners in the North-East of England, and Maurice was the younger brother of Gertrude Bell, the famous Arabist, whom Bulfin knew and would see more of in the Middle East in 1922.
6. *OH*, Mil Ops France and Belgium, Winter 1914–1915, 207.
7. Harington, Charles, *Plumer of Messines* (John Murray, London 1935) quoted on pp.72–3.
8. Bulfin, letter to Edmonds, 28 October 1925, TNA CAB 45/140.

9. Loch, letter to his wife, 16 March 1915, IWM Lord Loch Papers 1/2/3.

10. Ibid., 24 April 1915, IWM 1/2/4.

11. Bulfin, letter to Edmonds, 28 October 1925, TNA CAB 45/140.

12. *OH*, Vol III, 248.

13. Loch, letter to his wife, 27 April 1915, IWM 1/2/4.

14. Bulfin, letter to Edmonds, 28 October 1915, TNA CAB 45/140. His ADC's diary contains interesting details on the problems of finding suitable buildings and stabling for the divisional headquarters as well as the report centre further forward. As the Germans pushed V Corps further back to Ypres, 28th Division's report centre at Vlamertinghe received 'about 6 whizz-bangs over the house … one burst just outside the Orderlies door & made me jump like blazes.' They were forced into a 'little *estaminet*' and had to move their main HQ west to Chateau Couthove, north-west of Poperinghe. Other divisional HQs were having similar problems. Chateaux were often chosen because of the number of rooms for staff officers and clerks to work efficiently, as well as stabling and outhouses for horses and support staff. Not surprisingly, they did attract enemy attention.

15. Snow, Thomas D'Oyly, *The Confusion of Command: The War Memoirs of Lieutenant-General Sir Thomas D'Oyly Snow* (Frontline Books, London, 2011), ed. by Dan Snow and Mark Pottle, 113.

16. Ibid., 114.

17. Loch, letter to his wife, 2 May 1915, IWM 1/2/5.

18. Smith-Dorrien Papers, IWM 87/47/7.

19. *OH*, Vol. III, 295-6.

20. Loch, letter to his wife, 3 May 1915, IWM 1/2/5.

21. Snow, op. cit. 131.

22. Marden, Maj. Gen. Sir Thomas, *The History of the Welch Regiment in the Great War* (Western Mail and Echo Ltd., Cardiff, 1923) Part 2, 1914–1918, 347. Marden commanded 1st Welch during Second Ypres, and his description and critique of the battle are vivid.

23. Haldane Papers, National Library of Scotland, 10 June 1915.

24. Allenby Papers, LHCMA, GB009 KCLMA 1/6.

25. *ODNB* entry on Louis Bols by C. V. Owen, 479.

26. Loch, letter to his wife, 11 May 1815, IWM 1/2/5.

27. Dixon, John *Magnificent But Not War: The Second Battle of Ypres 1915* (Leo Cooper, Barnsley, 2003) 262.

28. Sandilands, Brig. H. R., *The Fifth in the Great War* (G. W. Grigg & Son, Dover, 1938) 99.

29. Bulfin wrote to Pereira in hospital in Rouen: 'I can't tell you how much I feel your departure … Let me thank you for all you have done under difficult circumstances. I knew your difficulties quite well and wished I could have lessened your anxieties … Get well soon and come back to us – we want you badly, but not a minute before you are fit.' 28 May 1915, Pereira Papers.

30. Terraine, John, *The First World War 1914–1918* (Macmillan, London, 1965) 67.
31. Ibid.
32. Bulfin, letter to Edmonds, 28 October 1925, TNA CAB 45/140.
33. Travers, Tim, *The Killing Ground: The British Army, the Western Front and the Emergence of Modern War 1900–1918* (first published by Allen & Unwin, London, 1987, reprinted by Pen & Sword, Barnsley, 2009) 20–1.
34. Stellenbosch was an army base during the South African war where officers were sent when relieved of command. The French had a similar expression – to be *Limogé* – referring to the town of Limoges. A later expression was to be 'degummed', from the French *degommé*.
35. Terraine, John, op.cit. xi.
36. Neillands, Robin, *The Great War Generals on the Western Front 1914–1918* (Magpie Books, London, 2004) 164.
37. Dixon, op. cit.
38. Correspondence between the author and John Dixon, 19 May 2016.

Chapter 8: 1915 Loos – 'A horrid nightmare' (pp. 124–147)

1. The opening two lines of Charles Sorley's untitled poem, found in his kit after he fell at Loos, aged twenty, on 13 October 1915. He was serving as a young captain with the Suffolks. John Masefield thought Sorley was 'potentially the greatest poet lost in the war'. His name is on the Memorial to the Missing at Loos, as well as on the memorial stone for First World War poets in Poets' Corner in Westminster Abbey.
2. Bulfin, letter to Edmonds, 11 December 1927, TNA CAB 45/120.
3. Asquith, H. H. *Memories and Reflections 1852–1927* (Cassell, London, 1928, 2 Vols.) Vol II, 106–7.
4. Joffre, *The Memoirs of Marshal Joffre*, transl. by Col. T. Bentley Mott and Lt. Col. S.J. Lowe (Geoffrey Biles, London, 1932) Vol. II, 380–1.
5. Kitchener to Hamilton, quoted in *Winston S. Churchill* ed. Martin Gilbert (Heinemann, London, 1972), Vol. III Companion, Part 2, Documents, May 1915–December 1916.
6. Lloyd, Nick, *Loos 1915* (The History Press, Stroud, first published 2006, paperback ed.) 35.
7. Haig diary, 20 June 1915.
8. Liddell Hart, Basil, *A History of World War 1914–1918* (Faber & Faber, London, 1936) 255.
9. GHQ to Haig, 23 August 1915, TNA PRO WO 95/157.
10. The 6th Battalion of Bulfin's own regiment was the first Kitchener battalion into battle in the First World War – at Suvla Bay in Gallipoli a month earlier in August. 'The long and varied annals of the British Army contain no more heart-breaking episode', bewailed Churchill of Suvla.

11. *GHG* 'Regimental Personalities' by General Sir Harold Franklyn, Vol. LXVI, No. 779, February 1959, 290–1. Franklyn, who served as a young officer under Arthur Hadow in the 2nd Battalion of the regiment in South Africa (*see* Chapter 3) thought Hadow was 'not a happy man and his only pleasure lay in the regiment to which he was devoted' and considered that being killed at Loos was 'a death which he would have welcomed'. He had also lost his twenty-one-year-old son, Gerald, only a few months earlier, killed in action at Givenchy on 15 June, serving with his father's regiment. Hadow's last letters to his wife, written up to the day he was killed, are amongst the most moving of the First World War, IWM Docs 11023.

12. Rudyard Kipling's only son, John (Jack), serving with the Irish Guards, was killed that day.

13. Lloyd, op. cit. 189.

14. 28th Division War Diary (General Staff), 23 September 1915, TNA WO 95/2268.

15. *The Complete Dispatches of Lord French* (Chapman & Hall, London, 1917), 24 September 1915.

16. Cumberbatch diary, 24 September 1915.

17. 28th Division War Diary, 25 September 1915.

18. Ibid.

19. *OH*, Mil Ops in France & Belgium, Vol. II, 352.

20. 28th Division War Diary, 26 September 1915.

21. Cowper, Colonel J. M. *The King's Own: The Story of a Royal Regiment* (Gale & Polden, Aldershot, 1957) Vol. II 1914–1950, 84–5.

22. Gough, General Sir Hubert, *The Fifth Army* (Hodder & Stoughton, London, 1931) 117.

23. James, Lawrence, *Imperial Warrior: The Life and Times of Field-Marshal Viscount Allenby 1861–1936* (Weidenfeld & Nicolson, London, 1993) 74.

24. Neillands, Robin, *The Great War Generals on the Western Front 1914–1918* (Constable & Robinson, London, 1999) 267.

25. Oakey, op. cit., note 120 on p.32.

26. The late Queen Mother's brother, Captain Fergus Bowes-Lyon, was killed in this action, serving in the Black Watch.

27. Gough, op. cit. 116.

28. Haig diary, 27 September 1915, TNA WO 256/5.

29. Cumberbatch diary, 26 September 1915.

30. Brig. Gen. Studd, letter to Cecil Pereira, from HQ 180 Bde, Warminster, 7 February 1916, Pereira Papers.

31. Private diary of Brig. Gen. C. E. Pereira, 27 September 1915, TNA WO 95/2278.

32. Ibid.

33. Ibid.

34. 2nd Buffs war diary, TNA WO 95/2279.

35. 85 Brigade War Diary, 28 September 1915, TNA WO 95/2268.

36. Col. Roberts letter to Cecil Pereira, 11 October 1915, Pereira Papers.

37. GHQ order 3 October 1915, signed by Chief of the General Staff (Lieutenant General William Robertson), TNA WO 95/159.
38. Lt. Williams, 2nd Buffs war diary, TNA WO 95/2279.
39. Cumberbatch diary, 29 September 1915.
40. Ibid., 30 September 1915.
41. Lloyd, op. cit. 194.
42. Cumberbatch diary, 30 September 1915.
43. Ibid., 1 October 1915.
44. 28th Division War Diary, TNA WO 95/2268.
45. Col. Roberts letter to Cecil Pereira, 11 October 1915, Pereira Papers.
46. Cumberbatch diary, 3 October 1915.
47. Ibid., 4 October 1915.
48. Ibid., 4 October 1915. The key page covering the events of 4 October is missing from 28th Division's War Diary held at TNA, WO 95/2268.
49. Bulfin, letter to Edmonds, 11 December 1927, TNA PRO CAB 45/120.
50. Haig diary, 4 October 1915, TNA WO 256/6.
51. Haig to GHQ, 4 October 1915, TNA WO 95/159.
52. 'Notes on Staff Work and Command in 28th Division', 6 October 1915, TNA WO 95/2268 and I Corps War Diary, October 1915, reports regarding 28th Division Operations, TNA WO 95/592.
53. 2nd East Yorks War Diary, report by Lieutenant Colonel W. A. Blake DSO, TNA WO 95/2275/1.
54. Bulfin report to I Corps, October 1915, TNA 95/2268.
55. Col. Roberts letter to Cecil Pereira, 11 October 1915, Pereira Papers.
56. Haig diary, 8 October 1915, TNA WO 256/6.
57. Ibid., 11 October 1915.
58. Cumberbatch diary, 11 October 1915.
59. Ibid., 11 October 1915.
60. Ibid., 12 October 1915. Wimereux was a major base hospital, near Boulogne.
61. Loch, letter to his wife, 14 October 1915, IWM 1/3/5.
62. Pulteney, Lt Gen Sir William, letter to Edith Londonderry dated 12 October 1915, quoted in Leask, Anthony, *Putty. From Tel-el-Kebir to Cambrai; The Life and Letters of Lieutenant General Sir William Pulteney 1861–1941* (Helion, 2015) 332.
63. Private diary of Brigadier General C. E. Pereira, 20 October 1915, TNA WO 95/2278.
64. Ibid.
65. Cumberbatch diary, 19 November 1915.
66. Spencer Jones has written a fair and well researched analysis in 'The Nadir of the Regular Army: 28th Division and the Battle for the Hohenzollern Redoubt, September – October 1915', forthcoming publication in *Journal of Military History*.
67. Bulfin, letter to Edmonds, 11 December 1927, TNA PRO CAB 45/120.
68. *OH*, Mil Ops in France & Belgium, Vol. II, 387.

69. Graves, Robert, *Goodbye to All That* (Penguin Modern Classics 1985 edition), 127.
70. Lloyd George, David, *War Memoirs* (Nicholson & Watson, London, 1933, 2 vols), Vol. 1, 487.
71. Bulfin, letter to Edmonds, 11 December 1927, TNA PRO CAB 45/120.

Chapter 9: 1916–1917 The Making of a Territorial Division: the 60th (London) Division (pp. 148–166)

1. Dalbiac, Col. P. H., *History of the 60th Division (2/2nd London Division)* (George Allen & Unwin, London, 1927) 33.
2. *GHG*, Vol. XXIII, No. 274, 1915, 170.
3. Dalbiac, op. cit. 34.
4. Ibid.
5. Letter from Military Secretary War Office to GOC-in-C Central Forces and Eastern Command 9/Gen.no./5250. (M.S.1) dated 13 December 1915, Calley Papers, 1178/465, Wiltshire and Swindon History Centre.
6. Letter from Bulfin to Calley dated 17 December 1915, Calley Papers, 1178/465, Wiltshire and Swindon History Centre.
7. Dalbiac, op. cit. 35.
8. Brig. Gen. Studd, letter to Cecil Pereira, from HQ 180 Bde, Warminster, 7 February 1916, Pereira Papers.
9. Ibid. 39. In Salonika, the 2/4th London Field Ambulance RAMC had a band trained by Private Ralph Vaughan-Williams. Most famous was 'The Roosters', which was started by Lieutenant H. H. Warren of the 2/17th Londons, becoming the 60th Division concert party in Salonika; it lived on as a successful professional company well after the war and into the Second World War.
10. Woodtown Park deeds, 17 February 1916.
11. One of the leaders at the GPO was George Plunkett, who had been at Stonyhurst with Maurice Dease, the first man to win the Victoria Cross in the First World War, posthumously during the Retreat from Mons in August 1914.
12. Dalbiac, op. cit. 40.
13. Knight, Jill, *The Civil Service Rifles in the Great War: 'All Bloody Gentlemen'* (Pen & Sword, Barnsley, 2004) 154, quoted from Charles Jones's diary.
14. Dalbiac, op. cit. foreword.
15. Bulfin, letter to Col. Wigram, HM King George V's Private Secretary, 25 September 1916, Royal Archives, Windsor Castle RA PS/PSO/GV/Q/832/292. The King also sent a message 'wishing the Division every success in future operations' in October following its posting to Salonika. He maintained a close personal interest in his Army throughout the war.
16. Knight, op. cit. 159, quoted from Private Henry Pope's diary.
17. Ibid. 161, quoted from Charles Jones's diary.
18. Elliot, Capt. W. R., *The Second Twentieth* (Gale & Polden, Aldershot, 1920) 44.
19. Dalbiac, op. cit. 59.

20. Ibid. 64.
21. Liddell Hart, Basil, *A History of the World War 1914–1918* (Faber & Faber, London, 1936) 204.
22. Terraine, John, *The First World War 1914–1918* (Macmillan 1965, Papermac ed. 1984) 86.
23. Liddell Hart, op. cit. 206.
24. *OH*, Military Operations 1916, 46.
25. Elliott, op. cit. 54.
26. Private papers of Lt. C. W. Dannatt, 2nd Queen's Westminster Rifles, IWM Docs. 6639.
27. Ibid. 56.
28. Dalbiac, op. cit. 65.
29. Ibid. 65.
30. Ibid. 67.
31. Knight, Jill, op. cit. 163.
32. *OH*, Military Operations, Macedonia, 1914–1917, 227.
33. Knight, op. cit. 64, quoted from Kenneth Wills's diary.
34. Dalbiac, op. cit. 71.
35. Ibid.71–2.
36. Knight, op. cit. 166.
37. *OH*, 229.
38. Knight, op. cit. 168.
39. Elliott, op. cit. 61.
40. Knight, op. cit. 171, quoted from Kenneth Wills's diary.
41. Ibid. 168, quoted from Charles Jones's diary.
42. An explosive charge placed in one or more connected tubes, used by combat engineers to clear barbed wire or minefields and devised by a Royal Engineer officer serving in Bangalore in 1912.
43. Knight, op. cit. 177.

Chapter 10: 1917 Palestine – 'Jerusalem by Christmas' (pp. 167–186)

1. Carver, Michael, *Harding of Petherton* (Weidenfeld & Nicolson, London, 1978) 27.
2. Wavell, Field Marshal Viscount, *Allenby: Soldier and Statesman* (Harrap & Co, London, 1946) 157.
3. Allenby Papers, LHCMA, 6/VIII, 43.
4. Meinertzhagen, Colonel R., *Army Diary 1899–1926* (Oliver & Boyd, London, 1960) 15 July 1917, 219.
5. Wavell, op. cit. 158. Meinertzhagen offered a more nuanced and critical assessment: 'Chetwode is an excellent soldier but must be driven. If he acts by himself his every action is bluff and he is a very nervous officer. Apart from this he is a soldier with sound ideas; what he lacks is the initiative and courage to carry them out as planned. That is just where Allenby will find a very useful and talented servant' (diary entry 15 July 1917).

6. 'Notes on Palestine Operations' dated 6 June 1917, an Appreciation prepared by General Chetwode, included as appendix to Garsia, Lt. Col. Clive, *A Key to Victory: A Study in War Planning* (Eyre & Spottiswoode, London, 1940).

7. Robertson papers, Allenby's letter to CIGS, 19 July 1917.

8. Bernard Fergusson, Wavell's ADC after the Great War, recorded: 'When he [Wavell] was a schoolboy at Winchester, his headmaster had written, not very tactfully, to his father, then a major-general … "there is no need for your son to go into the Army: he is really quite intelligent", an observation he used to quote with relish.' *Wavell: Portrait of a Soldier* (Collins, London, 1961) 95.

9. The private papers of Brigadier General F. M. Carleton DSO, IWM, Docs. 20718, letter to his wife 26 July 1917.

10. Elliot, Capt. W. R. *The Second Twentieth* (Gale & Polden, Aldershot, 1920) 94.

11. Massey, W. T., *How Jerusalem Was Won* (Constable & Co., London, 1919) 30.

12. Cyril Falls agreed with Wavell that Shea was the best infantry divisional commander, but added an amusing sketch of him as 'an extraordinarily melodramatic character. Afterwards in retirement, an enthusiastic Boy Scout and one of Baden Powell's senior lieutenants, he was to be seen in old age tottering to his London club in Scouts uniform, including short shorts and wide-awake hat, heedless of the amusement he created.' Falls, C., *Armageddon* (Weidenfeld and Nicolson, London, 1946) 60.

13. Allenby Papers, letter to CIGS, 19 October 1917. Falls described Palin as 'a sound man … sometimes a little slow' and Hare as 'no genius' but 'competent'. See Falls, op. cit. 69 & 71.

14. Correspondence to CID Historical Branch and Official Historian, 29 September 1929, TNA, CAB 45/78.

15. Private Papers of Maj. Gen. Sir Steuart Hare, IWM, Docs 18385, diary entry 13 September 1917.

16. Correspondence to CID Historical Branch and Official Historian, 28 March 1928, TNA, CAB 45/78.

17. Hare papers, diary entry 13 September 1917.

18. Commander XXI Corps Report on Operations to C-in-C dated 27 October 1917–1 January 1918, 20/1/1918, TNA WO 95/4491.

19. Shea papers, LHCMA, GB009, Box 4/2.

20. Correspondence to CID Historical Branch and Official Historian, 11 January 1929, TNA CAB 45/78.

21. Hare papers, diary entry 1 November 1917. Captious is defined as 'fond of taking exception or raising objections' (OD).

22. Wavell, op. cit. 177–8. The last comment reflects, to a certain degree, a riposte to those officers – the 'Gaza School' – who believed that a stronger concentration of forces could have achieved a complete breakthrough at Gaza and led to the destruction of the Turkish Army by the end of 1917. This is covered further at the end of Chapter 10.

23. Private Papers of Captain H. L. Milsom, IWM, Docs. 5826, 96/48/1.

24. Allenby, letter to his wife, 9 November 1917, LHCMA, Allenby Papers 1/8/23.
25. Falls, Capt. Cyril, *The Official History of the Great War: Military Operations in Egypt & Palestine, From June 1917 to the End of the War* (HMSO, 1930), (OH) Part I, 267.
26. Ibid.133.
27. Private Papers of Maj. Gen. G. P. Dawnay, IWM, Docs. 10403b, Box 69/21/2.
28. Wavell, op. cit. 184.
29. Dawnay papers. letter to his wife, 11 November 1917.
30. Thompson, Lt. Col. R. R., *The Fifty-Second (Lowland) Division 1914–1918* (Maclehose, Jackson & Co., Glasgow, 1923), 415.
31. Correspondence to CID Historical Branch and Official Historian, letter from Major Charles Grahame, brigade major 234 Brigade, TNA CAB 45/79, 6 July 1928.
32. Dawnay papers. letter to his wife, 14 November 1917.
33. Wavell, op. cit. 189.
34. *OH*, 194.
35. Milsom papers, 96/48/1.
36. *OH*, 212.
37. Thompson, Lt. Col R. R., op. cit. 471.
38. *Allenby in Palestine: The Middle East Correspondence of Field Marshal Viscount Allenby June 1917–October 1919* (Army Records Society, Vol. 22) Allenby's letter to CIGS 4 December 1917, 101.
39. Hare papers, letter from Garsia to Hare, 8 June 1920, IWM, 09/86/1.
40. *OH*, 32–3.
41. Wavell, A.P., *The Palestinian Campaigns* (3rd ed. London, 1931).
42. Garsia, Lt. Col. Clive, *A Key to Victory: A Study in War Planning* (Eyre & Spottiswoode, London, 1940) 25, 204, 210, 217. Curiously, Garsia asked Chetwode to pen the Foreword, and not surprisingly he wrote: 'I do not agree with him as regards the First and Third Battles [of Gaza], with the plans of which I had a great deal to do ... I unrepentantly continue to think that the ... Allenby plan in the Third was the only possible one.' Garsia also sought the views of Wavell, who in reading the manuscript responded: 'I do not, as you know, agree with your reading of the Gaza Battles, especially the Third' (226). Third Gaza was taught at Sandhurst and the Staff College after the war, and the success of the plan became the orthodoxy. Garsia considered it a 'strategical defeat' (223). For further coverage of the 'Gaza School' position, refer to CID Historical Branch and Official Historians, letters from Lt. Col. C. Garsia, 2 and 7 December 1929, TNA, CAB 45/79.
43. Diary of Dom Bede Camm, 17 June 1918, Downside Abbey Archives.
44. Wavell, op. cit. 190.

Chapter 11: 1917–1918 The Final Crusade – Jaffa to Beirut (pp. 187–209)

1. Sir Mark Sykes was one who advised Allenby to enter on foot. Sykes sensibly posted Muslim guards on the Dome of the Rock.

2. Falls, Capt. Cyril, *The Official History of the Great War: Military Operations in Egypt & Palestine, From June 1917 to the End of the War* (*OH*) Part I, 267.

3. For this deed, Lt. Col. Jason Anderson won a Bar to his DSO and Lt. C. H. Hills was awarded the MC.

4. *OH*, 273–4.

5. Allenby, letter to his wife, 20 December 1917, LHCMA Allenby Papers 1/8/38.

6. Massey, W. T., *How Jerusalem was Won* (Constable & Co, London, 1919) 244.

7. Storrs, Ronald, *Orientations* (Ivor Nicholson & Watson, London, 1937) 330–1.

8. *GHG* Vol XXV, No 297, January 1918.

9. *OH* 326. Lessons from the success of Plumer's 'bite and hold' tactics at Messines Ridge the previous summer seem to have been taken up in Palestine.

10. The 'Indianization' of the EEF was a process that had been initiated by Robertson back in December and was more a response to the heavy attrition of manpower on the Western Front in 1917 than to the German offensive of Spring 1918.

11. Bulfin, letter to Falls, 17 December 1929, TNA CAB 45/78.

12. Cumberbatch was posted from France to Egypt in March 1918. He maintained contact with Bulfin, cabling him before departure and then writing to him on arrival. Whilst he was serving for a short period as brigade-major of 162 Brigade in 54th Division he took part in the Berukin operation. Bulfin sought him out when visiting the division and later Cumberbatch had lunch with him at Corps HQ. After a month, Cumberbatch returned to the Delta, where he was employed as Brigade Major to HQ Training Centre. Although his health was poor he managed to enjoy an active social and sporting life in Cairo, often seeing Lady Allenby and her cousin (Cumberbatch diary 1918).

13. Bulfin service records, 22–30 March 1918.

14. Diary of Dom Bede Camm, a Downside monk serving as a chaplain in Egypt, 17 June 1918. 'He [Bulfin] wants me to write a letter of introduction to Cardinal Gasquet. He goes tomorrow to Taranto on a man of war and from there to Rome, and wants to see the Holy Father.' The day before they had enjoyed lunch together with Eddie when 'Gen. Bulfin was very kind to me and asked me up to Palestine when he returns and promised me the use of a car to see the Holy places etc' (Downside Abbey Archives). Given Pope Benedict XV's efforts to act as an impartial peace negotiator during this period, such an audience might well not have been approved. Unfortunately, access to the Vatican Archive is strictly limited.

15. Wavell, Field Marshal Viscount, *Allenby: Soldier and Statesman* (Harrap & Co, London, 1946) 224.

16. Bruce, Anthony, *The Last Crusade: The Palestine Campaign in the First World War* (John Murray Press, an imprint of Hodder & Stoughton, London, 2003) 223.

17. *OH*, Part II, 465.

18 Barrow, Gen. Sir George, *The Fire of Life* (Hutchinson & Co, London, 1942) 192. When writing to Falls, Bulfin pointed out: 'I have been a Brigade Major of Cavalry

myself and I was fully alive … to the natural eagerness of the mounted troops to get away.' Letter, 17 December 1929, TNA CAB 45/7.

19. *OH*, Part II, 465.
20. Falls, C., *Armageddon 1918* (Weidenfeld & Nicolson, London, 1964) 59.
21. XXI Corps Operation Order 42, dated 17 September 1918, OH Vol. 2, Appendix 24, 716.
22. Savage, Raymond, *Allenby of Armageddon* (Diamond Press, London, 1925) 254.
23. Falls, C., *Armageddon 1918* (Weidenfeld & Nicolson, London, 1964) 68.
24. Lawrence, T. E., *Seven Pillars of Wisdom* (Jonathan Cape, London, 1935; Penguin 1962) 636.
25. Private Papers of Private E. C. Powell, IWM Doc. G769.
26. Johnstone, Tom, *Orange, Green and Khaki: The Story of the Irish Regiments in the Great War1914–1918* (Gill & Macmillan, Dublin, 1992) 405.
27. *OH*, 509.
28. Wavell, op. cit. 240.
29. Storrs, op. cit. 374.
30. *OH*, 603, confirmed by Bulfin, letter to Falls, 17 December 1929, TNA CAB 45/7.
31. Allenby, letter to his wife, 15 October 1918, LHCMA Allenby papers 1/9/14.
32. Brémond, Général Ed., *Le Hedjaz dans la Guerre Mondiale*, 308–9. Aldington, Richard, *Lawrence of Arabia - A Biographical Enquiry* (Collins, London, 1955) 255.
33. 'Account of a Mission October – February 1919', report by Maj. Ronald Gladstone, 10 March 1919. Hull History Centre, U DDSY 2/4/188, 9. Ronald Gladstone, a fellow Green Howard, accompanied Sykes on his mission as his staff officer.
34. Lawrence, op. cit. 636.
35. Wavell, op. cit. 254.
36. Falls, *Armageddon 1918* 11–12.
37. Bulfin, letter to Falls, 17 December 1929, TNA CAB 45/7.
38. Bulfin, letter to Edmonds, 11 December 1927, TNA CAB 45/120.
39. Falls, *Armageddon 1918* 59.
40. Allenby's Dispatch, supplement to *London Gazette*, 25 January 1918.

Chapter 12: 1919–1939 The Shadows Lengthen (pp. 210–233)
1. Allenby, letter, March 1919, Allenby papers, LHCMA GB009, 2/5/9.
2. James, Lawrence, *Imperial Warrior: The Life and Times of Field-Marshal Viscount Allenby 1861–1936* (Weidenfeld &Nicolson, London, 1993) 180.
3. Ibid., 182.
4. Darwin, J., *Britain, Egypt and the Middle East: Imperial Policy in the Aftermath of the War 1918–1922* (New York, 1981) 155.
5. XXI Corps General Staff War Diary August 1918–May 1919, TNA WO 95/4492.
6. Ibid.
7. File on Huddleston's Force March–May 1919, report by Maj. R. G. Gayer-Anderson, Political Officer Beirut, 12 April 1919, TNA WO 95/4402, 4.

8. 'Report on operations carried out in Egypt from the commencement of the present uprising by Lt. Gen. Sir Edward Bulfin'. From C-in-C EEF to War Office, dated 17 May 1919, Appx B, TNA WO 95/4373.

9. Chirol, Sir Valentine, *The Egyptian Problem* (Macmillan & Co., London, 1921) 183.

10. Cheetham, telegram to Foreign Office, 19 March 1919, 196, TNA FO 371/3714.

11. Egypt: Milner Mission 1919–1920, GHQ's historical summary of events during unrest in March, April and May 1919, Vol X, TNA FO 848/10.

12. TNA FO 371/3714, Tel. 42227, 19 March 1919.

13. Ibid.

14. TNA WO 95/4373.

15. Wavell, Field Marshal Viscount, *Allenby: Soldier and Statesman* (Harrap & Co, London, 1946) 270

16. Cheetham, telegram to Foreign Office, 20 March 1919, 242, TNA FO 371/3714.

17. TNA WO 95/4373.

18. Cheetham, telegram to Foreign Office, 23 March 1919, 282, TNA FO 371/3714.

19. James, op. cit. 190.

20. Johnson, Rob, *The Great War and the Middle East: A Strategic Study* (Oxford University Press, 2016) 251.

21. 'Report on the work done by the RAF in Egypt during the present disturbances 19/3/1919-30/6/1919', TNA Air 1/21, file 15/1/102. Five squadrons of a hundred aircraft were involved. Lt. Mackie, a R.E. officer serving in Egypt at the time, noted that 'a boatload of Australians on their way home were recalled from somewhere in the Red Sea to help deal with the emergency. What these Australians said, and what they did to the Egyptians is not for me to write about.' (Private Papers of Lt D.McD. Mackie, 'Return to Bilbers and Egyptian Rebellion', 3, IWM 22357, box 78/57/1).

22. European War Secret Telegrams Series C. Vol. IX, 1 May 1919 - 30 April 1920. TNA WO 33/981, Tel 11045, 3 May 1919.

23. TNA Air 1/21. file 15/1/102, Light car patrol company report 17/4/1919. In another incident, Lt. Mackie recorded the bravery of some Sappers rescuing 'two maiden ladies of uncertain years' from a Christian mission station in the village of Bilbers (IWM, ibid, 2).

24. TNA FO 848/10, 159.

25. Gwynn, Maj. Gen. Sir Charles, *Imperial Policing* (Macmillan & Co., London, 1936) 79.

26. James, op. cit.190. TNA FO 848/10. Lt. Mackie considered the Gurkhas 'a trigger happy crowd … a beaming little brown (devil?) behind a machine-gun before anyone could stop him' mowing down some protesters (IWM ibid, 4).

27. Bishku, Michael B., *The British Empire and the Question of Egypt's Future 1919–1920* (University Microfilms, Ann Arbor, 1988), quoted in Notes, 75. Also quoted in TNA FO 371/3714, 466.

28. EEF GS War Diary May 1919, C-in-C's covering letter to Bulfin's report, TNA WO 95/4373.
29. TNA FO 848/10, 91.
30. Allenby, letter to Chetwode, 29 March 1919 from Cairo, Chetwode Papers IWM, P/183/1.
31. As part of the EEF's reduction through demobilization, XXI Corps was disestablished at the end of April. Bulfin took over the key formation left, XX Corps, continuing to base himself at Heliopolis. By the time of his departure in November, General Sir Walter Congreve VC had been appointed C-in-C. Walter Congreve had won his VC rescuing the guns at Colenso in 1899; his son, Billy, also won the VC and was the officer who witnessed 28th Division's difficulties on arrival in the Ypres Salient in early 1915. Billy was killed in July 1916 in France.
32. Bulfin had been in England on Christmas Day in 1914 and 1915, busily preparing 28th and 60th Divisions respectively for overseas service, but did not have time for leave.
33. Jeffery, Keith, *The British Army and the Crisis of Empire 1918–1922* (Manchester University Press, 1984).
34. Wilson papers, diary entry, 11 May 1920, IWM, HHW 1/29-1/30, Reel 9.
35. Sir Nevil Macready had been Adjutant-General for the last two years of the war and later Commissioner of the Metropolitan Police. He had also commanded troops in aid of the civil power in South Wales at the time of Tonypandy. He combined considerable military and police experience. Although David Lloyd George supported his appointment, Macready was not keen to take it up, 'a task which I instinctively felt would be affected by every variation of the political weathercock and in which it was doubtful if any satisfactory result could be attained'. Macready, General Sir Nevil, *Annals of an Active Life* (Hutchinson, London, 1925) Vol II, 425.
36. Conclusions of a Conference of Ministers held at 10, Downing Street, S.W.I, on Tuesday, 11 May 1920 at 11.30 a.m., TNA CAB 23/37/32, 230.
37. Macready, op. cit., 453, 459.
38. Wilson papers, diary entry, 11 May 1920, IWM, HHW 1/29-1/30, Reel 9.
39. Letter from Churchill to Lord Stamfordham, 13 May 1920, quoted in Martin Gilbert, *Winston S. Churchill* (Heinemann, London, 1977) Vol IV, Companion Part 2 Documents July 1919–March 1921, 1095.
40. Wilson papers, diary entry, 11 May 1920, IWM.
41. Letter from Churchill to Lord Stamfordham, 13 May 1920, quoted in Gilbert, op. cit. 1095.
42. Macready, op cit. 453. Townshend, Charles, *The British Campaign in Ireland 1919–1921: The Development of Political and Military Policies* (Oxford University Press, 1975) 75.
43. Hugh Tudor, who was appointed Police Adviser to the Irish Government on 15 May, had treated Churchill to an unnerving display of gunnery on the Western

Front in 1916. Gilbert, Martin *Winston S. Churchill* (Heinemann, London, 1971) Vol. III, 663-664.

44. The 'Auxiliaries', more accurately the Auxiliary Division RIC, were former First World War officers, who wore the distinctive Tam O'Shanter hat and were paid as sergeants. The 'Black and Tans' were officially the RIC Special Reserve and were temporary constables, recruited from war veterans (former officers were excluded). Initially, they were used purely for defensive duties, whereas the Auxiliaries were deployed offensively. Both committed atrocities, but the 'Tans' were not former criminals or 'jailbirds' as some thought.

45. *Hansard*, 4 May 1920, Vol. 128, 1875-7.

46. Author's conversation with descendants of Eamon Bulfin at Derrinlough, Birr, Co. Offaly, 25 November 2015.

47. Shea papers, KCLMA, GB009, file 4/2.

48. The Green Howards' title would remain until the regiment was merged, for the first time in its history, full circle into 'The Yorkshire Regiment' in 2006.

49. Letter from Col. Hugh Levin to Regimental Secretary RHQ The Green Howards 29 January 1970, relating Bulfin's account to him of his summons from HM King George V. Levin was a close friend of Bulfin and had been severely wounded serving with the 2nd Battalion at Gheluvelt on 29 October 1914, at the height of the First Battle of Ypres. Levin spent the remainder of the war as a staff officer at home. In 1919–1920 he was secretary to the War Office committee dealing with the renaming of regiments. The Royal Archives at Windsor Castle were unable to find any record of Bulfin's audience with the King, but there is no reason to doubt Bulfin's account as given to Levin.

50. *GHG* Vol. XXVIII, July–August 1920, 49. Catalogue of Graduates, Vol. V, 1931, Library of Trinity College Dublin.

51. Ibid., Vol. XXVIII, 1920, 84.

52. Ibid., Vol. XXIX, 1921, 'Reports in Historical Record 2nd Bn 1858–1942'.

53. Ibid, Vol. XXX, 1922. The Bishop of Cashel conducted a farewell service for the 2nd Battalion on its departure from Tipperary, when he complimented the men on their behaviour, adding that many locals were sorry to see them go.

54. Ibid., Vol. XXIX, Nov 1921, 129.

55. Longer, V., *Red Coats to Olive Green: A History of the Indian Army 1600–1974* (Allied Publishers, India, 1974) 175.

56. Gertrude Bell's letter to her father, 16 February 1922, Gertrude Bell Archive, Newcastle University.

57. Ibid.

58. The author has scoured the National Archives as well as the India Office files, held by the British Library, to find out whether Bulfin had been tasked with other responsibilities beyond his commissioner role, whilst in India and Iraq, but no evidence of such was found. One cannot help but question whether Bulfin's experience of the region was not put to a wider use.

59. 'Gen. Bulfin sent me on your book, which you kindly authorised him to do.' Simpson-Baikie letter to Smith-Dorrien 29 May 1920. Papers of Brig. Gen. Sir Hugh Simpson-Baikie, GB0099 KCLMA.

60. Hyndson, J. G. W., *From Mons to the First Battle of Ypres* (1932), Foreword by General Sir Edward Bulfin. The literary quote is from Milton's *Paradise Lost*, drummed into most schoolboys of his generation.

61. *The Times*, 29 January 1927.

62. Letter from John Faraday to Colonel Geoffrey Powell, 12 August 1976, with typed record attached, titled 'Captain Bulfin's Watch', Green Howards Museum. The 1929 troubles in Palestine, soon after, became a classic example of 'Duties in Aid of the Civil Power', clearly written-up in Gwynn's textbook, *Imperial Policing* (chapter XI).

63. Inside the watch case, Faraday, who had won an MC on the Western Front, had inscribed his own name and '29.8.29 Palestine', the date he had met Eddie at Safed. The watch was still keeping good time in 1976, over sixty years on from when Faraday recorded the events of August 1929, and now resides in the regimental museum.

64. 'News in a Nutshell', http://www.britishpathe.com/programmes/news-in-a-nut shell/episode/asc/playlist/158.

65. *GHG*, Vol. XLVII, 1939, 97. Fanny Bulfin, in writing to a correspondent on behalf of her husband in January 1936, replied: 'I am sorry to say my husband has aged very much during the last three months & his memory is not at all good especially for recent events tho' strange to say he remembers most things connected with the war perfectly.' Letter from Lady Bulfin to Major C. A. Forsythe-Major DSO, Hull History Centre, U DFM/2/2 (h), dated 12 January 1936.

66. Ignatius's son, Patrick, was commissioned in the Green Howards in 1925. Known in the regiment as Paddy, he served in Palestine at the time his cousin, Eddie, died. He later commanded a company during the 1940 Norwegian campaign and led the 1st Battalion through Sicily and Italy, being awarded the DSO. After the war, he commanded the battalion again, this time during the Malayan Emergency. On retirement he and his wife Peggy moved to Australia, where they ran a boarding kennels. They had no children. His full name was Patrick George John Mary Davies Bulfin (1904–1981).

67. In 2010 Sara Richer, Bulfin's great-granddaughter, was working at Strensall Barracks near York, when she met a Chelsea Pensioner finding his way to a Green Howard parade. On discovering who she was, he introduced himself as the regimental bugler at her ancestor's funeral.

68. *GHG*, Vol. XLVII, 1939, 113/4. Present at the Requiem Mass, held in Berkeley Square, London on 25 August, was Sir Cecil Pereira (*The Times* 26 August 1939), who had fought alongside Bulfin through much of 1915.

69. The full wording on the headstone is: 'Here sleepeth until the great reveille sounds, of your charity pray for the repose of the soul of General Sir Edward Bulfin KCB CVO LLD Colonel of The Green Howards, Alexandra The Princess of Wales's Own Yorkshire Regiment. Born in Dublin November 6 1862. Died at Boscombe

August 20 1939.' The reference to his colonelcy of the regiment reflected the great pride he took in this honour.

Chapter 13: Epilogue (pp. 234–241)

1. Keegan, John, 'Whole Stunt Napoo', *New Statesman*, 17 November 1978.
2. Parker, Peter, *The Old Lie: The Great War and the Public School Ethos* (London, 1987) 283–4.
3. The Lord Mayor of London hosted a dinner in the Mansion House on 6 November 1935 for the Archbishop of Westminster and the 'Catholic Hierarchy' of England, attended by the Duke of Norfolk and Bulfin amongst others. In his toast, the Lord Mayor commented, 'that they should be meeting on the Mansion House that night was a measure of the change which the last century had seen'. The first Catholic Lord Mayor since Henry VIII's reign was Sir Stuart Knill in 1892. *The Times* report, titled 'Catholics in England: Change in Public Feeling' dated 7 November 1935.
4. Perry, Nick, correspondence with author, 1 December 2015. The author's extensive search of London and Irish newspaper archives, in particular the widespread obituaries, revealed no mention of the link between Bulfin and his nationalist relations.
5. Aileen, sister to Eamon and Catalina, visited Edward and his family in England at least once and found the general 'a charming man' (correspondence between author and Michael Bulfin 3 November 2017) .
6. *Cairns Post*, obituary headline, 19 October 1939.
7. 'An Appreciation' from unnamed CO ('T. L. B.') to *The Times*, 23 August 1939, also quoted in *Stonyhurst Magazine* No. 341, July 1940.
8. BBC audio recording in 1964 of General Sir John Shea: 'Recollections of operations in command of 60th Division in Palestine', IWM 4227.
9. Gardner, Brian, *Allenby* (Cassell, London, 1965) quoted on p.116.
10. Falls, when writing about Megiddo, commented that 'Bulfin was the bludgeon, Chetwode the master of manoeuvre. Both sides were necessary in carrying through Allenby's plan. He knew his men and their respective virtues.' *Armageddon 1918*, 75. The bludgeon tag was also mentioned in his regiment's obituary in *GHG* and in 'An Appreciation' from unnamed CO to *The Times*, 23 August 1939.
11. *The Times* obituary, 22 August 1939, titled 'A Great Leader in War'.
12. Diary entry by Dom Bede Camm, 17 June 1918, Downside Abbey Archives.
13. Letter from Bell in Baghdad to her father, 16 February 1922, Gertrude Bell Archives, Newcastle University.
14. *The Times* obituary, 22 August 1939.
15. Letter from Allenby to Regimental Secretary RHQ The Green Howards, 20 March 1933, Green Howards Museum archives.

Bibliography

Primary Sources
Diocese of Westminster Archives, London
  Cardinal Manning Papers
Downside Abbey Archives
  Diary of Dom Bede Camm
  Letters from Gen and Mrs Bulfin to Father Ramsay, Head of Downside School
Green Howards Museum, Richmond North Yorkshire
  Green Howards Gazette
Hull History Centre
  Papers of Sir Mark Sykes
Imperial War Museum, London
Diaries of:
  Capt Hugh Cumberbatch
  Field Marshal Sir Henry Wilson
Papers of:
  Brig Gen F.M. Carleton
  Field Marshal Lord Chetwode
  Lt C.W. Dannatt
  Maj Gen Guy Dawnay
  Col Arthur Hadow
  Maj Gen Sir Steuart Hare
  Gen Sir Henry Horne
  Lt Col Lord Loch
  Lt D. McD. Mackie
  Capt H.L. Milsom
  Pte E.C. Powell
  Gen Sir Horace Smith-Dorrien
Liddell Hart Centre for Military Archives, King's College London
Papers of:
  Viscount Allenby
  Maj Gen Sir John Shea
  Brig Gen Simpson-Baikie
  Maj Gen Wintour
National Archives, Kew
Diaries of:
  Lt Gen Sir Edward Bulfin 11 August – 3 November 1914
  Brig Gen C.E. Pereira

Other papers, letters and war diaries, all listed in References
National Army Museum, London
Papers of:
  H.E. Belfield
  Maj Gen Pole-Carew
  Earl Roberts
National Library of Scotland
  Haldane Papers
Royal Archives, Windsor
  Correspondence from Gen Bulfin to King's Private Secretary
Stonyhurst College Archives
  Edward Bulfin school reports
  Stonyhurst Magazine
Wiltshire and Swindon History Centre
  Calley papers
  Methuen papers
Woodtown Park, Rathfarnham, Dublin
  Estate papers

Unpublished Works
Oakey, Iris, *Problems of Morale, Discipline and Leadership in the 28th Division January –
  October 1915* (MA Dissertation for University of Birmingham, Centre of First World
  War Studies, 2006)
Pereira Papers

Published Works
Aldington, Richard, *Lawrence of Arabia –A Biographical Enquiry* (Collins, London,
  1955)
*Allenby in Palestine: The Middle East Correspondence of Field Marshal Viscount Allenby
  June 1917–October 1919* (Army Records Society, Vol. 22)
Amery, L.S. (ed.), *The Times History of the War in South Africa 1899–1902* (Sampson
  Low, Marston & Co., London, 1906)
Anon, *History of the Prince of Wales's Own Civil Service Rifles* (Wyman & Sons, 1921)
Asquith, H.H., *Memories and Reflections 1852–1927* (Cassell, London, 1928, 2 Vols.)
Barnett, Corelli, *Britain and Her Army 1509–1970: A Military, Political and Social
  Survey* (Allen Lane The Penguin Press, London, 1970)
Barr, Niall and Sheffield, Gary, 'Douglas Haig, the Common Soldier, and the British
  Legion', chapter in *Haig: A Reappraisal 70 Years On* ed. by Bond, Brian and Cave,
  Nigel (Leo Cooper, Barnsley, 1999)
Barrow, Gen. Sir George, *The Fire of Life* (Hutchinson & Co, London, 1942)
Beckett, Ian, 'The Annual Confidential Report and Promotion in the Late Victorian
  Army', *British Journal for Military History*, Vol.1, Issue 1, October 2014.
Beckett, Ian, *Johnnie Gough VC* (Tom Donovan, London, 1989)
Beckett, Ian, *Oxford Dictionary of National Biography* entry on General Sir William
  Butler

Beckett, Ian, *The Victorians at War* (Hambledon Continuum, London, 2003)

Beckett, Ian (ed.), *The Army and the Curragh Incident 1914* (Army Records Society, 1986)

Beckett, Ian and Corvi, Steven (eds.), *Haig's Generals* (Pen & Sword, Barnsley, 2006)

Beckett, Ian, *Ypres: The First Battle 1914* (Pearson Education, Harlow, 2004)

Bishku, Michael B., *The British Empire and the Question of Egypt's Future 1919–1920* (University Microfilms, Ann Arbor, 1988)

Bolwell, F.A., *With a Reservist in France* (George Routledge & Sons, London, 1917)

Bond, Brian (ed.), *The First World War and British Military History* (Clarendon Press, Oxford, 1991)

Bourne, John, entry on Bulfin in the *Oxford Dictionary of National Biography*

Bourne, John, 'Haig and the Historians', chapter in *Haig: A Reappraisal 70 Years On* ed. by Bond, Brian and Cave, Nigel (Leo Cooper, Barnsley, 1999)

Bourne, John, 'British Divisional Commanders during the Great War: First Thoughts', *Gun Fire: A Journal of First World War History*, 29.

Brémond, Général Edouard, *Le Hedjaz dans la Guerre Mondiale* (Payot, Paris, 1931)

Briscoe, Diana (ed.), *The Diary of a World War 1 Cavalry Officer* (Costello, Tunbridge Wells, 1985)

Bruce, Anthony, *The Last Crusade: The Palestine Campaign in the First World War* (John Murray, London, 2003)

Bullock, David, *Allenby's War: The Palestine-Arabian Campaigns 1916–1918* (Blandford Press, London, 1988)

Butler, Elizabeth, *From Sketch-Book and Diary* (Adam & Charles Black, London, 1909)

Butler, Patrick, *A Galloper at Ypres* (Fisher Unwin, London, 1920)

Butler, Sir William, *Sir William Butler: An Autobiography* (Constable, London, 1911)

Carew, Tim, *The Vanished Army* (William Kimber, London, 1964)

Cary, A.D.L. and McCance, S., *Regimental Records of the Royal Welch Fusiliers* (Forster, Groom & Co, London, 1923) Vol. II, 1816–1914.

Carver, Field Marshal Lord, *The British Army in the 20th Century* (Macmillan, London, in association with the Imperial War Museum, 1998)

Carver, Michael, *Harding of Petherton* (Weidenfeld & Nicolson, London, 1978)

Cassar, George H., *Trial by Gas: the British Army at the Second Battle of Ypres* (Potomac Books, University of Nebraska Press, 2014)

Catholic Encyclopedia entry on General Sir William Butler

Cave, Nigel, *Vimy Ridge: Arras* (Leo Cooper, London, 1996, Battleground Europe series)

Charteris, John, *Field-Marshal Earl Haig* (Cassell, London, 1929)

Charteris, John, *At G.H.Q.* (Cassell, 1931)

Cherry, Niall, *Most Unfavourable Ground: The Battle of Loos 1915* (Helion, Solihull, 2005)

Chirol, Sir Valentine, *The Egyptian Problem* (Macmillan & Co., London, 1921)

Churchill, W.S., *Winston S. Churchill* ed. Martin Gilbert (Heinemann, London, 1972)

Coleman, Frederick, *From Mons to Ypres with French: A Personal Narrative* (Sampson, Low Marston & Co, London, 1916)

Collins, Maj. Gen. R. J., *Lord Wavell (1883–1941): A Military Biography* (Hodder & Stoughton, London, 1948)

Colvile, Maj. Gen. Sir Henry, *The Work of the 9th Division in South Africa 1900* (Edward Arnold, London, 1901)

Conan Doyle, Sir Arthur, *The Great Boer War* (London, 1901)

Conan Doyle, Sir Arthur, *The British Campaign in France and Flanders 1915* (Hodder & Stoughton, London, 1917)

Connell, John, *Wavell: Scholar and Soldier* (Collins, London, 1964)

Corrigan, Gordon, *Mud, Blood and Poppycock* (Cassell, London, 2003)

Corrigan, Gordon, *Loos 1915: The Unwanted Battle* (Spellmount, Stroud, 2006)

Cowper, Col. J.M., *The King's Own: The Story of a Royal Regiment* (Gale & Polden, Aldershot, 1957)

Dalbiac, Col. P.H., *History of the 60th Division (2/2nd London Division)* (George Allen & Unwin, London, 1927)

Danchev, Alex, 'Bunking and Debunking: The Controversies of the 1960s' in Bond, Brian (ed.) *The First World War and British Military History* (Clarendon Press, Oxford, 1991)

Darwin, J., *Britain, Egypt and the Middle East: Imperial Policy in the Aftermath of the War 1918–1922* (New York, 1981)

Davies, Frank and Maddocks, Graham, *Bloody Red Tabs: General Officer Casualties of the Great War 1914–1918* (Pen & Sword, Barnsley, 2014)

Dixon, John, *Magnificent But Not War: The Second Battle of Ypres 1915* (Leo Cooper, Barnsley, 2003)

Dixon, Norman, *On the Psychology of Military Incompetence* (Jonathan Cape, London, 1976)

Elliot, Capt. W.R., *The Second Twentieth* (Gale & Polden, Aldershot, 1920)

Falls, Cyril, *Armageddon 1918* (Weidenfeld &Nicolson, London, 1964)

Falls, Cyril, *The Life of A Regiment: The History of the Gordon Highlanders* Vol. IV 1914–1919 (University Press, Aberdeen, 1958)

Falls, Capt. Cyril, *The Official History of the Great War: Military Operations in Egypt & Palestine, From June 1917 to the End of the War* (HMSO, 1930)

Farrar-Hockley, Anthony, *Death of an Army* (Wordsworth Editions, Ware, 1998)

Farwell, Byron, *The Great Boer War* (Allen Lane, London, 1976)

Fergusson, Bernard, *Wavell: Portrait of a Soldier* (Collins, London, 1961)

Ferrar, Major M.L., *Officers of the Green Howards 1688–1931* (Belfast, 1931)

Ford, Roger, *Eden to Armageddon* (Weidenfeld & Nicolson, London, 2009)

The Complete Dispatches of Lord French (Chapman & Hall, London, 1917)

Gardner, Brian, *Allenby* (Cassell, London, 1965)

Gardner, Nikolas, *Trial By Fire: Command and the British Expeditionary Force in 1914* (Contributions in Military Studies, No. 27, Praeger, Connnecticut, USA, 2003)

Garsia, Lt. Col. Clive, *A Key to Victory: A Study in War Planning* (Eyre & Spottiswoode, London, 1940)

Garvin, J.L., *The Life of Joseph Chamberlain* (Macmillan, London 1934)

Gilbert, Adrian, *Challenge of Battle: The Real Story of the British Army in 1914* (Osprey, 2014)

Gilbert, Martin (ed)., *Winston S. Churchill* (Heinemann, London, 1972–7)

Gough, General Sir Hubert, *Soldiering On* (Arthur Baker, London, 1954).

Gough, General Sir Hubert, *The Fifth Army* (Hodder & Stoughton, London, 1931)

Graves, Robert, *Goodbye to All That* (Penguin Modern Classics, 1985 edition)

Guest, Herbert, *With Lord Methuen and the 1st Division* (Klerksdorp, South Africa, 1902)

Gurney, Russell, *History of the Northamptonshire Regiment 1742–1934* (Gale & Polden, Aldershot, 1935)

Gwynn, Maj. Gen. Sir Charles, *Imperial Policing* (Macmillan & Co., London 1936)

Hadaway, Stuart, *From Gaza to Jerusalem: the Campaigns for Southern Palestine 1917* (The History Press, Stroud, 2015)

Haig, Douglas, *War Diaries and Letters 1914–1918*, ed. by Gary Sheffield and John Bourne (Weidenfeld & Nicolson, London, 2005)

Hammerton, Sir John (ed.), *The Great War – I Was There* (Amalgamated Press, London)

Harington, Charles, *Plumer of Messines* (John Murray, London, 1935)

Harris, J.P,. *Douglas Haig and the First World War* (Cambridge University Press, 2008)

Headlam, Cecil (ed.), *Milner Papers* 1897-9 (Cassell, London, 1931)

Holt, Major and Mrs, *Holt's Battlefield Guide to the Ypres Salient* (Leo Cooper, Barnsley, 1996)

Home, Brig. Gen. Sir Archibald, *The Diary of a World War 1 Cavalry Officer*, ed. by Diana Briscoe (Costello, Tunbridge Wells, 1985)

Hughes, Matthew, *Allenby and British Strategy in the Middle East 1917–1919* (Frank Cass, London, 1999)

Hyndson, J.G.W., *From Mons to the First Battle of Ypres* ((Wyman & Sons, London, 1932)

Jacobsen, Mark (ed.), *Rawlinson in India* (Sutton Publishing, for the Army Records Society, 2002)

James, Lawrence, *Imperial Warrior: The Life and Times of Field-Marshal Viscount Allenby 1861–1936* (Weidenfeld & Nicolson, London, 1993)

Jeffery, Keith, *The British Army and the Crisis of Empire 1918–1922* (Manchester University Press, 1984)

Jeffery, Keith, *Field Marshal Sir Henry Wilson: A Political Soldier* (Oxford University Press, 2006)

Jeffery, Keith, 'The Irish Soldier in the Boer War', chapter in *The Boer War: Direction, Experience and Image*, ed. by John Gooch (Frank Cass, London, 2000)

Joffre, Joseph, *The Memoirs of Marshal Joffre*, transl. by Col. T. Bentley Mott and Lt. Col. S.J. Lowe (Geoffrey Bles, London, 1932)

Johnson, Rob, *The Great War and the Middle East: A Strategic Study* (Oxford University Press, 2016)

Johnstone, Tom, *Orange, Green and Khaki: The Story of the Irish Regiments in the Great War 1914–1918* (Gill and Macmillan, Dublin, 1992)

Jones, Spencer, *From Boer War to World War: Tactical Reform of the British Army 1902–1914* (University of Oklahoma Press, 2012)

Jones, Spencer (ed.), *Stemming the Tide: Officers and Leadership in the British Expeditionary Force 1914* (Helion, Solihull, 2013)

Jones, Spencer (ed.), *Courage without Glory: The British Army on the Western Front 1915* (Helion & Co, Sollihull, 2015)

Keegan, John, *The First World War* (Hutchinson, London, 1998)

Keegan, John, *The Face of Battle* (Jonathan Cape, London, 1976)

Keegan, John, 'Whole Stunt Napoo', *New Statesman*, 17 November 1978.

Kendall, Paul, *Aisne 1914: The Dawn of Trench Warfare* (The History Press, Stroud, 2012)

Kinnear, Alfred, *To Modder River with Methuen* (J.W. Arrowsmith, Bristol, 1900)

Kirby, Major E.L., *Officers of the Royal Welch Fusiliers* (privately published, 1997)

Kitchen, James E., *The British Imperial Army in the Middle East: Morale and Military Identity in the Sinai and Palestine Campaigns, 1916–18* (Bloomsbury, London, 2014)

Knight, Jill, *The Civil Service Rifles in the Great War: 'All Bloody Gentlemen'* (Pen & Sword, Barnsley, 2004)

Kruger, Rayne, *Good-bye Dolly Gray* (Cassell, London, 1959)

Lawrence, T.E., *Seven Pillars of Wisdom* (Jonathan Cape, London, 1935; Penguin 1962)

Leask, Anthony, *Putty. From Tel-el-Kebir to Cambrai: The Life and Letters of Lieutenant General Sir William Pulteney 1861–1941* (Helion, 2015)

Liddell Hart, Basil, *A History of World War 1914–1918* (Faber & Faber, London, 1936)

Lloyd, Nick, *Loos 1915* (The History Press, Stroud, 2006)

Lloyd George, David, *War Memoirs* (Nicholson & Watson, London, 1933)

LoCicero, Michael S., '"A Tower of Strength": Brigadier-General Edward Bulfin', chapter on Brigade Command in *Stemming the Tide: Officers and Leadership in the British Expeditionary Force 1914* (Helion, Solihull, 2013) ed. by Spencer Jones

Longer, V., *Red Coats to Olive Green: A History of the Indian Army 1600–1974* (Allied Publishers, India, 1974)

MacDiarmid, D.S., *The Life of Lt. Gen. Sir James Grierson* (Constable, London, 1923)

Macready, General Sir Nevil, *Annals of an Active Life* (George H. Doran, New York, 1925)

Mallinson, Allan, *1914: Fight the Good Fight* (Bantam Press, London, 2013)

Mallinson, Allan, *Too Important for the Generals: Losing and Winning The First World War* (Bantam Press, London, 2016)

Marden, Maj. Gen. Sir Thomas, *The History of the Welch Regiment in the Great War* (Western Mail and Echo Ltd., Cardiff, 1923)

Massey, W.T., *How Jerusalem Was Won* (Constable & Co., London, 1919)

Maurice, Major-General Sir Frederick, and staff, *History of the War in South Africa 1899–1902* (Hurst & Blackett, London, 1906)

McCourt, Edward, *Remember Butler; The Story of Sir William Butler* (Routledge and Kegan Paul, London, 1967)

Meinertzhagen, Colonel Richard, *Army Diary:1899–1926* (Oliver & Boyd, Edinburgh and London, 1960)

Menpes, Mortimer, *War Impressions Being a Record in Colour* (Adam & Charles Black, London, 1901)

Messenger, Charle,s *Call to Arms: The British Army 1914–1918* (Weidenfeld & Nicolson, London, 2005)

Miller, Stephen, *Lord Methuen and the British Army; Failure and Redemption in South Africa* (Frank Cass, London, 1999)

Moody, R.S.H., *Historical Records of the Buffs (East Kent Regiment) 3rd Foot 1914–1919* (Medici Society, London, 1922)

Murland, Jerry, *Battle of the Aisne 1914: The BEF and the Birth of the Western Front* (Pen & Sword, Barnsley, 2012)

Neillands, Robin, *The Great War Generals on the Western Front 1914–1918* (Magpie Books, London, 2004)

Neillands, Robin, *The Death of Glory: The Western Front 1915* (John Murray, London, 2006)

Newell, Jonathan, 'Allenby and the Palestine Campaign in Bond', Brian (ed.) *The First World War and British Military History* (Clarendon Press, Oxford, 1991)

Newell, Jonathan, *Learning the Hard Way: Allenby in Egypt and Palestine, 1917–1919* (*Journal of Strategic Studies*, Volume 14, No. 3, September 1991)

Norman, T., *Armageddon Road: A VC's Diary 1914–1916* (Kimber, London, 1982)

The Northamptonshire Regiment 1914–1918 (Gale & Polden), compiled under direction of the regimental history committee

O'Connor, Steven, *Irish Officers in the British Forces, 1922–45* (Palgrave Macmillan, London, 2014)

Pakenham, Thomas, *The Boer War* (Weidenfeld & Nicholson, London, 1979)

Parker, Peter, *The Old Lie: The Great War and the Public School Ethos* (London, 1987)

Pearse, H.W., *History of the East Surrey Regiment* (Medici Society, London, 1923)

Pemberton, W. Baring, *Battles of the Boer War* (Pan Books, London, 1969)

Perrett, Bryan, *Megiddo 1918 – The Last Great Cavalry Victory* (Osprey Military, Oxford, 1999)

Perry, Nicholas, *The Irish Landed Class and the British Army, 1850–1950* (Sage, 2011)

Powell, Geoffrey, *Plumer: The Soldier's General* (Leo Cooper, London, 1990)

Powell, Geoffrey and Powell, John, *The History of the Green Howards: Three Hundred Years of Service* (Pen & Sword, Barnsley, 2002)

Rawson, Andrew, *Loos – Hohenzollern* (Leo Cooper, Barnsley, 2003, Battleground Europe series)

Robbins, Simon, *British Generalship on the Western Front 1914–1918: Defeat into Victory* (Frank Cass, London, 2005)

Robertson, William, *From Private to Field Marshal* (Constable, London, 1921)

Rogan, Eugene, *The Fall of the Ottomans: The Great War in the Middle East 1914–1920* (Penguin Books, 2015)

Sandilands, Brig H. R., *The Fifth in the Great War* (G.W. Grigg & Son, Dover, 1938)

Savage, Raymond, *Allenby of Armageddon* (Diamond Press, London, 1925)

Schwink, Otto, *Ypres 1914: An Official Account published by order of German General Staff* (Constable & Co, London, 1919)

Schofield, Victoria, *Wavell: Soldier & Statesman* (John Murray, London, 2006)

Selby, John, *The Boer War: A Study in Cowardice and Courage* (Arthur Baker, London, 1969)

Sheffield, Gary, *The Chief: Douglas Haig and the British Army* (Aurum Press, London, 2011)

Sheffield, Gary & Todman, Dan (ed.), *Command and Control on the Western Front: The British Army's Experience 1914–1918* (Spellmount, Stroud, 2007)

Simkins, Peter, 'Everyman at War: Recent Interpretations of the Front Line Experience' in Bond, Brian (ed.) *The First World War and British Military History* (Clarendon Press, Oxford, 1991)

Smith-Dorrien, General Sir Horace, *Memories of 48 Years of Service* (John Murray, London 1925)

Snow, Thomas D'Oyly, *The Confusion of Command: The War Memoirs of Lieutenant-General Sir Thomas D'Oyly Snow* (Frontline Books, London, 2011), ed. by Dan Snow and Mark Pottle

Spears, Louis, *Liaison 1914: A Narrative of the Great Retreat* (William Heinemann, London, 1931)

Storrs, Ronald, *Orientations* (Ivor Nicholson & Watson, London, 1937)

Strachan, Hew, *The Politics of the British Army* (Oxford University Press, 1997)

Sutherland, John and Webb, Margaret, *All the Business f War: The British Army Exercises of 1913, the British Expeditionary Force and the Great War* (in association with the Towcester and District Local History Society, 2012)

Sykes, Christopher Simon, *The Man Who Created the Middle East: A Story of Empire, Conflict and the Sykes-Picot Agreement* (William Collins, London, 2016)

Terraine, John, *The First World War 1914–1918* (Macmillan, London, 1965)

Terraine, John *1914–1918: Essays on Leadership and War* (Western Front Association, 1998)

Thompson, Lt Col R. R., *The Fifty-Second (Lowland) Division 1914–1918* (Maclehose, Jackson & Co, Glasgow, 1923)

Townshend, Charles, *The British Campaign in Ireland 1919–1921: The Development of Political and Military Policies* (Oxford University Press, 1975)

Travers, Tim, *The Killing Ground: The British Army, the Western Front and the Emergence of Modern War 1900–1918* (first published by Allen & Unwin, London, 1987, reprinted by Pen & Sword, Barnsley, 2009)

Usherwood, Paul and Spencer-Jones, Jenny, *Lady Butler: Battle Artist 1846–1933* (National Army Museum, London, 1987)

Walker, H.M., *History of the Northumberland Fusiliers* (John Murray, London, 1919)

Wavell, A.P., *The Palestinian Campaigns* (3rd Ed. London, 1931)

Wavell, Field Marshal Viscount, *Allenby: Soldier and Statesman* (Harrap & Co, London, 1946)

de Wet, Christiaan, *Three Years War* (Archibald Constable, London, 1902)

Wood, Walter, *The Northumberland Fusiliers* (Grant Richards, London, 1901)

Woodward, David R., *Hell in the Holy Land: World War 1 in the Middle East* (University Press of Kentucky, 2006)

Index